CH00970929

Systematically Working with Multimodal Data

Systematically Working with Multimodal Data

Research Methods in Multimodal Discourse Analysis

Sigrid Norris

WILEY Blackwell

This edition first published 2019
© 2019 John Wiley & Sons, Inc.

All rights reserved. No part of this publication may be reproduced, stored in a retrieval system, or transmitted, in any form or by any means, electronic, mechanical, photocopying, recording or otherwise, except as permitted by law. Advice on how to obtain permission to reuse material from this title is available at http://www.wiley.com/go/permissions.

The right of Sigrid Norris to be identified as the author of this work has been asserted in accordance with law.

Registered Office
John Wiley & Sons, Inc., 111 River Street, Hoboken, NJ 07030, USA

Editorial Office
The Atrium, Southern Gate, Chichester, West Sussex, PO19 8SQ, UK

For details of our global editorial offices, customer services, and more information about Wiley products visit us at www.wiley.com.

Wiley also publishes its books in a variety of electronic formats and by print-on-demand. Some content that appears in standard print versions of this book may not be available in other formats.

Limit of Liability/Disclaimer of Warranty
While the publisher and authors have used their best efforts in preparing this work, they make no representations or warranties with respect to the accuracy or completeness of the contents of this work and specifically disclaim all warranties, including without limitation any implied warranties of merchantability or fitness for a particular purpose. No warranty may be created or extended by sales representatives, written sales materials or promotional statements for this work. The fact that an organization, website, or product is referred to in this work as a citation and/or potential source of further information does not mean that the publisher and authors endorse the information or services the organization, website, or product may provide or recommendations it may make. This work is sold with the understanding that the publisher is not engaged in rendering professional services. The advice and strategies contained herein may not be suitable for your situation. You should consult with a specialist where appropriate. Further, readers should be aware that websites listed in this work may have changed or disappeared between when this work was written and when it is read. Neither the publisher nor authors shall be liable for any loss of profit or any other commercial damages, including but not limited to special, incidental, consequential, or other damages.

Library of Congress Cataloging-in-Publication Data

Names: Norris, Sigrid, 1961– author.
Title: Systematically working with multimodal data : research methods in
    multimodal discourse analysis / Sigrid Norris.
Description: Hoboken, NJ : John Wiley & Sons, 2019. | Includes bibliographical
    references and index. |
Identifiers: LCCN 2018027393 (print) | LCCN 2018058184 (ebook) |
    ISBN 9781119168331 (Adobe PDF) | ISBN 9781119168348 (ePub) |
    ISBN 9781119168317 (hardcover) | ISBN 9781119168324 (pbk.)
Subjects: LCSH: Discourse analysis–Technology. | Discourse analysis–Study and teaching. |
    Modality (Linguistics)
Classification: LCC P302.865 (ebook) | LCC P302.865 .N67 2018 (print) | DDC 401/.41–dc23
LC record available at https://lccn.loc.gov/2018027393

Cover Design: Wiley
Cover Image: © Peshkova/iStock.com

Set in 10/12pt Warnock by SPi Global, Pondicherry, India

Printed in Singapore by C.O.S. Printers Pte Ltd

10 9 8 7 6 5 4 3 2 1

To Alan

Contents

List of Figures

List of Tables

Acknowledgments

The book has taken a substantial amount of time to write and I thank the editors at Wiley for their patience. Many people have been helpful along the way, but if I was naming everyone who had had an impact upon the many pages before you, these acknowledgments would turn into the longest chapter of the book. I think most people who have had contact with me over the last few years, who have asked a question with regard to multimodal data collection, data analysis, reliability of qualitative research, or the like, would have had an impact upon my writing of this book. Here, I would like to thank all of you for your interest, curiosity, and trust in me having an answer to these questions. I do hope that you will find at least some of your answers in the pages ahead and I hope that you will find the book useful. I know that I have promised many a reader that I would answer questions, that I would write a book that explained how I work with data, and I hope that you will not be disappointed.

There are also a few people who I will name and first, some members of the Multimodal Research Center, who have had the greatest impact upon my writing and who deserve special thanks. I thank Tui Matelau, Yulia Khan, and Ivana Rajic for their questions as they were working with the phases and steps and their support in writing this book; a particular thank you goes to Jesse Pirini, who read very early drafts of some sections and who found my writing of the how-to sections for data analysis incredibly useful. Special thanks also go to Jarret Geenen, who visited the Center in early 2017 and was a catalyst in my explaining some theory in great detail. Both Jarret's input with regard to the need for theory to be covered and Jesse's input during this early writing stage of phases and steps solidified my thinking. I would also like to thank Elina Tapio and Chloe Grace Fogarty-Bourget, who were visiting researchers at the Multimodal Research Centre and tried out some of the phases and steps for data analysis. They both had valuable feedback and questions with regard to the systematic approach. Further, I would like to thank Edgar Bernad-Mechó, another visiting scholar, who also tried out some phases and steps and who emphasized that I needed to include not only data analysis, but also to outline data collection and transcription in the same book.

Of course, all participants, in our projects have been of utmost importance. Without participants, we cannot do our work. But here, I am most grateful to the participants who are featured in this book. Every participant and every family featured has viewed the videos, tables, and images and permitted them to be published as shown. Featuring color images of real participants and being able to use excerpts of our data to give students and researchers hands-on experience makes this book special. Therefore, I would like to thank the following participants of the studies for their permission to publish their images, names and videos as part of this book: Abbie O'Rourke, Ali, the Budd Family and the Charko Family, Cameron Fraser, Dunja Vajsakovic, Isla Connors, Dina-Sara Vajsakovic, Edgar Bernad-Mechó, Hana Mlinac, Ivana Mlinac, Ivana Rajic, Jay Nam, Jake Connors, Jo Connors, Luke Norris, Melanie, Michael Evans, Rachelle Ferguson, Shymala Sidharth, Sophie Connors, and Brownderbag Tagaloa.

I would like to thank the Faculty of Design and Creative Technologies, the School of Communication Studies, and the AUT Multimodal Research Centre at Auckland University of Technology in New Zealand for funding the projects and making the writing of this book possible.

I would also like to thank Freiburg Institute for Advanced Studies (FRIAS), University of Freiburg, Germany and the People Programme (Marie Curie Actions) of the European Union's Seventh Framework Programme (FP7/2007–2013) under REA grant agreement no. [609305] for making the completion of this book possible.

Then, there is family. Family is always most important for my writing. Luke and Kevin, with their humor and light-heartedness as well as the many beautifully prepared meals, particularly by our nutritionist, Luke, always helped me to switch off. Alan, as always, has been more supportive than I can ever explain. He has accompanied me to many destinations from New Zealand to Germany, a ski resort in Austria, a monastery in Spain, the hills of Tuscany, Sicily, Florence, and Rome in Italy, to Chamonix as well as around Nice in France, to Los Angeles and San Francisco in the USA, to Budapest in Hungary, to Stockholm and Lingköping in Sweden, or to Aarhus and Aalborg in Denmark, all the while bearing with me as I was trying to write this book. He sought out hotels that allowed me to continue my writing and has been the kindest companion, who only once stopped me from finishing a section. This was in San Sebastián, where I was typing away, while he had been out and around town. When he came back to the hotel, I was still typing away, but he looked at me earnestly and requested I stop writing and have a look at the beautiful city. How right he was! We had an unforgettable afternoon and evening in San Sebastián and when we left the next morning, I was still happy that I had not finished the section. Now, whenever I come across the section that I did not finish in San Sebastián, I remember our wonderful time there. But this is only one beautiful memory during my book-writing travels and for me, Alan is visible in many parts of this book and I dedicate this book to him.

While so many people have had an impact upon my writing of this book, all shortcomings, of course, are my very own. I do hope that the book will be useful to many students, teachers, and researchers alike and I hope you will enjoy the many examples and forgive the shortcomings.

About the Companion Website

This book is accompanied by a companion website:

www.wiley.com/go/Norris/multimodal-data

The website includes:

- Videos
- Transcript

Chapter 1

Introduction

1.0

Introduction to the Book

Multimodal discourse analysis is an area of research that is becoming more and more widely used in applied linguistics, sociolinguistics, education, psychology, anthropology, business and other applied social sciences. There are a number of multimodal approaches that have sprouted up over the past 20 years (Bateman 2008; Forceville 1994; Jewitt 2002; Kress and van Leeuwen 1996, 1998, 2001; van Leeuwen 1999; Mondada 2006; Norris 2002a, 2004a; O'Halloran 1999; O'Toole 1994; Scollon 1998, 2001a, b; Stöckl 2001). Yet, Multimodal (Inter)action Analysis (Norris 2002a, 2004a, 2011a, 2013a) is the only interdisciplinary approach that has been developed specifically for the analysis of multimodal action and interaction. In this approach, emphasis is placed upon the actions that people take as opposed to the language plus particular non-verbal movements that they produce (Goodwin 1981; Mondada 2014; Scollon 1979), the cognitive work that they do (Anderson 1990; Collins and Quillian 1969; Fodor 1975; Kintsch 1988; Newell and Simon 1976; Tulving 1983) or the psychological expressions that they display (Ekman 1979; Ekman and Friesen 1969). Actions, of course, are embodied *and* cognitive, psychological *and* performed with language plus non-verbal movements. In fact, all of the components, the verbal, non-verbal, environmental, cognitive, and psychological come together in our approach to analyzing multimodal (inter)action (Norris 2013a, b). Through systematic analysis of actions and interactions, this approach allows us to gain new insight into human action and interaction in a holistic and comprehensive way, and this book demonstrates how to engage in systematic analysis of multimodal (inter)actions.

What This Book is About

This book illustrates the phases and steps used when engaging in a Multimodal (Inter)action Analysis. The Step-by-Step process outlined here is a guide that shows how you can systematically work with multimodal data. This systematic guide consists of five phases, four of which consist of a number of steps each and one of which consist of a great number of analytical tools. The book emphasizes our working with video data. However, multimodal (inter)action analysts also use this process when working with different kinds of data that include but are not limited to video data. This is shown to some extent in the chapter sections that demonstrate how to use the Step-by-Step guide with examples from an experimental study and a video ethnography. However,

Systematically Working with Multimodal Data: Research Methods in Multimodal Discourse Analysis,
First Edition. Sigrid Norris.
© 2019 John Wiley & Sons, Inc. Published 2019 by John Wiley & Sons, Inc.
Companion website: www.wiley.com/go/Norris/multimodal-data

because this book focuses upon video data and the holistic ways to analyze it, other data such as interviews or observational notes may be alluded to, but not worked with here in detail. However, it is important to note that for us, observational notes, text messages, emails, interviews, and diary entries also often are a part of the data collected and analyzed. But now, let us turn to what this book is about.

This book is written for undergraduate and graduate students as well as for emergent and established researchers wishing to engage in multimodal discourse analysis in a theoretically founded and interdisciplinary manner, integrating the verbal and non-verbal with object use and the embeddedness of people with the environment. Some sections of chapters are more geared towards undergraduate students, while other sections of chapters are more useful for Masters students, and again other sections are particularly important for PhD students and researchers wanting to engage in video ethnography. Some chapter sections are absolutely necessary to read for all readers, while other chapter sections are focused to this or that readership. Here, I would like to allude the reader to what is most necessary to engage in for whom to make reading choices and reading assignments easier and clearer for teachers and students alike. The gray boxes contain notes which give a quick overview of which chapters and sections are useful for whom and what to expect to find in them.

Systematically Working with Video Data: Phases I–V

Chapter 1: Systematically Working with Multimodal Data: Introduction

Note 1
Chapter 1 is a useful read, but *not a must-read for undergraduate or graduate* students starting out to learn how to conduct a multimodal discourse analysis. PhD students will definitely want to read Chapter 1.1.

Note 2
Chapter 1 introduces the reader to the book overall, presents a chapter-by-chapter outline, and offers the keen reader a vast amount of references in some of its paragraphs. Without going into too much detail, these references can be used as a guide to delve deeper into the background literature alluded to here.

Chapter 1, besides first giving a brief overview of what you can find in the chapters to come, quickly sums up other multimodal research areas and the literature background of Multimodal (Inter)action Analysis. Here, you will find an abundant amount of literature referenced and the deliberate reader may want to read some of the texts referred to here. The literature, although quite vast in these paragraphs, is not meant to be comprehensive. Other books and online references are a better place for comprehensive literature reviews (Norris 2015 a–e; Pirini 2017). Also, you will not find me lingering on what has been said or done in many of the referenced texts. Rather, I allude to them in order to lead you to other work if you are inclined to move deeper into the multimodality literature. Here, I wish to demonstrate some of the vastness that already exists in this area of relatively new research and guide the careful reader to see differences as well as similarities. When differences are pointed out, the reader needs to understand that differences are not negative, but rather simply developments from different theoretical thought. In fact, no method, including the one outlined in detail in this book, is perfect. No methods can analyze everything, and no method is necessarily better than another. Methods are tools and, just as you will use a different set of tools when you are working with jewelry than when you are building a house, you will use different tools to understand multimodal action and interaction than you will if you are interested in studying text-image relations. Just as jewelry tools are not better than tools that help you build a house, so are tools to study multimodal actions and interactions not better than tools that allow you to examine text-image relations. What is important is to use the right tools for what you intend to do. You will not do well with working on jewelry if you are using tools that are made to build a house. Similarly, you will lack ability to study human actions and interactions if you are using the tools made to study text-image relations. This book is about the tools that help you study the multimodality of human actions and interactions. Specifically, Chapter 2 guides you to first understand the theoretical thought behind why we think of multimodal action and interaction in the way outlined in this text.

Chapter 2: Philosophical and Theoretical Background

Note 3
Chapter 2 is an *absolute must-read for all instructors, PhD students and researchers particularly up to (and including) the part on the site of engagement.*

Note 4
The sections about the development of Scollon's philosophical thought are offered for the keen reader, who is inclined to wanting to know more about the origin of some of the philosophical and theoretical thoughts underpinning this book. This is not a must-read for undergraduate or Masters-level students, but useful for PhD-level students.

Note 5
Chapter 2 provides the theoretical underpinning for all to be learned in chapters to come. Without this theoretical understanding (up to and including the section on the site of engagement), the rest of the book will make relatively little sense, since all phases and steps outlined in the chapters to come build upon the philosophical and theoretical background offered in Chapter 2.

In Chapter 2, you find the philosophical underpinnings, which are the primacy of perception and the primacy of embodiment. Then, you find the theoretical underpinnings, the principle of social actions and the two sub-principles of communication and history, and an explanation of how the principle and sub-principles fit together. Besides the principles that underpin everything written in this book, Chapter 2 offers some basic theoretical concepts and links these to perception and embodiment. For example, here you find the definition and deep explanation of the unit of analysis, the mediated action. The mediated action, as you will see, consists of social actors (usually human beings) and mediational means/cultural tools (usually things, the environment, body parts, emotion, or knowledge). But of course, we can also have non-human actors. Just think of your dog or cat, and you can see how we could possibly see a pet as acting in similar ways as humans in our socialized world. But just as a dog may be thought of as a social actor, a human being can be thought of as a mediational means (just think of a translator). The chapter goes into quite some detail to demonstrate how our thoughts are theoretically founded. But of course, any social action is always mediated in multiple ways, i.e. any social action is a mediated action (just think of reading these pages and you will see that it is mediated by the written word, your knowledge of the English language, the book or screen, your eyes, to mention a few). Chapter 2 then discusses particular mediated actions, units that help us analyze people's actions and interactions in great detail. Here, you find sections on the lower-level mediated action, the higher-level mediated action, and the frozen mediated action. Each time, the various mediated actions are linked to perception and embodiment in order not to lose sight of our philosophical underpinnings. Then, Chapter 2 moves on to discuss practices and discourse, demonstrating that we do not only wish to work in micro analyses, but rather wish to produce links to intermediate and macro analyses. Again, you will find the links to perception and embodiment here. Once you have learned about practices and discourses, it is time for you to learn about the site of engagement, the window opened up by practices and discourses that make concrete mediated actions possible. After links for the site of engagement to perception and embodiment have been established, Chapter 2 delves deeper into previous thought on which this book rests. There, you can read about Scollon's development of thought. You can find out how Scollon referenced Vygotsky (a Russian social psychologist) and Nishida (a Japanese philosopher), and how Scollon's theory came about. This section is meant for the excited reader, who wishes to gain insight into how scholars develop their own thinking. However, this is not a section that is a must-read in order to understand the phases and steps demonstrated in later chapters. Throughout, Chapter 2 provides the reader with definitions, notes, and discussion points and at the end, Chapter 2 offers a summary and a section on things to remember. In Chapter 3, quite different from Chapters 1 and 2, you will find much less referencing. This is where the Step-by-Step process of systematically working with multimodal data begins, and this process has been developed by myself and is first outlined and demonstrated in detail in this very book.

Chapter 3: Systematically Working with Multimodal Data Phase I

In Chapter 3, we move into the nitty-gritty of systematically working with multimodal data, beginning with the 10 steps of Phase I. Chapter 3 is divided into four sections: Chapters 3.0, 3.1, 3.2, and 3.3. Chapter 3.0 is the most important part of the chapter, and the part that all students and researchers should read. Chapters 3.1, 3.2, and 3.3 cater to specific readers, so that Chapters 3.0 and 3.1 are particularly useful for undergraduate classes, Chapters 3.0 and 3.2 are particularly useful for Masters-level classes and research projects, and Chapters 3.0 and 3.3 are particularly useful for PhD seminars and PhD theses development. Chapters 3.0 and 3.2 or Chapters 3.0 and 3.3 are also useful for small to medium-sized research teams in which graduate students (Masters and/or PhD level) are involved.

Below, I outline each section of Chapter 3 in order to clarify the intended readership for each section and to foreshadow what can be expected in the individual sections.

Chapter 3.0: Phase I: Data Collection

Note 6
Chapter 3.0 is an *absolute must-read for all.*

Note 7
In Chapter 3.0, the reader is introduced to Phase I of systematically working with multimodal data. PHASE I is all about DATA COLLECTION and consists of 10 steps that the student researcher engages in consecutively. Twenty-nine tasks guide the class or researcher to proceed with thinking through and engaging in data collection in a systematic manner.

In Chapter 3.0, the student learns about data collection from developing a research topic and research questions to considering what we actually can call data. The chapter addresses aspects such as what we call naturally occurring data, discussing the observers' paradox (Labov 2006), and goes into some detail on ethical considerations that researchers and student researchers need to think about before setting out on data collection (Norris et al. 2014; Pirini et al. 2014). The chapter elucidates where to best place a video recorder, how to video record in practical situations, discusses the taking of field or observational notes and the interviewing of participants. Even though the book only touches upon these different kinds of data that can (and often will) be collected and primarily focuses upon how to analyze multimodal video data, the reader is every so often reminded that there are more data sources than simply video data. In order to help in data collection, it is explained in Chapter 3 how to best produce a data collection table that does not give too much information but does give us the information that is necessary about the collection of data. Further, the chapter illustrates how to keep track of camera, researcher and participant positions during video recording. Lastly, the chapter gives information on how to begin working with the video recorded material by collating multiple camera views (when used) and time-stamping the collated video in the left top corner.

Chapter 3.1: Systematically Working with Small Data Sets/Data Pieces: Phase I

Note 8
Chapter 3.1 is useful for all, but an *absolute must-read for undergraduate students.*

Note 9
Chapter 3.1 demonstrates with an example taken from YouTube how to proceed using the steps of Phase I outlined in Chapter 3.0. Chapter 3.1 guides the reader through actual data collection for a classroom project. With 14 tasks, the reader can easily follow the Step-by-Step process, moving straight into their own multimodal discourse analysis.

Chapter 3.1 offers the reader an example of how to utilize the steps of Phase I by explicating each individual step with an example found on YouTube. Here, the reader is shown exactly how a student may identify a theme or topic and develop research questions. The reader is guided to consider the notion of what data actually is, and when or in what ways, data is naturally occurring or not. With the practical YouTube example, Section 3.1 then discusses the notion of ethics, video recording and camera placement, the collecting of data and taking observational notes, and production of a data collection table with all the significant information without showing too much extraneous information. Section 3.1 then proceeds with the Step-by-Step process and the student researcher learns to consider themselves in relation to the YouTube video. With 14 tasks throughout this section, Chapter 3.1 in connection with the previous Section 3.0 is a useful teaching and learning tool that guides the reader through the data collection process of Phase I.

Chapter 3.2: Systematically Working with Medium-Sized Data Sets: Phase I

Note 10
Chapter 3.2 is useful for all, but an *absolute must-read for Masters-level graduate students.*

Note 11
Chapter 3.2 uses an example of an experimental study to practically demonstrate how to proceed using the steps of Phase I outlined in Chapter 3.0. Chapter 3.2 guides the reader through actual data collection for a medium-sized research project. Following this example and the 10 tasks provided, the reader can use the Step-by-Step process, moving straight into their own multimodal discourse analysis for a Masters research project.

Chapter 3.2 offers the reader an example of how to utilize the steps of Phase I by explicating each individual step with an example from an experimental study. Here, the reader is shown exactly how a graduate student may identify a theme or topic for a Masters research paper and develop research questions. The reader is guided to consider the notion of what data is, and when or in what ways, data is naturally occurring. With the practical example from an experimental study, Section 3.2 then discusses the notion of ethics, video recording and camera placement, the collecting of data and taking observational notes, and the production of a data collection table with all the significant information without giving extraneous information. Section 3.2 then proceeds with the Step-by-Step process and the student researcher learns to consider themselves in relation to the data. With 10 tasks throughout this section, Chapter 3.2 in connection with

the previous Section 3.0 is a useful teaching and learning tool that guides the graduate reader through the data collection process of Phase I.

Chapter 3.3: Systematically Working with Large Data Sets: Phase I

Note 12
Chapter 3.3 is useful for all, but an *absolute must-read for PhD students and researchers interested in conducting a video ethnography.*

Note 13
Chapter 3.3 uses an example of a video ethnography to practically demonstrate how to proceed using the steps of Phase I outlined in Chapter 3.0. Chapter 3.3 guides the emergent researcher through actual data collection for a large sized research project. Following this example and the 10 tasks provided, the reader can use the Step-by-Step process of Phase I, moving straight into their own multimodal discourse analysis for a PhD research project.

Chapter 3.3 offers the reader an example of how to utilize the steps of Phase I by explicating each individual step with an example from a video ethnographic study. Here, the reader is shown how a PhD student may identify a theme or topic for a PhD project and develop research questions. The reader is guided to consider the notion of what data is and when, or in what ways, data is naturally occurring. With the practical example from a video ethnographic study, Section 3.3 discusses the notion of ethics, video recording and camera placement, the collecting of data and taking observational notes, and the production of a data collection table with all the significant information without giving extraneous information. Section 3.3 then proceeds with the Step-by-Step process and the emergent researcher learns to consider themselves in relation to the data. With 10 tasks throughout this section, Chapter 3.3 in connection with the previous Section 3.0 is a useful teaching and learning tool that guides the PhD student and scholar through the data collection process of Phase I.

Chapter 4: Systematically Working with Video Data Phase II

In Chapter 4, we continue with the nitty-gritty of systematically working with multimodal data with Phase II. In this chapter, Phase II with its five steps is outlined in detail. Chapter 4 is divided into four sections: Chapters 4.0, 4.1, 4.2, and 4.3. As in Chapter 3, the beginning of the chapter, Chapter 4.0, is the most important part, and the part that all students and researchers should read. Chapters 4.1, 4.2, and 4.3 are continuations of the examples given in the previous chapter. Here too, these sections cater to specific readers, so that Chapters 4.0 and 4.1 are particularly useful for undergraduate classes, Chapters 4.0 and 4.2 are particularly useful for Masters-level classes and research projects, and Chapters 4.0 and 4.3 are particularly useful for PhD seminars and PhD theses development and scholars wishing to engage in video ethnography. Chapters 4.0 and 4.2 or Chapters 4.0 and 4.3 are also useful for small to medium-sized research teams in which graduate students (Masters and/or PhD level) are involved.

Below, I outline each section of Chapter 4 in order to clarify the intended readership for each section and to foreshadow what can be expected in the individual sections.

Chapter 4.0: Phase II: Delineating the Data

Note 14
Chapter 4.0 is an *absolute must-read for all.*

Note 15
In Chapter 4.0, the reader is introduced to Phase II of systematically working with multimodal data. PHASE II is all about DELINEATING THE DATA and consists of five steps that the student researcher engages in consecutively. Seven tasks guide the class or researcher to proceed with thinking through the delineation of data in a systematic manner.

In Chapter 4.0, the student or researcher learns how to understand and delineate the data. In order to do this in a systematic manner, the reader is guided to first identify a data set, developing a data set table. This data set table embraces other information than the data collection table produced in Phase I. Next, the student is guided in thinking through their own positioning in relation to the data set. Here, a first (overtly) theoretical notion, the site of engagement, is utilized. The following step focuses the student upon a particular data piece and the step right after this, again makes researcher-presence overt by utilizing the tool used previously, the site of engagement. Since, in this approach, we want to work in a data driven manner, the reader is then taught to reformulate a new research question that embraces the data, rather than the one that drove data collection in the previous phase. Phase II is complete once this reformulation has taken place.

Chapter 4.1: Systematically Working with Small Data Sets/Data Pieces: Phase II

Note 16
Chapter 4.1 is useful for all, but an *absolute must-read for undergraduate students.*

Note 17
Chapter 4.1 demonstrates with an example taken from YouTube how to proceed using the steps of Phase II outlined in Chapter 4.0. Chapter 4.1 guides the reader through the delineation of data for a classroom project. With nine tasks, the reader can easily follow the Step-by-Step process, continuing their own multimodal discourse analysis.

Chapter 4.1 is the direct continuation of Chapter 3.1. Chapter 4.1 offers the reader an example of how to utilize the steps of Phase II by explicating each individual step with the YouTube example used in the previous chapter. Here, the reader is shown exactly how a student may delineate their collected data by first identifying the data set, then understanding the site of engagement that includes the student researcher and the data set, before identifying a data piece and the student researcher in relation to the data

piece. Utilizing the theoretical notion of the site of engagement demonstrates the usefulness of the conceptualization and helps the student to understand the practical side of utilizing theoretical tools to analyze data. In the last step of Phase II, the student learns to formulate a new research question. This research question, different from the ones that drove data collection, will enable the student to proceed with data analysis in a data driven manner.

Chapter 4.2: Systematically Working with Medium-Sized Data Sets: Phase II

Note 18
Chapter 4.2 is useful for all, but an *absolute must-read for Masters-level graduate students*.

Note 19
Chapter 4.2 demonstrates with an example taken from the experimental study how to proceed using the steps of Phase II outlined in Chapter 4.0. Chapter 4.1 guides the reader through the delineation of data for a Masters-level project. With ten tasks, the reader can easily follow the Step-by-Step process, continuing their own multimodal discourse analysis.

Chapter 4.2 is the direct continuation of Chapter 3.2. Chapter 4.2 offers the reader an example of how to utilize the steps of Phase II by explicating each individual step with the experimental study example used in the previous chapter. Here, the reader is shown exactly how a graduate student may delineate their collected data by first identifying the data set, then understanding the site of engagement that includes the student researcher and the data set, before identifying a data piece and the student researcher in relation to the data piece. Utilizing the theoretical notion of the site of engagement demonstrates the usefulness of the conceptualization and helps the student to understand the practical side of utilizing theoretical tools to analyze data. In the last step of Phase II, the student learns to formulate new research questions. These research questions, different from the ones that drove data collection, will enable the student to proceed with data analysis in a data driven manner.

Chapter 4.3: Systematically Working with Large Data Sets: Phase II

Note 20
Chapter 4.3 is useful for all, but an *absolute must-read for PhD students and researchers interested in conducting a video ethnography*.

Note 21
Chapter 4.3 demonstrates with an example taken from the video ethnographic study how to proceed using the steps of Phase II outlined in Chapter 4.0. Chapter 4.3 guides the reader through the delineation of data for a PhD project. With nine tasks, the reader can easily follow the Step-by-Step process, continuing their own multimodal discourse analysis.

Chapter 4.3 is the direct continuation of Chapter 3.3. Chapter 4.3 offers the reader an example of how to utilize the steps of Phase II by explicating each individual step with the video ethnographic study used in the previous chapter. Here, the reader is shown exactly how a PhD student may delineate their collected data by first identifying the data set, then understanding the site of engagement that includes the emergent researcher and the data set, before identifying a data piece and the researcher in relation to the data piece. Utilizing the theoretical notion of the site of engagement demonstrates the usefulness of the conceptualization and helps the researcher to understand the practical side of utilizing theoretical tools to analyze data. In the last step of Phase II, the researcher learns to formulate new research questions. These research questions, different from the ones that drove data collection, will enable the researcher to proceed with data analysis in a data driven manner.

It is noteworthy here, that Phase II could easily become the first phase for those who already have collected data and have not used Phase I before and during data collection. This really is not a problem because the phases are only guides, not strict ways of working. While it may be easier and highly fruitful to work through all phases and steps (particularly for classroom use, a Masters or PhD thesis), researchers can also utilize the phases that are useful to them and leave out other phases. More important, however, is to point out that the larger the project, the less organized the phases and steps will be. Often, a large project begins and Phase I is utilized. But as the project continues, some data moves forward through other phases while data collection continues. Thus, what we find in a large project is that the phases are still separate, but they overlap as we work through the various collected data pieces and sets.

Chapter 5: Systematically Working with Video Data Phase III

Chapter 5.0: Phase III: Selecting Data Pieces for Micro analysis

Note 22
Chapter 5.0 is an *absolute must-read for all*.

Note 23
In Chapter 5.0, the reader is introduced to Phase III of systematically working with multimodal data. PHASE III is all about SELECTING DATA PIECES FOR MICRO ANALYSIS and consists of four steps that the student or researcher engages in consecutively. Six tasks guide the class to proceed with thinking through selecting a data piece for micro analysis in a systematic manner.

In Chapter 5.0, the student or researcher learns how to select a data piece for micro analysis. In order to do this in a systematic manner, the student is guided to first rephrase the general data driven research question developed in the last step of Phase II into a mediated action. Here, the reader is guided to utilize the theoretical framework to think through data. Then, the reader learns how to demarcate higher-level mediated actions and how to produce a higher-level mediated action table of the collected data.

In the next step, the reader learns to bundle higher-level mediated actions before narrowing the site of engagement. Here, the site of engagement, which was used in earlier steps to overtly illustrate the researcher in relation to the data set and data pieces, is utilized in order to narrow our view to a particular higher-level mediated action that is systematically selected for micro analysis.

Chapter 5.1: Systematically Working with Small Data Sets/Data Pieces: Phase III

Note 24
Chapter 5.1 is useful for all, but an *absolute must-read for undergraduate students*.

Note 25
Chapter 5.1 demonstrates with our example taken from YouTube how to proceed using the steps of Phase III outlined in Chapter 5.0. Chapter 5.1 guides the reader through the selection of data pieces for micro analysis for a classroom project. With seven tasks, the reader can easily follow the Step-by-Step process, continuing their own multimodal discourse analysis.

Chapter 5.1 is the direct continuation of Chapters 3.1 and 4.1. Chapter 5.1 offers the reader an example of how to utilize the steps of Phase III by explicating each individual step with the YouTube example used in the previous chapters. Here, the reader is shown exactly how a student may work with their data in order to systematically select data pieces for micro analysis. First, the student learns to rephrase the data driven research question developed in the last step of Phase II into a mediated action. This is an important step that then allows the student to work in a theoretically founded manner to select data pieces for micro analysis. The student then is walked through an excerpt of the YouTube clip to practically show how to demarcate higher-level mediated actions and how to develop a higher-level mediated action table. Here, the student is given a correct and an incorrect example. Both examples of higher-level mediated action tables, the correct and the incorrect one, are useful for the teaching and learning of what is needed here. In fact, if a student works in too detailed a manner in this Phase, the student will lose sight of what is important and easily get lost in their data. Thus, the correct way of working here, will determine a positive or a negative outcome for a later analysis. Once this point is understood, the student is walked through the development of a bundled higher-level mediated action table, and then is shown how to utilize the site of engagement, a concept used previously, in order to narrow our view to a specific higher-level mediated action for micro analysis.

Chapter 5.2: Systematically Working with Medium-Sized Data Sets: Phase III

Note 26
Chapter 5.2 is useful for all, but an *absolute must-read for Masters-level graduate students*.

> **Note 27**
>
> Chapter 5.2 demonstrates with our experimental study example how to proceed using the steps of Phase III outlined in Chapter 5.0. Chapter 5.2 guides the reader through the selection of data pieces for micro analysis for a Masters-sized project. With six tasks, the reader can easily follow the Step-by-Step process, continuing their own multimodal discourse analysis.

Chapter 5.2 is the direct continuation of Chapters 3.2 and 4.2. Chapter 5.2 offers the reader an example of how to utilize the steps of Phase III by explicating each individual step with an example of the experimental study used in the previous chapters. Here, the reader is shown exactly how a student researcher may work with their data in order to systematically select data pieces for micro analysis. First, the student researcher learns to rephrase the data driven research question developed in the last step of Phase II into a mediated action. This is an important step that then allows the student researcher to work in a theoretically founded manner to select data pieces for micro analysis. The student researcher then is walked through an excerpt of the experimental study to practically show how to demarcate higher-level mediated actions and how to develop a higher-level mediated action table. Here, the student researcher is given a correct and an incorrect example. Both examples of higher-level mediated action tables, the correct and the incorrect one, are useful for the teaching and learning of what is needed here. In fact, if a student researcher works in too detailed a manner in this phase, they will lose sight of what is important and easily get lost in their data. Thus, the correct way of working here, will determine a positive or a negative outcome for a later analysis. Once this point is understood, the student researcher is walked through the development of a bundled higher-level mediated action table, and then is shown how to utilize the site of engagement, a concept used previously, in order to narrow our view to a specific higher-level mediated action for micro analysis.

Chapter 5.3: Systematically Working with Large Data Sets: Phase III

> **Note 28**
>
> Chapter 5.3 is useful for all, but an *absolute must-read for PhD students and researchers interested in conducting a video ethnography.*

> **Note 29**
>
> Chapter 5.3 demonstrates with our video ethnographic study example how to proceed using the steps of Phase III outlined in Chapter 5.0. Chapter 5.3 guides the reader through the selection of data pieces for micro analysis for a PhD-sized project. With seven tasks, the reader can easily follow the Step-by-Step process, continuing their own multimodal discourse analysis.

Chapter 5.3 is the direct continuation of Chapters 3.3 and 4.3. Chapter 5.3 offers the reader an example of how to utilize the steps of Phase III by explicating each individual step with an example of the video ethnographic study used in the previous chapters. Here, the reader is shown exactly how a researcher may work with their data in order to systematically select data pieces for micro analysis. First, the researcher learns to rephrase the data driven research question developed in the last step of Phase II into a mediated action. This is an important step that then allows the researcher to work in a theoretically founded manner to select data pieces for micro analysis. The researcher then is walked through an excerpt of the video ethnographic study to practically show how to demarcate higher-level mediated actions and how to develop a higher-level mediated action table. Here, the researcher is given a correct and an incorrect example. Both examples of higher-level mediated action tables, the correct and the incorrect one, are useful for the teaching and learning of what is needed here. In fact, if a researcher works in too detailed a manner in this phase, the researcher will lose sight of what is important and easily get lost in their data. This is true for all multimodal analyses using this Step-by-Step process, but it is particularly important when working with large data sets. Thus, the correct way of working here, will determine a positive or a negative outcome for a later analysis. Once this point is understood, the researcher is walked through the development of a bundled higher-level mediated action table, and then is shown how to utilize the site of engagement, a concept used previously, in order to narrow our view to a specific higher-level mediated action for micro analysis.

Chapter 6: Systematically Working with Video Data Phase IV

Note 30
Chapter 6 is an *absolute must-read for all*.

Note 31
In Chapter 6, the reader is introduced to Phase IV of systematically working with multimodal data. PHASE IV is all about MULTIMODAL TRANSCRIPTION and consists of 11 steps that the students and researchers engage in consecutively. 29 tasks guide the class or the researcher to proceed with thinking through producing multimodal transcripts.

Phase IV: Transcribing Data Using Multimodal Transcription Conventions
In Chapter 6, the student learns how to develop multimodal transcripts, using multimodal transcription conventions. In the first step of Phase IV, the student learns to identify a mode. Here, the theoretical concept of mode is discussed, linked to lower-level mediated actions and to the notions of perception and embodiment. Here too, the student learns the connection between modes and transcription conventions outlined in this chapter. Including theoretical discussion, the reader begins to learn about transcription conventions throughout the chapter. Here, the researcher begins by examining the mode of layout. As an example, we examine the YouTube clip that we have been working with in Chapters 3.1, 4.1, and 5.1. However, the reader is here not expected to necessarily have worked with those sections. Rather, a reader who has been working with Sections 3.2, 4.2, and 5.2, just as a reader who has been working with Sections 3.3, 4.3, and 5.3, will be able to work with this example without having to refer to earlier discussions of this video clip. Here, the importance is to examine the mode of layout and to think

through how to best transcribe this in a systematic manner. Just as this YouTube example can be used as a one-off example, so can the other examples, some of which are taken from the Experimental study and some of which are taken from the video ethnographic study. Chapter 6 is special in the respect that various examples are given as one-off examples in order to learn transcription conventions. All videos of the examples used here can be found online and utilized to teach and learn transcription conventions. After the mode of layout, the reader learns to transcribe the modes of proxemics, posture, gesture, gaze, head movement, facial expression, object handling, and language. Finally, the reader learns how to put individual transcripts together in order to produce one final transcript. Only once a researcher has learned the transcription conventions, can they move on to use the conventions to analyze the higher-level action selected in Phase III Step 4. Here, it becomes very clear that transcription in this multimodal framework is analysis. Thus, it is of utmost importance to carefully transcribe, and to be careful to note down what and how we transcribe our data. As the reader will see once again in this chapter, the notion of mode is a theoretical concept that constantly has to be defined and re-defined. This means, that there in fact is *not* one way to transcribe a mode. Rather, there is only one way to transcribe a mode *defined in a certain and very clear manner*.

Chapter 7: Systematically Working with Multimodal Data Phase V

Note 32
Chapter 7 is an *absolute must-read for all*, but instructors may want to focus undergraduate students on particular analytical tools.

Note 33
In Chapter 7, the reader is introduced to Phase V of systematically working with multimodal data. PHASE V is all about ANALYTICAL TOOLS, how to use them and what to use them for and consists of four steps, seven analytical tools for micro analysis, and three analytical tools or tool sets that allow placing micro analytical findings into a larger perspective. 48 tasks guide the class or researcher to conduct analyses.

Phase V: Using Analytical Tools

In Chapter 7, the student learns how to utilize analytical tools. In the first step of Phase V, the student learns about the various analytical tools for micro analysis offered in this book. Here, seven analytical tools are explained in detail and then it is discussed how the analytical tools are linked to the concepts of perception and embodiment. In Step 2, the student learns to select analytical tools by honing in on exactly what can be learned from utilizing each of the seven analytical tools for micro analysis. Through practical examples and tasks, the student is guided to think through their data and the tools applicable to examine what they wish to examine. In Step 3, the student learns about two analytical tools and one analytical tool set that enable them to place their micro analytical findings into a larger perspective. Here, again, each tool or tool set is related to the concepts of perception and embodiment. In Step 4, the student is guided to think through the tools or tool sets in practical terms, helping them to make an informed choice as to which tools will allow them to gain the most interesting insight into their own data.

Chapter 8: Systematically Working with Multimodal Data

Note 34
Chapter 8 is particularly useful for instructors of different levels of classes.

A Quick Guide for Instructors

Chapter 8 presents suggestions for teachers of different levels of classes in separate sections. Thus, the undergraduate instructor can easily read how the book could be used; the Masters-level teacher can find ways of using the book in graduate school; similarly, the PhD seminar instructor can find suggestions of using the book. However, these are just some suggestions, and the book can be used in many different ways and also lends itself for self-study.

How to Use This Book

This book has been written for various audiences:

1) The upper undergraduate and postgraduate classroom where Multimodal (Inter) action Analysis is taught;
2) Masters-level and PhD-level research students and research teams that wish to engage in experimental studies; and
3) PhD-level research students and research teams that wish to engage in video ethnographic studies.

The introduction (Chapter 1), the philosophical and theoretical background (Chapter 2), the chapter outlining transcription conventions (Chapter 6), as well as all first sections in each Chapter (Sections 3.0, 4.0, and 5.0) will be useful for all students and researchers, who would like to work in this systematic way of conducting a multimodal discourse analysis.

For the undergraduate classroom, Chapter Sections 3.1, 4.1, and 5.1 will be most suitable. Here, the systematic way of working with multimodal data is explicated with a short video available on YouTube. Tasks throughout these sections will guide both teacher and learner, offering an easy-to-follow example for classroom use.

For the Masters research student, the PhD student, or the research team that sets out to collect and analyze experimental data, Sections 3.2, 4.2, and 5.2 will be most useful. In these sections, the systematic way of working with multimodal data is illustrated with an example from an experimental study of dyads working on tasks together via Skype. The tasks throughout these sections offer ways to develop and analyze an experimental study.

For PhD students and research teams that wish to engage in video ethnographic studies, Sections 3.3, 4.3, and 5.3 will be most suitable. Here, the book offers insight into developing an ethnographic study, collecting video ethnographic data, and illustrating how to systematically work with video ethnographic data with an example from a video ethnography of 17 New Zealand families (inter)acting with far-away family members via video conferencing technology. Here, tasks lead the way to a productive engagement with the text.

However, while the various sections are particularly relevant for specific audiences, when readers engage with all sections, the book facilitates greater understanding of how one systematically works with various kinds of multimodal data. While the reader will find some necessary redundancy, when proceeding to read the entire book, the reader will realize that the phases and steps outlined here achieve two important objectives:

1) The phases and steps allow for a systematic way to analyze complex multimodal data sets of any kind and any size; and
2) The phases and steps allow for the analysis of a great variety of data without structuring what can be analyzed or what can be discovered.

1.1

Brief Introduction to Multimodal Discourse Analysis

Section 1.1 offers a glimpse of research conducted in multimodal discourse analysis and related fields relevant for multimodal discourse analysis. Upfront, it is noteworthy to say that this brief introduction is by no means a comprehensive introduction, nor is it a true literature review. A literature review has no place in this book, which focuses upon how to conduct Multimodal (Inter)action Analysis in a systematic and replicable manner. Rather, this section very briefly introduces the reader to frameworks relevant to or related to multimodal discourse analysis and showcases some literature to indicate the vastness of the field on the one hand and to frame the book on the other hand. Further, this section very briefly introduces the reader to literature that underpins the framework offered in detail in the coming chapters. Most importantly is the fact that many references are alluded to so that the keen reader can follow some of the ones of most interest for their own studies. This section will be most useful for the PhD student and the researcher using the framework outlined in subsequent chapters. While it may be good to read this at the beginning, the tasks will illustrate that this section of Chapter 1.1 again will be of use to scholars after having conducted their project using the phases and steps outlined further in the book. The book begins by examining some of what other researchers, who are *not* working within the framework offered in this book, are looking at.

Multimodal Discourse Analysis: Some Other Research

Much research in multimodality from early on has examined texts or images or images in relation to texts (Baldry 2004; Bateman 2008; Forceville 1994; Kress 1993; Kress and van Leeuwen 1996, 1998, 2001; O'Halloran 1999; Royce 1998). This interest in texts and images continues to this day and research in this area has grown immensely (Bowcher et al. 2013; Djonov and van Leeuwen 2011a, b, 2013; Jones 2014; König and Lick 2014; Maier et al. 2007; Margolis 1999; Martinec 1998; McCloud 1993; Pahl 2007; Stöckl, 2001, 2005). But there has also been an interest in the study of art or three-dimensional space (Abousnnouga and Machin 2010; Al Zidjaly 2011a, b; Hofinger and Ventola 2004; O'Toole 1994, 2004; Stenglin 2009; Stöckl 2005; Ventola 2004). Similarly, a great interest in the moving image has emerged (Bateman and Schmidt 2014; Iedema 2003; Maier 2012; Metz 1974; Weis and Belton 1985; Wildfeuer 2012). Just as interest in music and

Systematically Working with Multimodal Data: Research Methods in Multimodal Discourse Analysis,
First Edition. Sigrid Norris.
© 2019 John Wiley & Sons, Inc. Published 2019 by John Wiley & Sons, Inc.
Companion website: www.wiley.com/go/Norris/multimodal-data

other semiotic modes such as color is growing, we are seeing an increase in the study of the online dimension (Djonov and van Leeuwen 2011a, b; Jones 2009; Kress and van Leeuwen 2002; Machin 2013; O'Halloran 2007; O'Halloran et al. 2012; Rowsell et al. 2013; Unger-Hamilton et al. 1979; Van Leeuwen 1999). Much of this work (Jewitt 2002, 2008, 2009; Jewitt and Oyama, 2001) related to images and texts originated from theoretical thoughts developed by Halliday (1973, 1974, 1978, 1985) and was continued by Kress (1993, 2000, 2005, 2009), Kress et al. (2001), Kress and Van Leeuwen (1996, 2001), and Van Leeuwen (1983, 1984, 2005, 2009). While the area of multimodal research stemming from the work of Halliday is focused upon texts and images, there is also quite a body of work stemming from conversation analysis and other discourse analytical frameworks and related areas emerging (Ferre 2014; Fox and Artemeva 2011; Haddington et al. 2013; Kastberg 2007; Kusmierczyk 2013; Mondada 2006, 2014, 2017; Müller et al. 2013; Tapio 2014; Whalen et al. unpublished manuscript, 2002; Zemel and Koschmann 2014). The area of research that this book belongs to is quite differently focused upon the study of human action and interaction.

Task 1: For PhD Students and Researchers

Of course, you will have done a literature review in order to find that the framework outlined in this book is useful. But once you have conducted your study and are writing up your findings after having completed all phases and steps outlined in this book, do come back to Chapter 1.1 and find some different literature here as your stepping stones to position your study in a larger frame of multimodal discourse analysis. In the above paragraph, you find some of the most relevant literature as well as some less known literature. Only take these as a starting point and please be aware that there is *much more* literature for you to engage with than is alluded to here. But the small glimpse above is offered as a starting point.

Multimodal Discourse Analysis: Research Underpinning This Book

This book originates from work that has been conducted in the past 15–20 years. Much thought has gone into the development of the multimodal framework and the many analytical tools offered in this text. The analytical tools discussed have been tested in various research projects and reported upon in much literature (Norris 2002a, b, 2004a, 2005, 2006, 2007, 2008, 2009a, b, 2011a, b, c, 2012a, b, c, 2013a, b, c, 2014a, b, c, 2015a, b, c, d, e, f, 2016a, b, 2017a, b; Norris and Jones 2005a, b, c, Norris and Maier 2014a, b, c; Norris and Makboon 2015, Norris and Pirini 2017; Norris et al. 2014; Makboon 2013, 2015; Geenen 2016, 2017, 2018; Makboon 2013, 2015; Pirini 2013a, b, 2014a, b, 2015, 2016, 2017; Pirini et al. 2014; White 2010).

Task 2: For PhD Students and Researchers

In Chapters 7 and 8 you will find some of the readings mentioned in the above paragraph. Many of these additional readings will be relevant again, when you are writing up your thesis and/or research findings. Thus, come back to this paragraph, then.

Mediated Discourse Theory

While other directions of multimodality, as mentioned previously, originated from Halliday's work (1973, 1974, 1978, 1985) with regard to a systemic functional grammar or from a conversation or discourse analysis direction, the direction of multimodality that this book originates from lies in diverse directions from linguistics, particularly socio- and anthropological linguistics and is greatly indebted to the work of Scollon (1997, 1998, 2001a, b, c) as well as Scollon and Scollon (2003). Many other scholars, for example Engeström (1987), Jones (2004, 2005), Jocuns (2007), Murray et al. (2014), Rish (2015), Lou (2017), or Wohlwend et al. (2017), to name but a few, are using mediated discourse theory for the analysis of mediated action in a variety of contexts.

Task 3: For PhD Students and Researchers

Since Scollon's work is so important for Multimodal (Inter)action Analysis, it is of utmost importance for PhD students and researchers to gain a strong grounding in Scollon's mediated discourse analysis.

As an important area that underpins Multimodal (Inter)action Analysis, we find much work focused upon language (Auer 2005; Auer and Pfaender 2011; Chafe 1992, 1994; Ciccourel 1980; van Dijk 1977, 1980; Duranti and Goodwin 1992; Ehlich 1993; Erickson 1980, 1982, 1990; Erickson and Schultz 1977; Fasold 1990; Garfinkel 1967, 1974; Garfinkel and Sacks 1970; Jefferson 1974; Labov 2006 [1966]; Lakoff 1972; Levinson 1983; Merritt 1976; Mey 2001; Milroy 1987; Pike 1967; Sacks 1973, 1974; Sacks et al. 1974; Sapir 1921, 1933; de Saussure 1959; Searle 2001; Sperber and Wilson 1986; Whorf 1956; Winograd 1972). In particular those who predominantly studied the spoken word highly influenced the development of the multimodal framework explicated in this book (Bamberg 2006; Bamberg and Georgakopoulou 2008; Goodwin 1979, 1986, 1994, 1995, 1996, 2000, 2001; Goodwin and Goodwin 1992; Goodwin and Heritage 1990; Hamilton 1998; Holmes and Marra 2002; Schiffrin 1977, 1981, 1985, 1986, 1987, 1988a, b, 1990, 1994; Schiffrin et al. 2001; Tannen 1979, 1984, 1989a, b; Tannen and Wallet 1997). But just as this socio and anthropological direction was influential, so was the sociological work of Goffman (1959, 1974), the work of Hymes (1972a, b, 1974a, b) and Gumperz (1981, 1982) as well as Hall (1983); and interdisciplinary work (see Engeström and Middleton 1998). Moreover, work into intonation (Bolinger 1964; Ladd 1980; Ladefoged 1975), particularly that of Ladefoged was influential, as was the work in practice theory (Bourdieu 1977, 1990, 1998; de Certeau 1984).

Task 4: For PhD Students and Researchers

The above section illustrates the importance of some early literature for multimodal discourse analysis. Thus, when conducting your literature review be careful not only to take note of current literature, but also look back in time to see what was written previously.

Much work in nonverbal behavior and work in the language and gesture area are important in this framework. Some of such work may be that of Efron (1941), Rüesch and Kees (1956), Hall (1959, 1966), Goffman (1961, 1963, 1979, 1981), Scheflen (1964, 1974), Argyle and Dean (1965), Condon and Ogston (1967), Kendon (1967, 1972, 1974, 1977, 1978, 1980, 1981, 1982, 1990, 1992, 1994, 1997, 2004), Birdwhilstell (1970), Bateson (1972), Kendon and Ferber (1973), Kahneman (1973), Halliday (1973, 1974, 1978, 1985), Heims (1977), Goodwin (1980), McNeill (1981, 1992), Exline and Fehr (1982), Dittman (1987), Frielund et al. (1987), Streeck (1988, 1993, 1994, 1996), Dray and McNeill (1990), Haviland (1993, 2000), Altorfer et al. (2000), Jossen et al. (2000), Käesermann et al. (2000), as well as Krahmer et al. (unpublished manuscript) and Holler and Wilkin (2011), all of which are examples of work in these areas.

Task 5: For PhD Students and Researchers
Here too, the first paragraph above illustrates the importance of some early literature. While much current literature has sprung up, it is important not to dismiss earlier writings, many of which can help us form new ideas and put current work into perspective. The task here is to review some of the earlier research that focused upon the nonverbal area that is important in your own work. The above section only highlights a few interesting pieces of writing and should be viewed as a stepping-stone to delve into earlier writing.

Task 6: For PhD Students and Researchers
Once you have a good grasp of earlier research, you will want to move forward in time and gain a good grasp of current research in nonverbal communication relevant to your own study. This literature is easy to find and is not further alluded to here.

Philosophy and Theory

Besides writings in linguistics, the nonverbal, and related fields, philosophy, and theory played a large part in the development of the framework taught in this book. Heidegger (1962), Kant (1973), Piaget (1976, 1978), Schafer (1977), Giddens (1979), Nishida (1990), Kozulin (1990), Bakhtin (Holquist and Emerson 1981) and Wertsch (1981, 1985a, b, 1998) played a role in developing this thought. Habermas (1984, 1999a, b), Descartes (1984) and Yuasa (1987) were important in my thinking. So were Hegel (1988), Husserl (1991, 1999, 2006), as well as Nishitani (1991) and the work of Foucault (1993), Latour (1994, 1996, 2005), Schatzki (1996), Lemke (1998, 2000a, b, c, d, 2002), Luhmann (1998), Wittgenstein (1998), and Heisig (2001), Wodak (2001), Reckwitz (2002), and Michiko (2002) just to mention a few.

Others that were influential are Mead (1974), who played a special role since he quite strongly purported that we needed to make the link between people's identity and society. Further, the work of Eco (1972), Schegloff (1972), Sklar (1977), Vygotsky (1978, 1986), and even work in chemistry (Christen 1980) played a role. But so did the work of Bruner (1986, 1990), Butler (1990), Trudge (1990), Lave and Wenger (1991), Van Lier (1995, 1996), Chalmers (1996) as well as Carter (1997) and Kozulin (1990), Habermas

(1999a, b), Raskin (2000), Van Leeuwen and Jewitt (2001), Finnegan (2002), Levine and Scollon (2004), Garrod and Pickering (2009), Hasko (2012), or Loenhoff and Schmitz (2015), which all helped in developing the line of thought that we call Multimodal (Inter)action Analysis.

As you will note, this paragraph is quite a mixture of thinkers. You find Western philosophers, Eastern philosophers, Western, and Eastern theoreticians. You will also find, when you read this literature, that there are many divergent views presented. Not all of the views outlined in these works will sync with the thoughts expressed in the current book. However, that does not make these works less valuable. Rather, it is sometimes especially because of other works that do not fall into the same area of thought that we can position our own thinking and can develop a new line of thought.

Task 7: For PhD Students and Researchers

The references in the above paragraphs are not well ordered. In order to gain a deeper understanding of the literature about philosophy and theory noted above, try to arrange the references in categories such as Eastern philosophy, Western philosophy, social theory, etc. Then discuss.

Timing and Rhythm

An interest in timing and rhythm has been around for quite some time. For example, Bücher (1899) was already interested in rhythm. Quite some time after that, Erickson (1980, 1990), or Scollon (1981, 1982) had a keen interest in the rhythmic organization in interaction. More recently, Bernieri and Rosenthal (1991), Auer et al. (1999), Van Leeuwen (1999), Norris (2009b, 2017a), Gill (2011), Machin (2013), Behrends et al. (2012), or Breyer et al. (2017) are some of a great number of researchers working in the area of rhythm and timing.

Task 8: For PhD Students and Researchers

The above illustrates the importance of some literature in the area of timing and rhythm. Noteworthy here, again, is that we need to be careful not to dismiss literature that was produced at a much earlier time. Quite often, this literature is relevant and sometimes the ideas addressed are good to revisit and maybe rethink in light of more current knowledge. Thus, read Bücher (1899) and discuss his thoughts in light of today's literature on rhythm and timing.

Chapter 2

Background

2.0

Philosophical and Theoretical Background

A strong coherence between philosophical, theoretical, and analytical framework ensures reliability of the research that is being conducted. Quite often, philosophical foundations of theories that underpin analytical frameworks are not made evident. Or, in some cases, a philosophical underpinning is explicitly referred to, but no clear theoretical background is discussed. Either way, these shortcomings become apparent when conducting research as research missing the clear development of all of these facets is not as reliable as research that makes a strong connection between the empirical framework, its theory, and philosophy.

This chapter outlines the basic philosophical and theoretical underpinnings of Multimodal (Inter)action Analysis. I begin with philosophy and then turn to theory, demonstrating how the philosophical notions discussed are theoretically taken into account. In this way, I explicate here a linear direction from philosophy to theory to (later) empirical framework. However, during the development of the empirical framework, the theory outlined/utilized and the philosophical notions embraced was in no way linear: the empirical framework was purely data driven (Norris 2002a, 2011a); the theoretical concepts used were fruitful because of empirical findings that were in need of explanation and analysis and the philosophical notions began with grounded common sense on the one hand and a strong connection to Eastern and Western phenomenology (Hegel 1988; Nishida 1958; Yuasa 1987) on the other hand. Philosophical notions needed to prove useful and co-embrace empirical data analysis, just as theory needed to be taken into account and co-developed through empirical data analysis. A strong interconnectedness between all of these facets now helps our understanding. While the original development of all of these facets was circular and/or is produced in tandem, once developed, the analytical framework rests upon firm theoretical foundations and is enhanced through a coherent philosophical basis. Therefore, Multimodal (Inter)action Analysis is a framework in which all three facets come together to build a coherent philosophical, theoretical, and analytical framework.

This chapter begins with two important philosophical concepts for multimodal discourse analysis, the notion of *perception* and the notion of *embodiment* (Merleau-Ponty 1963, 2012; Nishida 1958; Yuasa 1987). Taking Merleau-Ponty's, Nishida's and Yuasa's work as my base, I view these two notions in ways that are proven through empirical

Systematically Working with Multimodal Data: Research Methods in Multimodal Discourse Analysis,
First Edition. Sigrid Norris.
© 2019 John Wiley & Sons, Inc. Published 2019 by John Wiley & Sons, Inc.
Companion website: www.wiley.com/go/Norris/multimodal-data

analysis (Norris 2004a, 2011a). Certainly, the work of these scholars is not the only philosophical underpinning for this framework. See also Hegel (1988) and other phenomenologists (Heidegger 1962; Husserl 1991, 1999, 2006; Smith 2016) as well as the philosophical thought espoused in the last part of this chapter. The notions discussed here are of particular importance when beginning to work with multimodal data.

The chapter then moves on to theory, illustrating just how these philosophical concepts are embedded in multimodal mediated theory. For this, the chapter outlines the unit of analysis, the *mediated action* (Scollon 1997, 1998, 2001a; Wertsch 1998) and the derived units of analysis (Norris 2004a), the *lower-level mediated action, the higher-level mediated action* and the *frozen mediated action*. Since multimodal mediated theory, building on mediated discourse theory (Scollon 1998, 2001a), postulates that actions and interactions link to history, the chapter then discusses the concepts of *practice* and *discourses* as conceived of in multimodal mediated theory. Here, the chapter naturally turns to the notion of a *site of engagement*, which is the concept that allows us to bring the concrete mediated actions (lower-level, higher-level, or frozen) together with practices and relevant discourses. Each section in the theory part of this chapter shows how the philosophical notions of perception and embodiment discussed in the first part of the chapter link to the theoretical concepts.

For those who would like to delve deeper into the philosophical underpinnings of mediated discourse analysis (Scollon 1998, 2001a) upon which our multimodal framework rests, a discussion of Scollon's philosophical thought is offered in the last part of this chapter. This part gives the reader some background of how Scollon developed some of his thought, particularly emphasizing the philosophical ideas that he grappled with and which emerged through his reading of Vygotsky and Nishida.

Philosophical Underpinnings

The French philosopher Merleau-Ponty (1963, 2012) as well as the Eastern philosophers Nishida (1958) and Yuasa (1987) insisted upon the primacy of perception and/or embodiment; it is the primacy of perception *and* embodiment that we take as our philosophical underpinning when studying people acting and interacting. However, exactly how I think of these notions, is close to, but not exactly the same as in the writings of Merleau-Ponty, Nishida, or Yuasa. In essence, my philosophy is thus: actors perceive the world, objects and others through their bodies as they are acting and interacting. Body, mind, and world are not separated, even though they may be perceived as separated by the individual actor. I postulate that in fact body, mind, and world are so closely interlinked that they are never separated in action and interaction. Because of this, we perceive the world as that which we encounter by being a part of the world in an embodied way. This non-separation between body, mind, and world is close to the understanding of non-separation in Eastern philosophy. However, in Eastern philosophy, the individual's ability to perceive the non-separateness has to be achieved through meditation and other practices. While I agree with this notion of bringing the non-separated together in Eastern philosophy, I would like us to think about the non-separateness of body, mind, and world as a given, whether it is so perceived by an individual or not. The reason for this is that in (inter)action, particularly when examining it multimodally, we see how body, mind, and world come together.

When thinking about an example, the philosophical underpinnings become clearer. Imagine for a moment that you are not in a body. That thought is impossible for us to consider as we are the body itself. Now consider yourself without cognition. Again, an impossibility to consider because it takes cognition in order to consider it. Next, imagine that you had no feelings. As you might guess, that too is impossible since we always have some kind of feelings even if it simply is the feeling of indifference. Now, imagine that your body existed without a world. Again, an impossibility, since our bodies – and thus we – are completely dependent upon the existence of the world. Now think of yourself without any other human being and once again, you will find that such a way of thinking is impossible. But let us think further. If you are sitting, imagine yourself in that same position for a moment without a chair (or whatever you might be sitting on). Certainly, you will not be able to hold that posture for very long. Sitting requires something to sit on. Or if you are standing, imagine that there is no ground to stand on. Of course, if that was the case, you would be dropping and dropping quite fast into some hole until you would hit some ground and probably break your ankles. At which point, others would help you and see to it that you go to a doctor. Thus, standing without a surface is impossible. While we quite often seem to forget that the world is an incredibly important part of us, that other people are an incredibly important part of us, we may think that we live mostly in our own heads, that verbal thoughts are most important in our lives, that verbal thinking is who we actually are, or that language is the mode that is most important in communication. Thinking about the above scenarios quickly makes clear that when we leave out the most essential aspects to our own being, namely the body, the world, and other people, we in fact miss most of what makes us who we are, most of what allows us to act and most of what carries us and communicates when we interact.

When taking these philosophical underpinnings seriously, we will have to admit that there is more to acting and interacting than language and verbal thought. But not only is there more, there are some more fundamental aspects to acting and interacting. For example, when I am tired because I have walked too long through a city, I can easily sit on a bench and my action of sitting there communicates my resting to others, without words. When, on the other hand, I yell out just how tired I am, but there is nobody and no world, no bench to sit on, and no ground to stand on, all the words in the world cannot express my tiredness. Not to mention the fact that neither I nor anyone else would exist in such a circumstance. Certainly, this does not mean that language is not informative or that it is not important. Language most certainly is very important as it makes us human. But language is not the only important thing as we find when taking the philosophical position of primacy of perception and primacy of embodiment seriously.

Note 1

With these philosophical underpinnings, our primary interest is the human being; i.e. actor(s) as they act and interact.

Primacy of Perception

Let us consider the philosophical position *primacy of perception* in more detail. Perception is of such importance to the human being (as well as to animals, but we will leave them out in our discussion and focus on people here), because only that which we can perceive does exist for us. This means, only those aspects in the world – including other people, objects, countries, or anything else imaginable – are real for you if you have perceived them. For example, a kind of bird that you have never perceived simply does not exist for you. This kind of bird only comes into existence *for you* if you have been told about it, have read about it, have seen it, have seen a picture of it, have imagined it, or have perceived it in some other way. Only once you have perceived this kind of bird in some way, does the bird actually exist for you. Up until then, it simply does not exist *for you*. Let us take another example. We all know about far away galaxies, about black holes, and about the minute atomic structures that we are made of. Very few of us have ever actually seen any of these. Yet, we all have perceived them in some way. Either we have heard about them in school, or read about them in books or on the Internet, or have watched movies that were made about them. Perception thus goes far beyond sight. Perception encompasses any kind of learning, imagining, or knowing.

Of course, when taking perception – the way we perceive ourselves with the world, the objects and others – seriously, we find that we also perceive more than just language. When encountering a new person, we perceive much about the person long before the person can even say a word. Our non-verbal perception of the other is just as important and sometimes more important, than anything the person says. This does not mean that we necessarily perceive the other correctly. All it means is that we perceive the other as it fits our very own previous experience. Our perception is ours. But our actions that are based on our perception move beyond our own. Let us think about this: you encounter a new person and this person looks and acts a lot like somebody you once knew during your childhood. Of course, you know that this person is not that person, but you will nevertheless be inclined to attribute similarities to this new person. This perception thus stems from your own history of having met a person that looked, or in some ways acted, similarly a long time ago. You may be very surprised as you get to know this new person that the two in fact have nothing at all in common. But your first impression, your first perception of this person still appeared quite real and correct to you at the time. Yet, now that you have found out that two people can seem to be alike and may in fact not be alike at all, next time you meet someone looking or acting like another person that you have previously met you will not make the same perceptual mistake. Next time, you will wait, watch, act, and interact with that new person and try to find out who they really are. You see, you have learned to perceive differently. Perception is based upon your experience and through much experience we learn to pay better attention to what *is* rather than to what *we think is*. Perception allows us to understand ourselves, others, objects, and the environment we interconnectedly live with. Perception is dependent upon individual development, history and culture. But, of course, we are not simply made of perception, but rather are living, feeling, thinking, and acting bodies. Because of this, we embrace the philosophical position of primacy of embodiment.

Note 2

Perception, as used here, moves us beyond pure sense-perception. It includes previous experience, emotion, imagination, history and culture.

Primacy of Embodiment

Let us consider the philosophical position *primacy of embodiment* in more detail. The notion of embodiment refers to the fact that we live as bodies, that these bodies are interconnected with the environment, objects within, and with others. Without body, there is no person (or animal, but again, we will continue to focus on humans here); without environment, there is no body, since bodies cannot live in a vacuum; without others there is no body, because we cannot grow and live without the care of and without (inter) acting with others. Therefore, the human body and the environment always co-exist; the human body always co-exists with other human bodies, without any of these being primary, which means that all three, body, others, and environment, have to exist at the very same time and therefore take on the same importance. Certainly, we can think of people living all by themselves once they have grown up. However, it is because of previous experiences with other people that this is even possible. In the mind of a hermit, the hermit still sees themselves in connection with others. Embodiment is thus more than simply the notion of body as part in an action. Rather when speaking of embodiment, we want to always consider the connectedness between body, world, and others.

When thinking of embodiment in this philosophical way, we can see that disconnecting the person from the environment or from others is in fact impossible. Following from this philosophical position, it is impossible to investigate people as they act or interact through language and/or non-verbal modes alone. The reason for this is that people do not communicate with each other by acting and interacting only verbally, but act and interact with each other with and through their entire bodies *and* the environment they inhabit. Imagine for a moment that you are waiting for a friend at a café. You sit at a little table, have a half empty cup of coffee in front of you and you are texting on your mobile. Here, you are communicating with and through the environment about having a cup of coffee in a café. You are communicating to others that you are engaged on your mobile and you are communicating through language as you are texting. Certainly, all of these messages are of a different kind and have different relevance for different people. The people sitting around you in the café may just see you as another guest having a cup of coffee; the waitress might already know that you are waiting for someone as you may have told her that somebody else will take up the other seat at the table; the person you are texting will read your message and answer it; your friend on arrival will see that you have already ordered and have had half of your cup of coffee and may apologize for being late as they approach the table. Here, it is not words that your friend reads as communicative, but the fact that you have already ordered, have received and consumed half of your cup of coffee by the time they enter the café. Embodiment in this sense thus goes far beyond the notion of language, gesture, gaze, or posture as embodied actions. Here, it is the situatedness in the café at a little table with a half empty cup of coffee that tells your friend (and others) of your embodied experience of drinking coffee.

When taking embodiment – our body and its interconnection with the world – seriously, we find that it is not only our verbal thoughts, writing, and speaking that is of importance when communicating; rather that our bodies and their situatedness in the environment are of equal importance when considering communication. But how can we understand this kind of deep embodiment when we are trying to examine people acting and interacting with a specific focus on language? The answer is quite easy:

When a person is writing, the writing can only be accomplished through both pen and paper, a computer, mobile, sand and stick, or other devices. Without a writing utensil, object, or device, words cannot be written. Or, when a person speaks, they can only do so through their own bodies, lips, teeth, tongue, larynx, and air. Without air, there is no spoken language. Here we see that even spoken language is not in fact producible without the environment, the air we breathe. But let us take it further. We can only gesture in an environment. Without an environment, gesturing would not only be impossible (because we would not exist), but gesturing would also make no sense. What we here call embodied actions always include not only the body or parts thereof, but also always include aspects of the environment. Gestures only have meaning in relation to bodies and environment. The philosophical position that takes both perception and embodiment as primary, requires a theory that connects the body to the environment on the one hand and realizes a difference in perception in action and interaction for different individuals. Multimodal mediated theory is this theory.

Note 3

When studying action and interaction, we need to take physical bodies *and* the environment into consideration.

Discussion Point 1

What is an individual? How can we define the *individual* when taking the outlined thoughts as our philosophical underpinning?

Theoretical Underpinnings: One Principle, Two Sub-Principles

The Principle of Social Action

Multimodal mediated theory is built on one principle: the principle of social action, a principle first outlined in Scollon (1998) (more about Scollon's theoretical framework is discussed in later sections of this chapter),[1] What this means is that in multimodal mediated research, we believe that human beings always perform social actions.

When you think about this, you will realize that you do things all day long: you get up in the morning; you brush your teeth; you have breakfast; you converse with your family; you go to work or school; you ride the bus, ride your bike, or drive your car; you walk to the office or the classroom and you speak to friends or colleagues that you meet on the way. All of these things that you do are actions. All of these actions are social. While it will be easy for you to see that you perform actions all day long, it may be less obvious that all of your actions are social. But what does it mean for an action to be social?

For one thing, humans are social animals. All that this really means is that as humans we need other humans in order to survive in the first place. A sea turtle does not need

---

1 The difference between Scollon's (1998, 2001a) mediated discourse theory and the way we use the principles in multimodal mediated theory is *only* a differentiation of primacy of social action.

a mother sea turtle to make sure it survives. What a sea turtle needs is the right environment and a bit of luck. Humans are different. Human babies need a parent or a caregiver, who can keep them safe. The human brain after birth is not developed enough for a human to live without help. But what does this have to do with the actions that you perform from morning to night as an adult in your world here and now? A whole lot, in fact. You learn from very little on how things are done in our human world. You eat a certain way and you eat certain foods. You eat them not just because you like them, but you like them because others around you like them or dislike them or because they show that they think you should like them or not. You develop your own ways of doing things in accordance with and in opposition to, others around you. You are a social being. So, when you drive alone in your car, you act like you have learned to act. Or, to give you a different example, if you are home alone, you act either just like you always act, no matter if someone is present or not, or you act differently because nobody else is present. Either way, you act in relation to others: you act in some social way. But now you will say that this is some kind of trick: I say everything you do is social; in fact, yes, that is exactly what I am saying. Everything you do is social because you are doing it in relation to others. Everything you do is social because you have learned doing it (and may even have long forgotten that you ever learned it). Even the most "a-social" behavior is social because it is and can only be, "a-social" in relation to what we term social.

So, in multimodal mediated research, we claim that there is one thing that is most important to all humans and to any aspect of being human and that is the social action. Whatever it is you wish to study about humans, it should always bring you back to what these humans do: the social action. This point is so vital, I believe, that I have made it our one and only theoretical principle. Within this principle, I have highlighted two facets as sub-principles: the principle of communication and the principle of history.

Note 4

Our focus is always the action that is being performed (and *not* the language spoken, a text, or any other mode).

The Sub-Principle of Communication

The sub-principle of communication is not a principle in its own right. It is a sub-principle that is subsumed under the principle of social action. What this means is that humans always act in the world, that all actions are social, and that all actions communicate in some way or form to others. Going back to our example of your day above, we can say that you get up in the morning and you brush your teeth. When you come to the breakfast table, your very presence communicates to the others that you have risen and your clean teeth and fresh breath communicate to others that you have brushed your teeth. There is nothing that you have to say in order to communicate these messages. They are apparent in your presence and your breath. While most people will not even think about these actions as being communicative, they certainly are communication. Just try not to get up in the morning when you have to go to school or work and see what happens. Or try not to brush your teeth and see what others say or do.

Thus, whatever social actions we perform, these social actions communicate messages to others. In fact, they cannot not communicate. Of course, now you will try to think of actions that you can hide from others; of course, there are actions that you can and that you do hide. These actions may not communicate directly, or not as directly as the ones discussed above. But they still do communicate in some way. Just think of a bowel movement. This is usually not something we discuss with others. As adults we usually perform this action on our own. However, now imagine, you did not go to the toilet. What would happen then? Negative examples, like this, illustrate that there is a communicative function even in these kinds of action that we think of as very private, not as social at all, and certainly not as communicative. Sometimes, we simply communicate by our actions that everything is fine. That, by itself, is an important message for others. However, as we will see later, these messages are not necessarily sent intentionally and they are also not necessarily taken up intentionally. First, however, let us look at the second sub-principle: the sub-principle of history.

Note 5
All actions are communicative.

The Sub-Principle of History

The sub-principle of history, just like the sub-principle of communication, is not a principle in its own right. It too is subsumed under the principle of social action. What this means is that humans always act in the world, that all actions are social, that all actions communicate in some way or form to others and that *all actions embed history*. Going back to our example of your day above, we can say that you have breakfast and converse with your family. The things that you eat for breakfast have a history. You eat them, because you like eating them and because, most likely, you eat them often for breakfast. At the same time, when you converse with your family, this conversation has a history. There are likely certain things that you all like to talk about in the morning. There are certain things that you may not like to discuss at the breakfast table. Similarly, the way you speak, the way the other family members speak, all have a history. It is a way that you or they usually speak. If one of you has a cold, tonal quality may be pointed out; a scratchy voice may be commented on and may be traced back to someone else's scratchy voice: more history.

Thus, whatever social actions we perform, they all communicate and they all have some kind of history. Our actions have a history. In fact, they cannot not have a history. Even if you are doing something completely new, it will not be new to everyone in the world. It will have some kind of antecedent; it will have some kind of origin in some other action; it will be taken up because of, or in opposition to, some other action. There has to be some kind of relation, positive or negative, somewhere. It is exciting to think of social actions in this way. Where did something that you do day in day out start? How did you change from performing a certain action to doing something very different? Where is the continuity in the discontinuity? These are questions that you can ask about everything, every action that any person may perform. And these are questions that will lead you to new discoveries.

Note 6
All actions have a history.

Principle and Sub-Principles: A Perfect Fit

The principle of social action bases all of our theoretical thought on actions that people take in the world. Through this principle, we are reminded that all humans act all day long. We get up in the morning (an action), make coffee or tea (an action), converse with a family member (an action), go to school, university or work (an action), and so on. Even when we sleep, we perform an action (the action of sleeping), or when we do absolutely nothing, we are performing an action (that of sitting somewhere and staring out of a window for example). In fact, we cannot ever not act.

Besides the emphasis on action, the principle reminds us that all actions are social. The reason that all actions are social is that actions are learned in social environments. Whatever humans do has been based on other actions that other humans have performed. Now, if you think of an action that no one has ever performed before you, you will soon realize that your creative and new action has actually developed because of other actions that you or other individuals have performed before you. In this way, your completely new and highly creative action also is a social action. It grows out of some kind of social environment that you are going against or that you are developing or that you are changing. All of these are social in nature and are always based on and in relation to other actions.

All actions have a history. They either derive directly from some previous action, or they derive indirectly from a previous action, or they derive in opposition to an action. Whatever it may be, it derives from some kind of history. Many actions that humans take are not new and oppositional in nature. Many actions are habitual, learned, and performed in alignment with other actions and fitting in particular social groups. It is these actions that are embedded in history and reproduced daily, which on the one hand, are the most easily viewed as social action. It is also these actions that are, on the other hand, the most difficult to change. Social change is a slow and difficult process. It is difficult primarily because all actions are historical and social in nature.

Discussion Point 2
In what way do the principle and the two sub-principles focus our research projects?

Discussion Point 3
In what way do these principles diffuse our focus, hinting at the complexity of the study of human action and interaction?

Multimodal Mediated Theory: Basic Theoretical Concepts

Multimodal mediated theory is an extension of mediated discourse theory as espoused by Scollon (1998, 2001a, b, c) and used by many researchers (Al Zidjaly 2011a, b; Geenen 2013a, b, 2017, 2018; Geenen et al. 2015; Johnston 2004; Jones 2014; Jones and Norris

2005a, b, c, d; Lou 2017; Pan 2014; Pirini 2014a, b, 2016, 2017; Randolph 2000; Rish 2015; de Saint-Georges 2004; de Saint-Georges and Norris 2000; Wohlwend et al. 2017). The basic concepts from mediated discourse theory remain intact, but many of them are extended, some refined, and others are newly developed (Norris 2004a, 2013a, 2014b, 2017b) in order to allow for a multimodal discourse analysis that embraces the above explicated philosophical and theoretical positions. The theoretical concepts explained below also are analytical concepts used for the analysis of empirical data. However, here in this chapter, we will focus on the theoretical aspects of the concepts and in later chapters we learn their applicability. In order to gain a deep understanding of multimodal mediated theory, let us begin by examining embodiment and perception in theoretical terms.

Embodiment and Perception: Multimodal Mediated Theory

As explained above, our philosophical position is that the body–mind is connected to and interdependent with the environment. Bodies are not units that act and interact with each other in and by themselves, neither are brains cognitive units that act and interact with each other in and by themselves, nor are minds psychological and/or embodied units that act and interact with each other in and by themselves. Actions and interactions that individuals engage in are always produced by the body (including cognition and emotions) *and* the environment and objects within. Actions and interactions that individuals engage in are produced and understood through individuals' perception in always multiple ways. This complex connection between body, environment, and perception is the foundation of multimodal mediated theory and is expressed first of all in the unit of analysis, the mediated action.

Unit of Analysis: The Mediated Action

The mediated action, first developed by Vygotsky (1978) has undergone some re-theorizing by Wertsch (1998), Scollon (1998), and then Norris (2004a). Below, we begin with Wertsch's (1998) definition, but then take up Scollon's (1998) understanding of the definition of mediated action as our stepping stone. Scollon (1998) insists on always multiple mediation of an action; a few years later, the mediated action is further re-theorized (Norris 2004a) and developed into three units of analysis. This last re-theorizing developed mediated discourse theory into multimodal mediated theory for two reasons:

1) A change to the philosophical position as explained above occurred (Scollon's philosophical thought is discussed further in the last part of the chapter);
2) Through a delineation of three units of analysis, a change in analytical focus occurred.

The three newly theorized meditated actions, the lower-level mediated action, the higher-level mediated action and the frozen mediated action as units of analysis developed in Norris (2002a, 2004a) permanently bind together the philosophical notions of perception and embodiment discussed above. These units of analysis, as the mediated action defined by Wertsch (1998) and Scollon (1998), ensure that we never lose sight of the interconnectedness of people with the environment and the objects within; it is this connection that is built into the theory throughout.

But let us begin by understanding the definition of the original unit of analysis, which continues to underlie all three units (the lower-level mediated action, the higher-level mediated action and the frozen mediated action). The mediated action is defined by Wertsch (1998) and taken up by Scollon (1998) as *social actor(s) acting with/through mediational means/cultural tools.*

Social Actors

In mediated discourse theory (Scollon 1998), we speak of people as social actors. The reason for this is that we want to emphasize the social aspect of people acting and interacting as the essence of our theory. By calling people social actors in multimodal mediated theory, we emphasize that the social is an incredibly important aspect when studying people acting and interacting.

Definition 1

Social actor = Person, human being

Mediational Means/Cultural Tools

In mediated discourse theory (Scollon 1998) we call aspects of the environment, objects, language, numeracy, and even body parts such as arms or hands *mediational means* or *cultural tools* when used by social actors in action or interaction. The terms *mediational means* and *cultural tools* are used interchangeably because all *mediational means* used in action or interaction *mediate* the action in some particular way; all mediational means are used in action or interaction in some cultural way, i.e. cultural tools.

Definition 2

Mediational means	=	Cultural tools
Mediational means	=	Anything needed to perform the action
Cultural tool	=	Anything needed to perform the action

The Mediated Action

As mentioned above, the mediated action is defined by Wertsch (1998) as *social actor(s) acting with/through mediational means/cultural tools.* What this means is that each action that people perform is mediated in (always multiple (Scollon 1998)) ways. The mediated action, defined as above is our fundamental theoretical unit of analysis. This fundamental unit then was refined in Norris (2004a) and delineated into three theoretical – and analytical – units of analysis. These are the lower-level, the higher-level, and the frozen mediated action.

But before going into too much detail about the various kinds of mediated actions, let us think through the notion of a social actor a little further.

Non-Human Social Actors

Generally speaking, as mentioned above, we are interested in the actions and interactions that human beings perform. However, other than human beings, a pet can also be thought of as a social actor. When thinking about a cat, a dog, or a horse, we may find that these (and also other animals) are sometimes treated by their human owners as social actors. For example, the cat may be given perceived agency when the owner remarks "oh, you want to be left alone today" and then steps away from the room in which the cat is lounging around. Or, you may find a dog perceived as a social actor when the owner is trying to feed the dog medication and the dog refuses to take it in any way offered. Similarly, the owner of a horse may show they perceive their horse as a social actor when remarking "I see, you really want to run this morning" and allowing the horse to fall into a gallop. What is important is the way the animal is treated and reacts in a given interaction with the human social actor. If the animal displays some kind of agency, such that the animal is able to initiate an interaction, deny an interaction and react in socially organized ways but (to some extent) with their own ways of doing and being that shows some kind of identity, then we may want to classify the animal as a social actor in a given interaction with a human. This certainly is a gray area, but when you watch and analyze interactions between humans and animals, you will quite easily see when you can make the argument that the animal interacts in some social way when interacting with the human.

A computer as well as other objects or institutions (quite differently from actor-network-theory (Latour 1994, 1996, 2005)) are not seen as social actors in Multimodal (Inter)action Analysis. A computer, no matter how much Artificial Intelligence may be embedded, is not an actor that acts with their own identity. Many computer scientists will agree that a computer has to be programmed by a human and that the actions that the computer (or robot) produces are not the same as those of humans. A computer is not really able to initiate an interaction, deny an interaction, and react in socially organized ways and with their own ways of doing and being that shows some kind of identity. For example, when you think of a robot that mows your lawn, the robot is pre-programmed to come out of its shed, mow the lawn and to go back into the shed. You do not need to be present. The robot initiates its own actions based upon the programming. But the robot cannot deny the action: It cannot say or think "oh, no, today, I don't feel like mowing the lawn. Today, I'll just sit in my shed and play a computer game." A dog, on the other hand, can deny an action. A dog may refuse to go out when it is raining. A robot also does not display an identity. One lawn mowing robot of the same brand will be like the others, whereas one dog of the same breed may be quite different from the other dogs of that breed depending upon their socialization. A dog can have an identity. But, of course, not all dogs are treated like social actors and not all dogs have the ability to develop their own social identity.

Thus, just as animals can be viewed, treated, and react like social actors (and we can make the claim that they can be analyzed as social actors in those circumstances), animals can also be viewed, treated, and react like mediational means. But not only animals can be treated and react like mediational means. Humans can be mediational means as well (Randolph 2000).

Humans and Animals as Mediational Means

Just as animals can sometimes be classified as social actors, human beings, and animals can sometimes be classified as mediational means. As an example, in an interaction between two politicians from different countries not speaking the others' language, we usually find a translator or two to be present. In a case like this, the translators are not viewed as participating in the interaction between the politicians. Rather, they are viewed as the means to make this conversation possible. Thus, they are viewed and engage in the interaction as mediational means: the translators cannot initiate a topic shift, saying "why don't you discuss this important point now"; or react to one of the politicians, disagreeing with their stance. Translators are solely there to make the interaction between the two politicians possible, i.e. they are viewed, act, and react as mediational means.

When thinking about animals as mediational means, we can easily see how working dogs are used as mediational means. They are not supposed to have much of an identity (other than the genetic identity bred into the breed), as they are supposed to help the human being do a specific job. Just try to react to or engage with a security dog at an airport as if it was a pet and you will see that the handler will not be pleased if the dog reacts positively to you. The dog is meant to ignore such actions and a well-trained dog will act like its handler's mediational means and pay no attention to you. Similarly, horses may be viewed and engaged with as mediational means. Certainly, here too, there will be gray areas so that the dog handler interacts with the dog differently when not working, or the dressage rider may interact with the horse playfully when not performing. But when performing, the horse is not to initiate their own action, or refuse an action initiated by the rider. Here, the horse is used as a mediational means that is to perform as the rider wishes without showing their own social identity.

Multiple Mediational Means/Cultural Tools in a Mediated Action

As Scollon (2001a) has pointed out, there are always multiple mediational means/cultural tools in a mediated action. The graph in Definition 3 illustrates this notion.

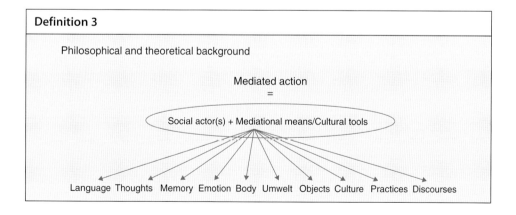

Definition 3

Philosophical and theoretical background

Mediated action
=

Social actor(s) + Mediational means/Cultural tools

Language Thoughts Memory Emotion Body Umwelt Objects Culture Practices Discourses

When looking at an example, this may become clearer. In a YouTube video (https://www.youtube.com/watch?v=OUISmCzLPTA) taken from the *Game of Thrones* series, the women are feeding a baby dragon. Some of the multiple mediational means are the piece of meat for the dragon, the women's knowledge that a dragon eats meat, the

Figure 2.1 Mediated action: feeding a baby dragon.

thought that they should feed the baby dragon, Daenerys Targaryen's hand, when she drops the piece of meat on the wall, the wall itself, where the feeding is accomplished, the women's gaze, their smiles as the dragon cooks the meat and many more (Figure 2.1).

Discussion Point 4

Continue with listing the multiple mediational means involved during the feeding of the baby dragon. For this, you may want to watch the YouTube clip at https://www.youtube.com/watch?v=QUISmCzl PTA

Discussion Point 5

Think about how the dragons are perceived in *Game of Thrones*. Are they more viewed as social actors, more like mediational means, or simply as beasts that would not fit either of these categories? Is it the same throughout the series or does it also change?

Lower-Level Mediated Action

The lower-level mediated action is defined as a *mode's smallest pragmatic meaning unit*. The term *pragmatic* is defined here as *in use* (i.e. language in use, gesture in use, object handling in use, layout in use). This, for example denotes a social actor acting with/

through mediational means/cultural tools such as the mode of spoken language. Or, to say it in a different way, an individual speaking one utterance. The utterance is defined by Chafe (1992, 1994) as a breath unit (and can be anything from a backchannel response of *mhm* or *OK* to a breath unit of many words). Or, as defined in Norris (2004a), it may be an individual producing a postural shift (a social actor acting with/through the mediational means/cultural tool of the mode of posture). Thus, an utterance is the smallest pragmatic meaning unit for the mode of spoken language; a postural shift is the smallest pragmatic meaning unit for the mode of posture. Pragmatic meaning units of a mode are the lower-level mediated actions that people perform and that individuals can easily perceive in action and interaction. For example, an individual perceives a pointing gesture (a lower-level mediated action) that another person performs. Or, an individual perceives how another is taking a step (a lower-level mediated action of the mode of walking). Of course, you will notice that even when taking a step, mediation is multiple: it takes the body, especially the legs and feet to take a step; it also takes a surface to take a step on; an environment (room, street, forest, or such) to take a step in.

Lower-level mediated actions, while theoretically, analytically, and in interaction practically distinguishable, never are produced alone. Any one of us, no matter what we do, always produces multiple lower-level mediated actions at the very same time. Some of these lower-level mediated actions may begin simultaneously and end simultaneously. But quite often, lower-level mediated actions have different starting and ending points as we will see in detail in later chapters, particularly in Chapter 6. In regards to theory, we want to understand the links to the philosophical notions of (i) Perception (what can a social actor perceive when acting and interacting); (ii) Embodiment (in what way does the lower-level mediated action connect body and environment).

Definition 4

Lower-level mediated action = Smallest pragmatic meaning unit of a mode

---

Note 7

1) Lower-level mediated actions have a clear beginning and ending point.
2) Lower-level mediated actions are always mediated in multiple ways.
3) Lower-level mediated actions are never performed alone.

Lower-Level Mediated Actions: Perception

A lower-level mediated action can be experienced and perceived by the person producing it; a lower-level mediated action can be experienced and perceived by others. The reason for saying "can be" is the fact that, quite often in action and interaction, individual lower-level mediated actions are not always individually experienced or perceived either by the performer, nor by others. Quite often, lower-level mediated actions are chained together in actions and interactions and quite often they are intricately interlinked with other chains of lower-level mediated actions. However, they are still units that have a clear beginning and ending point and are thus distinguishable by an analyst. Sometimes, a lower-level mediated action is also very much experienced and perceived in action and interaction. Think about the lower-level mediated action of a pointing gesture for example. The person pointing at something is certainly experiencing and perceiving their own pointing and the people seeing the person pointing are certainly experiencing and perceiving the gesture and will often follow such a gesture by producing the lower-level mediated action of a gaze shift, gazing in the direction of the pointed finger. A pointing gesture, as all lower-level mediated actions, has a beginning and an end-point. The fact that lower-level mediated actions have a clear beginning and ending, gives them theoretical significance. Even though lower-level mediated actions are not typically perceived as individual actions, they can be distinguished by a performer if you for example showed a slowed video to an individual who had performed the action. The reason for this is that these units can be perceived by all. This ability to perceive a lower-level mediated action gives it practical applicability because everyone can learn to distinguish these units.

Lower-Level Mediated Actions: Embodiment

Every lower-level mediated action that a person performs, experiences, and perceives is necessarily embodied and mediated in multiple ways. Without a person performing, experiencing or perceiving, a lower-level mediated action is not possible. Imagine an individual speaks an utterance (a lower-level mediated action of the mode of spoken language). Speaking the utterance is the action. This action is mediated by the speaker's body in multiple ways, i.e. the overall body size, the speaker's cognition, emotion, lung, larynx, tongue, teeth, lips, etc. Many aspects of the body are involved when producing sound and many aspects of the body play a role in the way the utterance is produced. The action of speaking an utterance is also mediated by the environment, i.e. the air which the individual inhaled and which is now expelled by the lungs in order to produce sound, the air outside of the individual that begins to vibrate and thus communicates the sound waves, the larger environment (such as the room or the forest that the speaker inhabits at the moment when speaking, which allows the speaker either to be heard clearly or not). Further, the action of speaking is mediated by the language itself, which in turn had been learned through social interaction often long before the speaker utters the utterance. Therefore, the utterance is mediated by memory, as well as by social norms (even if the speaker goes against social norms with the utterance itself) and other social conventions. The same is true for any lower-level mediated action that a social actor performs and/or experiences and perceives. We always find a great multiplicity of mediation in any kind of lower-level mediated action. This multiplicity of mediational means/cultural tools builds the glue in lower-level mediated actions that connect the body (including cognition and psychology) to the environment, the social, and the cultural. But, one lower-level mediated action is never produced alone. This brings us to the next concept, the higher-level mediated action.

Discussion Point 6

A lower-level mediated action is defined as the smallest pragmatic meaning unit of a mode (postural shift, a simple movement of the body from facing left to facing right with or without steps, is such a shift). Discuss why this can be termed the smallest meaning unit for the mode of posture. Then list the multiple mediational means/cultural tools that mediate this lower-level action.

Higher-Level Mediated Action

The higher-level mediated action is defined as the *coming together of a multitude of chains of lower-level mediated actions.* A higher-level mediated action is produced through chains of lower-level mediated actions at the very same time as the higher-level mediated action produces the chains of lower-level mediated actions. This means that a higher-level mediated action and the discernible chains of lower-level mediated actions mutually produce each other. Neither the higher-level mediated action, nor the multiple chains of lower-level mediated actions are primary. Let us look at an easy example where we only focus on one social actor, namely you: when you Skype with someone, you are producing a higher-level mediated action. This higher-level mediated action is made up of many chains of lower-level mediated actions that you are producing such as speaking many utterances, gesturing at intervals, or moving your head and posture and changing your proxemics to the device. Your higher-level mediated action of interacting via Skype makes these various chains of lower-level mediated actions come about. But, at the very same time, it is these chains of lower-level mediated actions that produce your higher-level mediated action of communicating via Skype. What this theoretical understanding of a higher-level mediated action means is the following: neither the lower-level mediated action, nor the higher-level mediated action is prior. They come about simultaneously, co-producing each other. But now, let us consider an example that is a bit more complex: we will again look at you as you are Skyping with a friend. But this time, we will consider you *and* your friend in the interaction. Here, you are producing the higher-level mediated action of Skyping through the multiple chains of lower-level mediated actions and the lower-level mediated actions are produced through your producing the higher-level mediated action as explained above. Your friend also produces a higher-level mediated action of interacting with someone on Skype and here the other is you. The production of a higher-level mediated action and the simultaneous production of the multiple chains of lower-level mediated actions proceed in theory just like they did when we discussed these actions by looking at you. But, and you will agree, your friend produces a different higher-level mediated action and different chains of lower-level mediated actions than you do. Thus, here we see how two people, engaged in the ostensibly "same" higher-level mediated action of Skyping with each other:

1) Produce different chains of lower-level mediated actions and
2) Both produce a different higher-level mediated action.

Both lower-level and higher-level mediated actions are thus always linked to specific social actors, namely the individuals who are acting in their own embodied ways and are therefore experiencing and perceiving in their very own ways. Simultaneously, both social actors are acting together and reacting to one another, so that the higher-level mediated action is not only individual but also mutually contingent. Important here is that higher-level mediated actions produced together exhibit both individual *and* joint aspects, so that we can say that each social actor produces and perceives a different higher-level mediated action *at the very same time* as the specific higher-level mediated action is jointly produced.

While lower-level mediated actions can be delineated relatively easily by their beginning and end-points, higher-level mediated actions are not as straightforward. Often beginning and end-points of higher-level mediated actions can be determined in various ways. Their determination depends upon the focus of study. As an example, when you are Skyping with your friend, the beginning of the Skype conversation may be considered when you open up your laptop or mobile and load the Skype app. Or, the beginning of your Skype conversation may be considered when your friend answers the call. Similarly, establishing end-points are dependent upon the focus of study. Maybe we want to consider the end of the call when the first person hangs up. Or we consider it to be the end of the call when the Skype app has been closed by one or both participants. Thus, it is important to be clear what we as researchers are investigating in order to know what we want to consider as the beginning and end-points of the higher-level mediated action that we are studying. But we will learn more about just how to do this in the following chapters. In regards to theory, we want to understand the links to the philosophical notions of (i) Perception (what can a social actor perceive when acting and interacting); (ii) Embodiment (in what way does the higher-level mediated action connect body and environment).

Definition 5
Higher-level mediated action = The coming together of many chains of lower-level mediated actions.

Note 8
The beginning and ending points of a higher-level mediated action under study have to be determined by the analyst. Usually several possibilities exist.

Note 9
Lower-level and higher-level mediated actions co-produce each other and neither is theoretically or practically prior.

Higher-Level Mediated Actions: Perception

A higher-level mediated action is perceived by the person producing it, a higher-level mediated action can be perceived by others. As chains of lower-level mediated action come together to build the higher-level mediated action on the one hand and the higher-level mediated action simultaneously produces the chains of lower-level mediated action on the other hand, the higher-level mediated action is perceived by the performer. When others are present, this higher-level mediated action can be perceived by others in whole or in part. The person performing the higher-level mediated action certainly perceives what it is they are doing; when others are present and paying attention to the higher-level mediated action that is being performed by the person, they too experience and perceive the higher-level mediated action. As we will see in later chapters, the notion of attention is quite important, but we will leave a detailed explication and discussion of what is meant by attention for later chapters. Here, we continue to focus upon the interconnection of philosophy and theory. Next, let us consider the philosophical notion of embodiment and see how this concept connects to the higher-level mediated action.

Higher-Level Mediated Actions: Embodiment

Since every lower-level mediated action that a person performs and perceives is embodied and mediated in multiple ways, each higher-level mediated action, which is the coming together of chains of lower-level mediated actions, is therefore necessarily embodied and always mediated in numerous ways. This multiplicity of mediational means/cultural tools, which builds the glue in lower-level mediated actions and connects the body (including cognition and psychology) to the environment, the social and the cultural, is also multiplied in higher-level mediated actions. Thus, each higher-level mediated action binds the physical body (including cognition and psychology) through mediation to the environment, the social and the cultural in always numerous ways. But, of course, we not only find people acting and interacting in real time in our world. We also find things that tell of previously performed actions. It is these kind of actions that we call frozen mediated actions in multimodal mediated theory.

Discussion Point 7

How exactly is it possible that lower-level mediated actions and higher-level mediated actions co-produce each other simultaneously?

Frozen Mediated Action

The frozen mediated action (Norris 2002a, 2004a) is defined as an action embedded within an object or the environment that tells of the previously performed actions. For example, a house tells of people having built it at some point in time. These actions of the builders are embedded in the house itself. While we may not know who actually performed the action of building the house, we are all quite sure that someone (the social actor(s) having performed the action) had to build the house (the mediated action(s) embedded) with and through a whole host of mediational means/cultural tools (such as cement, wood, glass, as well as hands, building tools and so on). When speaking about a house, we may find someone say "when they built this house, they really could have put in larger windows." A sentence such as this one demonstrates how we often think about things. Someone placed something somewhere, someone left something else in an odd place, or someone did not mow the lawn in some city where we do not know anybody. We always know that someone had to have done something (or not have done something) for things to be where or how they are now. What we see are mediational means/cultural tools such as the house itself. What we read off of the object are the actions that had to be performed in order for the object to be where and in the state that it is now. Most often, we read off most recently performed actions that are frozen in the objects as for example someone just moved into the house. Yet, we can often easily trace other, older actions as well, as the example with the windows above shows. Here, we read higher-level mediated actions off of the objects. But the concept of frozen mediated action is also useful when thinking of lower-level mediated actions. For example, one can read a brushstroke in a painting, or markings on a piece of paper. In regards to theory, we want to understand the links of this theoretical concept to the philosophical notions of (i) Perception (what can a social actor perceive when acting and interacting); (ii) Embodiment (in what way does the frozen mediated action connect body and environment).

Frozen Mediated Actions: Perception

When encountering an object, we do not only perceive the object itself, but quite readily assign mediated actions to the object as frozen within. In the Louvre, for example, the painting of Mona Lisa had hung at almost eye level years ago. When I went back many years later to visit her again, I remarked "oh look, they've put her up there now" as they had placed her at a different wall and way above eye level. What I had perceived here was the fact that some social actors re-positioned the painting of Mona Lisa. I had perceived the mediated action frozen in the new positioning of the painting. Thus, when encountering things in our everyday lives, we quite often read mediated actions off of them. This perceiving of the actions that it took for a painting to be placed in a new spot or the actions that it took to build a bridge, or the actions that it took to furnish an apartment is the focus of this theoretical notion that we call *frozen mediated action*. But how does this concept link to the philosophical notion of embodiment?

Frozen Mediated Actions: Embodiment

As mentioned above, a frozen mediated action can either be a lower-level mediated action or a higher-level mediated action. Since every lower-level mediated action that a person performs and perceives is necessarily embodied and always mediated in multiple ways, since each higher-level mediated action that an individual performs and perceives is necessarily embodied and always mediated in numerous ways, each frozen mediated action that a person performs and perceives is therefore necessarily embodied and always mediated in multiple ways. Here, too, it is the multiplicity of mediation that builds the glue in frozen mediated actions and connects the body (including cognition and psychology) to the environment, the social and the cultural. Of course, when you are the one seeing an object and you are the one who is perceiving a frozen mediated action embedded, then you are the social actor experiencing this frozen mediated action. At the same time, you are also assigning this frozen mediated action to another social actor (even if to an unknown social actor) who must have performed the action that you are now reading off of the object. Thus, each frozen mediated action also binds physical bodies (including cognition and psychology) through mediation to the environment, the social and the cultural in numerous ways. But, of course, embodied actions and interactions with all of their lower-level, higher-level and frozen mediated actions do not simply come about only because of and in the moment that they arise. We do not simply know how to act and interact in different circumstances and with different people on a momentary basis. We do not just perform embodied actions and interactions in a moment when we perceive the object, when we read frozen mediated actions of various objects and read them off mostly quite correctly. Rather, we have learned our embodied actions and our perceptions through a history of experience; this history of experience is embedded in practice.

Discussion Point 8

Frozen mediated actions can be read off of objects and/or the environment. In the examples above, we think about vision as the sense and gaze as the mode to perceive frozen mediated actions. What other ways of perception can you think of to read frozen mediated actions off of objects and the environment?

Practices and Discourses

Practice (Bourdieu 1977, 1990, 1998; de Certeau 1984; Norris and Jones 2005a; Scollon 1998, 2001a) has been defined in various ways. Scollon's (1998, 2001a) definition is the one we use in multimodal mediated theory. Scollon defined practice as *an action with a history*. In Scollon (2001a), he analyzed how a child learned the practice of handing. Handing, when analyzed in isolation, is a lower-level mediated action (Norris 2004a) when it is being performed and as Scollon showed, a child learns to hand different things to different people, turning handing into a practice. Each time the child hands something to someone, the child draws on the acquired history of handing, therefore, the definition of *practice as an action with a history*.

Thinking of practice in these concrete ways allows us to disambiguate what may seem ephemeral. A practice is learned; a practice changes with each performed concrete mediated action, i.e. each time the child hands something, the practice of handing develops in some way; each concrete mediated action that is performed grows out of the practice. Thus concrete mediated actions and practices merge into one another *and* enhance or inhibit one another (Norris 2014b). But practices are not only instantiated by and through the performance of lower-level mediated actions. Higher-level mediated actions (such as the higher-level mediated action of having coffee with someone or the higher-level mediated action of taking a university course) also form, develop, and link to practices. Again, it is the concrete higher-level mediated action that a specific social actor performs that produces the practice at the same time as the practice brings about the concrete higher-level mediated action. When a person performs the concrete higher-level mediated action of having coffee with a particular friend, the practice of having coffee with friends is developing. Simultaneously, the extent to which the practice of having coffee with friends is developed has a bearing on how the concrete higher-level mediated action of having coffee with this particular friend emerges. Therefore, the practice of having coffee with friends mediates the concrete higher-level mediated action of having coffee with a particular friend.

Definition 6

A practice is a mediated action with a history.

Discussion Point 9

Drawing on what was said about individual and joint production of mediated actions above, think about in what ways a practice can be individual or needs to be collective. Here, also consider your earlier discussion of what is meant by an *individual* in this framework.

Discourses (Fairclough 2001; Fairclough and Wodak 1997; Norris 2014b; Wodak 1989, 1995, 2001) are practices of a larger scale that quite often are linked to institutions (such as the discourse of schooling) or may be linked to a society or culture (such as the discourse of a green city). Discourses often appear on the one hand as ephemeral and on the other hand as a given or norm. But just as any practice, any discourse comes about through concrete mediated actions and is reinforced and/or changed through concrete mediated actions. More about practice can be found below in the section on Scollon's thought.

But now let us see how the concept of practice links to the philosophical notions of perception and embodiment.

Practice: Perception

A practice is an action with a history. Higher-level and lower-level mediated actions are (or can be) perceived by the person producing them as well as by others. Practice, or recurrent mediated actions, are often perceived tacitly. A concrete mediated action may be perceived as produced well due to the long historical development of the action, i.e. the learned practice. Think of playing the guitar as a practice, an action with a history. The more you play, the more often you perform the mediated action of playing the guitar, the better the mediated action is performed. While the concrete action is (or can be) perceived quite concretely, the practice is perceived more tacitly and often is experienced as something that *just feels right*. This feeling then, is our way of perceiving the practice.

Next, let us consider the philosophical notion of embodiment and see how this concept connects to practice as an action with a history.

Practice: Embodiment

Just as lower-level, higher-level, and frozen mediated actions bind physical bodies (including cognition and psychology) to the environment, the social and the cultural, practice, which arises through concrete mediated actions, binds physical bodies (including cognition and psychology) to the environment, the social and the cultural. It is with and through embodiment that practices (actions with a history) arise, develop, change, and intersect. When thinking about this theoretical thought, you may want to think about your ways of having dinner. While when, where, and what you eat will no doubt be different on different days, you will likely have developed a kind of practice of eating dinner. Even though your concrete dinners will differ, you will be easily able to explain how your practice of dinner developed through concrete mediated actions. Now, when you think further, you will see that your practice of having dinner is quite strongly and clearly linked to your body and the connection to the environment and objects within. Because practices emerge from concrete mediated actions and these mediated actions clearly link to embodiment, practices necessarily also link to embodiment. In fact, we cannot even perceive a practice without embodiment. Now that we have a good understanding of the mediated action and practice, it is time to consider the notion site of engagement.

Site of Engagement

The site of engagement was first developed by Scollon (1997), where he defined it as the window opened up that makes concrete actions possible. At the site of engagement, concrete actions are made possible through their intersection with practices (Scollon 1998) and discourses (Norris 2014b). The site of engagement allows the analysis of these different aspects from concrete actions and their modal make-up to the practices that the social actors performing the actions draw upon and reinforce (or contradict) and the discourses that play a role in the concrete mediated actions. As such, the site of engagement embeds the social actors, all mediational means/cultural tools and the environment in which the mediated actions are taking place in + the many (often different) practices that social actors draw on, engage in, or change + the various discourses that come into play in the very moment when and as social actors are acting.

Site of Engagement: Perception

Everything happens at a site of engagement and certainly, all social actors perceive what they are doing, what others do, where they are acting and how. Thus, the site of engagement is that coming together of all of our perception, the conglomeration of everything discussed above.

Site of Engagement: Embodiment

Just as the site of engagement is the conglomeration of all of perception discussed above, so is the site of engagement the conglomeration of embodiment discussed thus far. The site of engagement is the very moment, the very place and the very people that are acting and interacting in embodied ways.

Definition 7
A site of engagement is the window opened up through practices and discourses that make concrete mediated actions possible.

2.1

Development of Scollon's Philosophical Thought

Philosophy (Thesaurus: attitude, viewpoint, idea, thinking, way of life, values, beliefs) is often viewed as informing the social sciences – such as Marxist philosophy informs critical discourse analysis and parts of mediated discourse analysis. Yet, philosophy is seldom clearly expressed when we read about theory or methodology. Often, at least in mediated discourse analysis, the philosophical underpinnings are implicit, referred to with a reference here or there, but seldom if ever, clearly put forward. The reason I believe is that Scollon, the founder of mediated discourse analysis and an avid reader, was (as he said quite often himself) influenced by this or that notion in philosophy without really being all too clear just how or why he thought the way he did. Certainly, this is a wonderful weakness that probably all great thinkers exhibit; it was one that Scollon often discussed. However, while he was influenced by many great thinkers without being all too sure just how his own thought developed, Scollon was quite meticulous in his referencing; thus giving us a chance to retrace some of his thought.

As Scollon was developing his thought, always trying to stay grounded in the real world, he developed mediated discourse analysis. I remember, as one of the lucky students who were first taught mediated discourse analysis by him, that he himself doubted that he had in fact developed a theory. He had, as he claimed, developed some theoretical notions, but predominantly, he thought of mediated discourse analysis as a methodology. Yet, he also emphasized the fact that theory was most important if we wanted to understand human communication. Another important point that he made from the first class onward was that mediated discourse analysis was a starting point. It was not a finished framework. In his own mind, he thought of mediated discourse analysis as a work in progress; he asked his students who wanted to work with this starting point to be critical of mediated discourse analysis, to never view it as a bible and to always critically examine the theoretical and methodological notions that he had brought forward. Scollon himself was probably mediated discourse's greatest critic. He knew the flaws that were embedded in the framework. He knew he had muddled some notions and he knew that much more work was needed to sort out notions and terminology. One of Scollon's biggest fears in regard to mediated discourse analysis was that some of his disciples might canonize what he had written. Doing so, he argued, would destroy the possibility of gaining new knowledge, rather than helping in the pursuit of it. I have heeded his advice and have constantly tried to critically use and constantly develop his concepts as well as my own and do hope that the reader will take up this challenge as well.

Systematically Working with Multimodal Data: Research Methods in Multimodal Discourse Analysis,
First Edition. Sigrid Norris.
© 2019 John Wiley & Sons, Inc. Published 2019 by John Wiley & Sons, Inc.
Companion website: www.wiley.com/go/Norris/multimodal-data

Discussion Point 1

In what way does Scollon's insistence on staying grounded in the world continue in multimodal mediated theory?

Scollon Referenced Vygotsky *and* Nishida

Vygotsky was a Soviet psychologist and Nishida a Japanese philosopher. How are these two directions of thought embedded in Scollon's mediated discourse analysis? As readers, we gain our own understanding of ideas, concepts, and terms. This is true for each reader, as we link our own knowledge of the world and our own historical body (Scollon 1998; Scollon and Scollon 2003) to what we read. Thus, we take a term to be – quite often – what fits our own world, rather than actually taking a term to mean what the author meant. This was the same for Scollon. It is the same for myself and it is the same for you. Even if you do not wish to read in this way, you are actually bound by your own knowledge, your own perception and your own embodiment in the world.

   Because of this limitation, I have been reviewing concepts and re-read much of the literature that mediated discourse is based on, going back to antecedent and also peripheral literature, in the hope of finding thought that Scollon never mentioned, but may have read. Since we know that Scollon was meticulous in regard to referencing, I believe he referenced the literature that he thought he was directly basing his framework on.

Discussion Point 2

Think about how modes come about through mediated actions. Modes have to be personal as well as social (based in groups). If we think about modes in this way, how does that explain why readers read as Scollon did?

Scollon and Vygotsky: Some Musings

Scollon referenced Vygotsky's (1978) *Mind in Society*. The thought that was outlined in Vygotsky's *Mind in Society*, however, was only a part of Vygotsky's thought. Further, it was only a part of what Scollon had read of Vygotsky's thought. However, what can be said is that Scollon was primarily interested in the notion of mediation. Scollon takes Vygotsky's notion of mediation as a stepping stone. From Vygotsky, Scollon then jumps to Wertsch (1981) and from there, Scollon leaps to his own way of thinking about mediation: Speaking about texts, Scollon suggests:

> …what is crucial is to see texts as mediational means – the tools by which people undertake mediated action…In a mediational view of action, texts are cultural tools or mediational means.
>
> *(Scollon 1998, p. 14)*

Scollon, quite differently from Vygotsky, uses the terms "cultural tools" and "mediational means" interchangeably. He makes no distinction between psychological and other tools. While Vygotsky, certainly did make this distinction:

> The most essential feature distinguishing the psychological tool from the technical tool, is that it directs the mind and behaviour whereas the technical tool, which is also inserted as an intermediate link between human activity and the external object, is directed toward producing one or other set of changes in the object itself.
>
> *(Vygotsky 1981, p. 140)*

Thus, Scollon embraced the notion of mediation, but firstly disregarded Vygotsky's difference between psychological and technical tools and secondly used both notions (mediational means and cultural tools) as interchangeable. This is no mistake, either. This is well-thought through intent. Scollon, who grounds his thinking in action that real people take in the world along with Wertsch (1998), moved beyond Vygotsky's focus on the mediation of signs and symbols, without, however falling into the trap that the Kharkovites had fallen into:

> Kharkovites devoted their entire attention to activities, thus bringing them closer to the Piagetian programme with its emphasis on the internalisation of sensory-motor schemas…As a result the notion of symbolic psychological tools and the role of culture embodied in them, became underrepresented in Soviet psychology…
>
> *(Kozulin 1990, p. 247)*

Scollon guarded against this from happening by using double terminology: mediational means/cultural tools, either using both concurrently or using one term in one sentence and the other in the next, always emphasizing that all mediational means *also* are cultural tools. In Scollon's framework, mediational means and cultural tools are used interchangeably. As such, it was a direct response to those directions of thought that, like Piaget, prioritized cognition and internalization of schemata. In mediated discourse theory, Scollon (1998, 2001a), takes the mediated action, developed by Wertsch (1998), as the unit of analysis. The mediated action in Scollon's work (as well as in Multimodal (Inter)action Analysis outlined in this book) is the social actor(s) acting with or through mediational means or cultural tools. Mediational means/cultural tools are objects *and* what Vygtosky would call psychological tools such as language or math.

Discussion Point 3
How does multimodal mediated theory guard against the pitfalls of prioritizing cognition and internalization of schemata?

Scollon and Nishida: Some Musings

Scollon referenced Nishida's (1958) concept of *historical body*. He had picked up an English translation of Nishida (1958), which was probably one of the first when he was in Korea. Back then, the young Scollon was in the process of developing his understanding of a broad range of literature. Scollon and Scollon (2003) understood Nishida's concept of historical body to mean:

> Different people play the same role differently depending on their history of personal experience inscribed in what the philosopher Nishida calls the *histori-cal body*. A lifetime of personal habits come to feel so natural that one's body carries out actions seemingly without being told. Bourdieu referred to this phenomenon as *habitus* but we prefer *historical body* because it situates bodily memories precisely in the individual body.
>
> *(Scollon and Scollon 2003, p. 13)*

This is a beautiful definition (or explanation) of the term *historical body* and it allowed Scollon to say just what he wanted to say. He wanted to demonstrate the groundedness in the body, when performing mediated action. In order to do this, he called upon Nishida and used a term that seemed to clearly explicate just what he was trying to show. But Scollon actually used the term to mean what *he* intended to say, namely that experience is inscribed in the individual's body. Experience, as Scollon thought of it, never was *individual*, it was always linked to and enmeshed with society but was *inscribed in the individual body*.

Yet Nishida was trying to make a different point with his term *historical body* and I believe it is one that is often misunderstood. Yuasa (1987) writes:

> "A historical body" is a body in the self qua *basho* which is beyond the body in its everyday dimension; that is, the historical body has overcome the disintegration into subjectivity and objectivity. When the self acts as a historical body, it enters into the *basho* vis-a-vis nothing, transcending the dimensions of the ego-consciousness or bright consciousness. Consequently, transcending the standpoint of self-conscious-ness, the self has "immersed" itself into the "historical world," that is into beings' total interconnectedness in the world as the life-space. In this sense, the body's function is not the ordinary sense of "action," that is, it differs from the bright consciousness, from the everyday self in which one moves the body in accordance with the will's choices and decisions. But as Nishida says, insofar as it is viewed as "the expressive world's self-determination," we "act or function" in some higher sense.
>
> *(Yuasa 1987, p. 70)*

Scollon, of course, was not the only one interpreting Nishida's term historical body as he did. The online *Stanford Encyclopedia of Philosophy*, for example, states:

> Gradually Nishida came to recognize the importance of embodiment for human interaction and communication and introduced the notion of the expressive or historical body. The body is not primarily a physical object and product of the natural world, but a historical subject and co-creator of the world.
>
> *(http://plato.stanford.edu/entries/nishida-kitaro/, accessed 29 June 2013)*

This understanding is maybe a little bit closer to Nishida's thinking, but it still is only a Western reading of something very unfamiliar, that is then resemiotised (borrowing Iedema's 2001 term) into an understanding that appears to "make sense" to the Western reader rather than reflecting what the Eastern philosopher in fact stated.

Certainly, Nishida is not an easy read. His writing is difficult and unfamiliarly circular for the Western reader. The reader needs to have a very good grasp of Eastern philosophy, needs to be able to read between the lines and needs to be well familiar with Western philosophical thought as Nishida takes up much of Western thought and resemiotizes it *into* Eastern philosophical thought and at the same time intermingles it with Buddhist thought.

While I cannot explain why the Stanford Encyclopedia of Philosophy takes the term historical body to mean what is claimed above (and I think that a revision is in order there), I can explain why Scollon defined the term *historical body* as he did. Scollon read the translation of Nishida's (1958) *Intelligibility and the philosophy of nothingness* for the first time not long after it appeared. At that time, he was highly interested in Zen Buddhism. He took a copy home and carried it around the world, re-reading it or parts of it at times. As an aside, I can say that it was this very copy that I first read. He lent it to me when I was writing my PhD dissertation; I took from it that *historical body* meant what Scollon said it meant. Or to put it another way: I read Nishida (1958) much like Scollon had read Nishida (1958). Nishida actually does not say all that much about historical body in this book. He briefly and quite vaguely touches upon historical body. In one sense it appears that it could mean what both Scollon and later I, read as a "…history of personal experience inscribed in what the philosopher Nishida calls the historical body…" (Scollon and Scollon 2003, p. 13). Nishida, writing about the historical body notes:

> This means…that we form ourselves as viewpoints of the world…Man's action originates from mirroring the world through acts of expression…It means the comprehension of things by the self-expressing Self and from the standpoint of the present unity of opposites. This is the standpoint of concrete logic; here is the true and the real…The scientific standpoint does not deny this standpoint, but remains there, consistently.
>
> *(Nishida 1958, pp. 197–198)*

In the above quote, I have only given some of the many sentences that Nishida used in his way of writing. These are the parts that a Western reader would extract from the pages to make sense of what Nishida is trying to say. These sentences appear to a Western reader to be the essence of his writing in these pages. Our eyes are trained to get to the point as quickly as possible. If you would compare a Westerner's reading style to climbing a mountain, the fastest and straightest way up with the eyes on the track would be a good description. However, when you realize that Nishida has a style of writing that is maybe best described as someone climbing a mountain by slowly walking around the mountain and only incrementally moving upward, thereby lingering to gaze on the side of the path, not however, on the path itself, then you begin to understand some of what Nishida is trying to say. With this in mind, I offer the reader another few paragraphs, this time as written and without chopping off the redundancies and intricacies so notorious in Nishida's writing.

So historical life makes itself "concrete"; the world becomes something that truly moves by itself. I do not want to say that this evolution is merely a continuation of biological life, nor that it is merely negation of biological life. It means that the historical world is through and through unity of opposites. Biological life already contains the contradiction; but biological life is still in affordance with the environment and not yet truly "from the formed to the forming". At the extreme limit of the contradiction, the evolution leads to the life of man. Of course, this is the result of the work of the historical life from many millions of years. At the extreme limit of acting life from the formed towards the forming, a stage is reached where the subject lives by submerging into the environment and the environment is environment by negating itself and becoming subjective. Past and future, contradicting each other, join in the present, and the world, as unity of opposites, progresses from present to present, forming itself; i.e. the world is productive and creative. The body is no longer a mere biological body, but a historical one.

(Nishida 1958, p. 196)

The contradiction lies in the very fact that we are acting-intuitioning and that we are productive-bodily. Therefore, we are progressing as unity of opposites, from the formed to the forming and we transcend the "given," as something formed. It is so expected that we finally reach something that has transcended [even] action-intuition, [and] the body. This [transcending], however, must start from here and return here.

The world in which past and future, negating each other, join in the present and which, as present of the unity of opposites, forms itself, is through and through un-bodily and is represented in symbols. It is intellectual. But this does not mean that it is completely separated from our historical body.

Everything that is given to us in the world of unity of opposites is given to us as a "task". Our task in the world is "to form". In this we have our life. We are born with this task. That which is given is not merely to be negated, or to be mediated; it is given to be "completed". It is something bodily given. We have not been born with nothing, but with our body. It can be said that a task is put before us by the historical nature through the fact that we are born with a body. In this task is contained an infinite number of tasks (like the eye of an insect), as unity of opposites. The fact that we are born with a body, means that we are born and loaded with human tasks. That which is truly and directly given to our human acting Self confronts us objectively as an earnest task.

Reality is enveloping and conditioning us. Reality is neither merely material, nor mediating; it speaks to our Self: "Do this, or die!" The truly given is where the world, as one single present of unity of opposites, confronts me. The truly given, or true reality must be something that is to be found. We have that which is truly given to us, when we know where the contradiction of reality is.

(Nishida 1958, pp. 198–199)

As you can see, Nishida is not exactly an easy read for the Western reader. However, when you read the above paragraphs and read not only what is there, but also glance at that what is alluded to, but not quite spelled out, it becomes apparent that Nishida is not just speaking of the historical body as "...history of personal experience inscribed in...the historical body..." (Scollon and Scollon 2003, p. 13). Rather, Nishida treats the historical body as something that the body is a part of, but that in fact goes beyond the body itself.

Discussion Point 4

Which parts in the above paragraphs allude to the fact that Nishida has more than just the biological body and the experiences of a person in mind?

The glossary in the book notes that the body has two meanings in Nishida's writing, namely:

1) The biological body,
2) the "historical body" i.e. society or people. See "historical species."
(Nishida 1958, p. 243)

When reading the glossary entry, it appears that the term historical body is actually closer to Bourdieu's habitus. For this reason, Scollon speaks of either historical body or habitus, at times distinguishing and at times using the terms interchangeably.

The reason I found that that was actually not how Nishida meant the term historical body came about when I began to read much more of Nishida's writing. In doing so, I began to wonder. I did not actually wonder why Scollon had defined the term historical body as he did. I knew the answer to this and as I just mentioned, I agreed with his definition and I still do, even though now, I would suggest to those working in mediated discourse analysis to reference Scollon (1998), rather than Nishida when referring to the term *historical body*, because we use the term as Scollon used it and not at all as Nishida did. I see no flaw in Scollon defining the term as he did. It was useful for Scollon to do so at the time and it is a useful term, *our historical body* as understood and defined by Scollon. So why discuss it at all if there is no real problem here?

Rather than this being a problem, I began to see it like a mystery. What I was wondering about was this: while Scollon did not use the term historical body in Nishida's sense, I found by reading Nishida's writings that mediated discourse appeared to be quite grounded in Nishida's complex, circular, and creative world. Reading Nishida, I could not help but realize that mediated discourse theory was built – at least in part – on Eastern and particularly Buddhist, philosophy. Suzie Scollon tells me that Ron Scollon never read any other works by Nishida. Therefore, I will not suggest that he in fact consciously embedded these notions into mediated discourse theory, but I will suggest that this Eastern Buddhist philosophical thought coming out of Japan had some profound influence on Scollon's thinking.

Discussion Point 5

How does the *Stanford Encyclopedia of Philosophy* entry on Nishida tell us that our understanding is grounded in our experience?

Scollon's Theory: Some Musings

The multimodal framework discussed in this book has a strong theoretical underpinning. This theoretical underpinning is summed up in one theoretical principle, the principle of social action, with its two sub-principles, the principle of communication and the principle of history. While Scollon (1998) first conceived of three distinct principles, I have collapsed these three into one principle: the principle of social action. I have subsumed the other two principles as sub-principles to the principle of social action. The reason for collapsing the three principles into one is that both the principle of communication and the principle of history are, in fact, already embedded in the principle of social action. As Scollon (1998) himself has noted, the three principles as stated are tautological. In other words: there are no social actions that are not communicative in some way; there are no social actions which are not based on and do not embed history in some way. While the notion of communication and the notion of history are certainly very important, these are not actually principles in their own right, but rather are a sub-category to the principle of social action.

Scollon's Practice: Some Musings

Scollon speaks of practice as a count noun (see also Norris and Jones 2005b), giving as one of his examples the practice of handing. Because practice is used often and in different ways, this book offers more insight into how Scollon used it and how we use it in our multimodal framework. The thought here goes like this: a mediated action is a one-time concrete action that a social actor takes, while a practice is the mediated action with a history. In other words, you hand a crayon to your Mom (a mediated action) or you hand anything to anyone (a practice).

In respect to practice, I have been wondering: there are many different uses of the term practice. Scollon (1998) asserts that mediated discourse grew to some extent out of Lave and Wenger's (1991) notion of a community of practice. Yet we, Scollon (1998, 2001a) and others (Jones and Norris 2005c), make the point that the way we use practice is vastly different from the way Lave and Wenger use the term. In mediated discourse theory, practice is a count noun. It is an action with a history. In Lave and Wenger, a community of practice is a loose grouping (of weavers for example) who have a particular way of being weavers. Within the community of practice, we find novices and peripheral members, as well as central members. While Scollon's term practice resides somewhere on some intermediary level between the individual and the group or society, Lave and Wenger's term practice more clearly describes the organizational or institutional structures and how individuals move through and within them.

Scollon also referred to Bourdieu's (1977) theory of practice; practice theory is certainly an important and useful theoretical model. In essence, practice theory (Bourdieu 1977, 1990; Foucault 1993; Giddens 1979, 1984) primarily stems from a sociological point of view and has uncovered that constellations of human groupings develop, enforce, and re-enforce, but also invent and re-invent their – sometimes very particular – practices (or ways of doing things). The main point is that practices are routinized ways of behaving, thinking, and feeling. Related praxeological theories (Butler 1990; Garfinkel 1967; Latour 2005) and Schatzki's philosophy (1996) also build specifically on this notion of practice. Utilizing this notion, we can investigate institutions or organizations and their particular practices, or can examine particular groups in society and their practices. Thereby, we may find that the grouping that we were looking at is actually made up of various groups with differing practices; or we may find that a certain group is in fact not bound in the way that we had thought prior to embarking on a research project, as we find that their practices extend into areas that we were unaware of before. Reckwitz (2002) explains:

> … a practice represents a pattern which can be filled out by a multitude of single and often unique actions reproducing the practice (a certain way of consuming goods can be filled out by plenty of actual acts of consumption). The single individual – as a bodily and mental agent – then acts as the "carrier" (Träger) of a practice – and, in fact, of many different practices…

> A practice is social, as it is a "type" of behaving and understanding that appears at different locales and at different points of time and is carried out by different body/minds… routinized actions are themselves bodily performances… include also routinized mental and emotional activities which are – on a certain level – bodily, as well…

> They necessarily imply certain routinized ways of understanding the world, of desiring something, of knowing how to do something…A "practice" thus crosses the distinction between the allegedly inside and outside of mind and body…

> For practice theory, objects are necessary components of many practices – just as indispensable as bodily and mental activities. Carrying out a practice very often means using particular things in a certain way.
>
> *Reckwitz (2002, pp. 250–252)*

Thus, the term *practice* is here used quite differently from the way that Scollon used it (at least the way he used it most of the time). His thought had been that a practice is an action with a history. That is how I have used it for many years and so have others in the field. This action with a history can be thought of on various levels of action from handing to complex actions that are performed in a group, making up the practices that Bourdieu (or Reckwitz above) talked about. Yet in a way, I think Scollon was closer to de Certau's (1984) notion of practice, who for example, speaks of the practice of cooking, rather than Bordieu's notion of practice.

Certainly, there was a very good reason why Scollon defined a practice as an action with a history. He wanted to express that we can understand, read, and perform a variety of actions that are of the same kind (i.e. handing, no matter who or what you are handing, it always remains handing). Of course, Lave and Wenger, Bourdieu, de Certeau, and others also have a very good reason to use the term practice in the way that they do. Their use of the term practice, in fact, is closer to the common use of the term practice (as in: custom, tradition, or routine) and it is particularly this common-world use that Bourdieu and others wanted to emphasize.

However, there *is* a difference. Practice theory developed the theoretical notion by taking the common understanding of the term practice, i.e. habit, tradition, way of doing things, or routine as a theoretical model and explored the world through this theoretical model. Scollon found this model useful and highly important, but was also unhappy with the model as it was not clear to him just how knowing of and exploring practices through practice theory was going to lead to more than a better, but still ephemeral, understanding of what groups actually do. He was trying to understand the world in a more concrete way and was interested in developing theory that was grounded in the real world on the one hand *and* was deployable through methodological tools on the other hand. While practice theory was and is working on an abstracted level, practice theory does not offer a methodology that allows researchers to truly capture and describe scientifically what the theoretical notion of practice alludes to. Therefore, he postulated that practices (even on the larger level) were nothing else but actions with a history. However and I think this is where Scollon's notion of practice gets muddled, he used the term practice both in the theoretical sense as it is used in practice theory and also used the term practice (as action with a history) in his own sense. In other words, I think what Scollon was really getting at was that a practice (in practice theoretical terms) can be analyzed and understood by investigating the actions with a history that are being performed by those who engage in the practice.

Scollon's postulation was ground-breaking and highly useful. However, it was also confusing to those who had not had the chance of being able to discuss his thoughts at length in person. The confusion comes about because Scollon sometimes merged the differently defined notions of practice.

Discussion Point 6

How is Scollon's definition of practice (as an action with a history) more grounded in the real world than the definition of practice (as in custom, tradition, or routine) used by practice theorists?

Philosophical and Theoretical Background: Summary

In this chapter, Sections 2.0 and 2.1, we have learned how our philosophical underpinnings, the primacy of perception and the primacy of embodiment, link to our theoretical underpinnings. Perception and embodiment take an important role in Multimodal (Inter)action Analysis. Their role is grounded in Western and Eastern philosophy and grounded in Scollon's (1998, 2001a) mediated discourse theory and further developed in multimodal mediated theory.

With the unit of analysis, the mediated action, we bind the individual to the social, the cultural, and the psychological as well as to the physical environment. The unit of analysis, developed by Vygotsky (1978), further defined by Wertsch (1998) and re-defined in mediated discourse analysis by Scollon (1998), has undergone a change in multimodal mediated theory. Here, the unit of analysis is refined and developed into three units of analysis: the lower-level mediated action, the higher-level mediated action, and the frozen mediated action. Through the theorization of these units of analysis, we are able to analyze micro actions in great detail, analyze larger (or higher-level) actions in great detail and can also analyze objects in the environment or the environment itself. All of these analyses come together in Multimodal (Inter)action Analysis, so that the three units of analyses bring with them great explanatory power.

Practice is defined in multimodal mediated theory just as it is defined in Scollon's mediated discourse theory, namely as an action with a history. We can speak of practices on a lower level, a higher level and also in respect to objects. Thus, once again, a concept from mediated discourse theory has undergone a change. While previously, such distinction was not possible, we can now see the various levels of practice from the minute to the macro.

The site of engagement, first defined by Scollon (1997, 1998) as the window opened up through converging practices that make a concrete mediated action possible, also has undergone some change. This change did not only come about because of the refinement of the analytical unit, the mediated action, or the incorporation of discourses into the concept. Rather, the unit of analysis, the site of engagement is utilized as an analytical tool that always brings us back to the concrete moment, without, however, losing sight of the larger picture, the converging practices and discourses (Norris 2014b).

The last part of the chapter delved deeper into Scollon's thought. This, I believe is an important part, as without Scollon's thought, multimodal mediated theory would not have come about. Therefore, his way of thinking is a central background for all who are studying Multimodal (Inter)action Analysis.

Philosophical and Theoretical Background – Things to Remember

Things to Remember 1
Our primary interest is in how people act and interact. In order to understand this, we take perception (what each social actor perceives) and embodiment (who and how we are with others and with the environment) very seriously.

Things to Remember 2
Because of our view of the primacy of perception, we are greatly interested in attention, emotion, memory, imagination, thought, as well as manual actions.

Things to Remember 3
We wish to keep the complexity alive that shows how we are interconnected with each other, the environment and objects within.

Now that we have thought about philosophy and theory, in the next chapters we will delve into data collection and analysis.

Chapter 3

Systematically Working with Multimodal Data Phase I

3.0

Phase I: Data Collection

Video data usually is the prerequisite for conducting a multimodal discourse analysis.[1] However, video data may not be the only data that we will want to collect as will become evident below.

Collecting video data is easier than ever before. Mini video recorders and video apps in mobile phones allow us to collect video data anywhere and of anything without much intrusion. At the same time, people in today's world are much more used to videotaping themselves and others. This chapter begins with developing a research theme or topic and a research question. This is necessary before we can think about data collection, but this also naturally leads us into the nitty gritty of video data collection. Here, the chapter critically discusses video data collection and addresses questions such as "What is data?" "What are naturally occurring interactions?" "Which ethical considerations are important when working with participants?" and "What is fair use?" The chapter then discusses limitations of video recording and delves into the questions of "How much data is enough?" and "Where do we place the camera(s) when video recording participants?"

The ease of video recording and the common practice of people recording themselves, friends, and family members has also changed the way people react to being video recorded. This leads us to consider the observer's paradox (Labov 2006 [1966], p. 86), an effort to "observe how people speak when they are not being observed"; and in line with this, to examine the question "(Where) does the researcher come into the picture?" (Norris et al. 2014).

Lastly, the chapter reflects upon using readily available video as data and addresses pre-edited content from YouTube, TV, or movies.

Note 1
The objective of Phase I is to guide us in data collection.

---

1 See Norris (2011a) for ways to work multimodally if you cannot collect video data.

Systematically Working with Multimodal Data: Research Methods in Multimodal Discourse Analysis, First Edition. Sigrid Norris.
© 2019 John Wiley & Sons, Inc. Published 2019 by John Wiley & Sons, Inc.
Companion website: www.wiley.com/go/Norris/multimodal-data

So, Where Do We Begin?

The following Step-by-Step process is a guide that shows how you can work systematically with your video data. This chapter discusses Phase I of the guide. Phase I, data collection, consists of 10 steps. In Sections 3.1–3.3, each step is exemplified by various examples: Section 3.1 demonstrates how to utilize the steps in Phase I for collecting a YouTube video as data. Section 3.2 shows how the steps in Phase I can be used for an experimental study; and Section 3.3 illustrates how the steps of Phase I can be used in a larger video ethnographic study.

Throughout, readers will find tasks that will help familiarize themselves with using the steps of Phase I; and the reader will also find tasks that guide them to think through and discuss theoretical and analytical questions. Most importantly, the tasks will help the reader to better understand how to employ the Step-by-Step guide in a most fruitful way in order to examine their own video data.

Phase I: Data Collection

Before collecting data, you need to worry about only one thing. What are *you interested in*? The answer to this question will lead you to the question: *What exactly is it that you wish to collect*?

Step 1: Identifying a Theme or Topic

When setting out to conduct a multimodal discourse analysis, you will first want to think about your genuine interest. This very personal interest will lead your research in class projects, theses, and dissertations, as well as in larger scale projects. What is it that you are interested in? While the question is open and inviting, it is also a daunting question, exactly because you could essentially study anything that has to do with people's actions and interactions. Thus, let us begin in a general way. Are you interested in art, creativity, culture, family, gender, identity, knowledge, learning, migration, music, organizations, power, sports, or technology? These are just a few themes/topics that can be considered. Of course, we can also combine some of these and/or other themes and may wish to think about migrant identity or culture and ethnicity.

Task 1
Brainstorm in small groups and write down a list of themes/topics that may be of interest to you.

Task 2
Individually, pick three of the themes/topics that you are most strongly interested in.

Now that you have gathered a selection of themes/topics that you may wish to conduct research on, you will want to think about where you can find these themes/topics.

For example, if you are interested in gender in families, you already know that you will need data that show how family members act and interact. Or, if you are interested in organizations, you know that you need data that gives you insight into the workings of people in organizational settings. But what kind of data will you need if you are interested in technology? Since we are working in discourse analysis, you may want to have a look at how people interact with and through technology. For example, you may want to see how people use video conferencing technology. Or you may want to have a look at how people play games. Of course, you may not only want to think about people doing things in real time. You may also want to think about films, YouTube clips, or TV shows that can give insight into your favorite themes/topics. Thus, now you will want to link your three interests of themes/topics to specific instances of actions and interactions that will allow you to study these themes/topics.

Task 3
What kind of actions and interactions will be useful for you to study in order to gain insight into each of your three themes/topics?

Task 4
Which one of the three choices is the most interesting and/or the most doable for your project?

Once you have selected a theme/topic and the actions and interactions that you would like to study – be they real time by actual participants or performances produced for films or TV – it is time to delve deeper and develop some questions that you would like to answer.

Step 2: Developing Research Questions

Developing a research question or a number of research questions is important because your questions will drive your data collection and/or your thinking about the data that you are interested in studying. Because of this, you will want to take some time to contemplate what exactly you want to understand. Certainly for larger research projects as theses or dissertation projects and large scale research projects, a thorough literature review is in order at this point. A literature review of the theme/topic and your chosen direction of data will help you determine your research questions, which will be derived in part by the lack of research conducted in a particular area and in part by your interests. However, for class projects with a focus on multimodal discourse analysis, where the analysis part is emphasized, research questions can be used in order for the student to later conduct a relevant literature review of the theme/topic and kind of data used. Generally, one can say the smaller the project, the more concrete the research questions should be, whereas in large projects, research questions need to be developed that allow for the collection of more data and thus should be kept more general in the beginning.

Note 2 – BA or MA Thesis Ideas

One can develop a whole range of mini-projects that are doable for a BA or an MA project. Let us say you are interested in culture or ethnicity. You may want to analyze how cultural and ethnic stereotypes are produced and re-produced in the program *Orange is the new black*. Or you could see how identity of a specific character is developed through the use of objects in a soap opera such as *Offspring*. One can also analyze how the child actors in *Stranger Things* are produced as more knowledgeable, or in charge, in juxtaposition to adults. Or one could examine how the opposite female roles of the *Stark Sisters* is produced multimodally in *Game of Thrones*. These are just a few ideas and maybe this will give you a point to start from in order to develop your own possible thesis projects. For class projects, a YouTube video or the like as shown in Section 3.1 would be a good size.

Task 5

Brainstorm about possible mini- or large scale projects and find something that really interests you.

Task 6

Develop a fitting research question.

Task 7

Read some pertinent literature to begin gaining a good understanding of the area that you intend to study.

Given that the researcher, no matter if working on a small or a large sized project will read relevant thematic literature to situate their study, let us continue thinking about data. Before delving into data collection, there are a few things that we need to consider. For example we may want to think about what actually can be called data and what can not. We may also want to contemplate some ethical considerations before setting out on data collection.

Step 3: Considerations Before Setting Out on Data Collection: What Is Data?

For a multimodal discourse analysis, we can collect video data of people acting and interacting in any setting. As researchers, we may wish to collect video data of people in their everyday lives; we may wish to collect video data of people in an experimental setting; or we may wish to collect available online data in the form of YouTube clips, TV series, or movies.

However, just as readily available online content is not data per se, the pure recording of hours of naturally occurring interaction is not data as such. The collection of video recordings in the first instance is the collection of raw footage. People film people as they act and interact or browse to find a YouTube clip to watch.

Raw footage only becomes data once a particular researcher or research team is working with the footage by sorting and logging it, naming clips, and determining what it is that will be/has been collected. Sharable data-bases of video recordings, for example, are actually data-bases of raw footage for other researchers even if an individual in charge of the data-base has sorted, logged, and named the clips. Any raw footage only becomes data when the actual researcher or team of researchers analyzing the data is/are work ing with the recordings.

Why is it important to make this distinction between raw footage and data? The answer is simple: if we did not make a distinction between the two, the entire Internet would be data and everyone watching it would be a researcher working with this data. Of course, we all know that is not the case. People browse, learn, and inform themselves on the Internet, or watch video clips for entertainment. But people gen- erally do not conduct a video analysis as they use the Internet. Similarly, many peo- ple video record their own and other's actions and interactions. They store, edit, share, and watch each other's content. However, people generally do not analyze their footage in the same way as a discourse analyst interested in how people act and interact or a social scientist interested in how people store, edit, and share their video recordings.

As soon as we speak of data, some form of analysis has already occurred and many more steps of analysis are about to occur. While every kind of video recording can become data, the mere collecting or even editing and sharing of video recordings does not warrant calling the videos *data*. Thus, calling video recordings data entails a quali- tative shift from what has been collected to what is going to be analyzed.

As soon as we begin to speak of data and data sets, we have shifted our point of view from simply watching content to selecting content for analysis. This shift in point of view can occur and re-occur at different times for different projects. For example, when a researcher sets out to collect video recordings of specific actions and interactions of participants, the researcher can already speak of collecting data because the focus is on *collecting in order to analyze* certain actions. Or, when a researcher sets out to examine a large data-base in order to collect video recordings of particular actions for analysis, they can speak of collecting data. Just as a researcher examining the Internet for YouTube clips *to undergo analysis*, the researcher can speak of collecting data. The important distinction is the specific research question or theme or topic that drives the data collection and the focus on analysis of what is being collected.

Task 8
What is the difference between filmed or online videos and data?

Task 9
For whom are video corpora data?

Step 4: Considerations Before Setting Out on Data Collection: What Are Naturally Occurring Data?

Collecting data of people acting and interacting is a wonderful experience for any researcher interested in studying people. Everyday interactions are the sites where we can find naturally occurring actions and interactions. But even experiments lend themselves to finding naturally occurring actions and interactions. The difference here is the degree of naturalness. What is meant here by *naturally occurring* actions and interactions is the way people do things: Two people may be asked to perform a task in a structured research project and may be sitting in an unfamiliar place; however, the way these people interact in the given circumstance will naturally occur, i.e. they will behave in ways that are natural for them in that given situation. When contemplating this for a moment, you will realize that we cannot behave vastly differently from our normal ways. If the task calls for writing something on a piece of paper, the participants will write as they usually do. They will sit in ways that they usually sit and they will talk as they usually talk. They may use their best handwriting and sit as straight as they can, but they still behave in their very own ways. Participants may also try to change their speech, but these attempts – just as sitting up very straight if that is not their regular way of sitting – usually do not last very long, as doing so, unless the participant is an actor, will result in stilted ways of acting and interacting and become obvious to others including the researchers. However, even if this should happen, the data still is naturally occurring because the participants are only able to change their own ways in their very own ways: their repertoire of language use, sitting, or handwriting has to actually exist in the participants' repertoire in order for the participants to be able to act in this way.

In video ethnographic or ethnographically informed studies, participants are often closely connected to other participants in the study, resulting in a natural way of participants keeping each other in check. For example, when you are collecting video data in a classroom or in a family setting, participants react to deliberate changes by others with sentences like "why are you acting so strange," making it quite impossible for participants to change deliberately for the camera without being noticed. Recording participants with close ties to others in a network can thus ensure that participants act most naturally. However, as mentioned above, the naturalness of data collected is always and only a matter of degree.

Task 10
Why we can speak of naturally occurring data in semi-structured or structured experiments?

Task 11
How does recording of families or networks strengthen the naturalness of participants' actions and interactions?

Step 5: Considerations Before Setting Out on Data Collection: Ethics

In today's world, where people self-record and freely share their footage unedited or edited online, ethical considerations when collecting data may not appear to be as relevant as at earlier times. However, research ethics is just as important as ever and researchers, particularly those working with participants, have much to consider before setting out on data collection, during data collection, and during data analysis. In fact, it matters little if a research project has to go through ethical approval by a stringent ethics board or if the researchers are on their own to consider ethical research. The questions that need to be asked and contemplated are the same in either case. Ethics is part of good research practice and thus, it needs to be addressed by every researcher before setting out to collect data.

Working with Participants: Consent

Working with people is amazing, but working with people also requires researchers to be in tune with those who are being studied. Generally, researchers know that the things that do not feel right are the things that one should avoid in research. For example, if a potential participant does not wish to participate in a study, they need to be taken seriously and never be forced to participate. Of course, nobody (including the researchers themselves) likes being forced to do things they do not wish to do. In small scale projects or studies in which only a few participants are needed to be recorded at a time, this is usually not an issue because participants are sought and selected based on their own wish to participate. However, when video recording large groups as for example in a classroom study, not all individuals may wish to participate. Here, it is important to ensure the rights of those who do not wish to participate just as much as the rights of those who do wish to participate. In a classroom study, in which we collected video data over two weeks, several students did not give their consent (or their parents did not give their assent) to participate. Here, we used yellow vests to distinguish those students who were not participating from those who were. Then later, during analysis, we were clear which students we could analyze and show in the data analysis pieces when writing up the findings and which students we were not to analyze and thus needed to blank out in our analysis pieces (i.e. all students wearing yellow vests). Figure 3.1 shows one of the classrooms with children that were not participating hidden behind light blue ovals.

While making sure that the rights of non-participants is taken into account takes special care, it is important to always honor participants' and non-participants' rights. Besides the right to participate and the right *not* to participate, we may want make sure that participants are informed about and happy with being recorded, the data being analyzed and written about, their faces shown (or not) and video excerpts used for classroom, conference, and publication-use.

Of course, each project differs and with it ethical considerations will differ. Participant consent/assent is very important when recording in private or semi-private spaces such as homes, schools, or offices, whereas consent is not always necessary when filming people in public spaces. When it is and when it is not necessary to gain consent from participants in these public spaces can easily be determined by answering the question: Are you interested in what *a specific individual* does? If the answer is yes, then you will want to gain their consent. If the answer to this question is no, however, then consent is not usually needed in public spaces.

Figure 3.1 Ethical considerations: people have a basic right *not* to take part in a study.

Figure 3.2 Recording in public places where we were not interested in particular individuals' actions: no need for consent.

In a study in which we recorded people in public spaces to see how certain Pokémon stops drew people to play the game, we did not need consent (Figure 3.2).

However, even here, in a study where we did not need consent from people, we are careful to hide faces of those who are close to the camera. Here we were not interested in the individuals, who were playing the game, but rather in the *Pokémon stop* and how it was drawing people who played.

But, of course, we were not only interested in the place. We also wanted to examine what is actually happening at Pokémon stops; and for this we enlisted the help of an individual participant whom we followed and recorded specifically. Because of our

Figure 3.3 A specific individual recorded in public places: a need for consent. Reproduced with permission of the participant.

specific interest in this participant's actions and interactions, we did ask for and gained consent from this participant. Here consent was necessary, even though we recorded in public places (Figure 3.3).

Quite often private and public spaces are blurred. As a rule of thumb, the researcher can simply put themselves into the potential participants' position. If someone would record you in these circumstances and not tell you, would you mind? The answer to this question will always be your moral compass as we as people have a pretty good understanding of what is morally correct and what is not. But besides employing your own moral compass, you will want to discuss your ethical considerations with other researchers. These kinds of discussions always open up many interesting questions regarding gray areas that are well worth discussing and deliberating over.

The most important aspect when studying people is that you will want these people to feel good about their involvement in the study. Or, if you do not have to seek ethical consent from people, you may want to make sure that these people will not feel intruded upon. Hiding people's faces (as shown in Figure 3.2) is one way of making sure that the people recorded do not feel negatively about having been involved in your data collection since they would likely not even readily recognize themselves.

Working with Participants: Informing Them About Your Findings
When feasible, particularly when studying specific individuals, it is nice when you inform your participants of your findings. Your findings will often be something that your participants would never have suspected and thus they become intrigued by what you have to say. By showing participants your findings, they feel valued and, simultaneously, you minimize your power position by giving something back to your participants. Your findings are because of *and* about your participants, and so, they will love to see what you did.

Working with people means building and developing relationships. The better you can build relationships, the easier it will be for you to find participants. The very best outcome in working with people is when they ask to take part in your next study as well – and when that happens, you know that you are on the right track ethically.

Task 12
Why is the gaining of consent/assent important when collecting video data of participants?

Task 13
How would you go about developing a strong relationship with your participants?

Fair Use or Permissions: YouTube, TV, Movies

Fair use and permission seeking is something that needs to be understood by all researchers and students. Just as it is important to think through the need for consent/ assent when studying participants, it is important to think through the need for gaining permissions to use ready-made content. Luckily, the use of excerpts of ready-made content is often exempt from the need to gain permissions when using it for educational purposes. However, when it is and when it is not exempt from the need to gain permission needs to be thought through by students and researchers alike. Since there is much information online, I suggest using some time to familiarize yourself with the policies in order to be clear about where your project sits.

Task 14
Look up fair use policies for educational purposes.

Task 15
Discuss when permission seeking is necessary and how much data you can safely use in your project to fall under the fair use policy.

Step 6: Video Recording and Camera Placement

When video recording participants, the number and placement of recording devices becomes important. The possibilities are almost endless. We can use a great number of cameras and may record 360°. We can mount cameras on any kind of surface and can achieve almost any kind of angle. A bird's eye view seems like an all-seeing researcher, and 360° recording appears like all-encompassing. However, the usefulness of these possibilities depends upon your particular study and we will also want to consider limitations of video recording.

Limitations of Video Recording

Video recordings give us an amazing and realistic account of actions and interactions that we can watch, re-watch, and analyze in great detail. However, we need to be careful and critically assess what it is that we are recording. Any video recording, no matter how complete it may appear, is *incomplete*. Video recorders only record at a specific time in a specific place. Most actions and interactions that surround the ones being recorded are not recorded at all. Video data is thus always and only a snapshot. As researchers, we will want to be aware of these limitations and open them up for scrutiny and critical discussion, rather than trying to conceal these limitations by recording vast amounts of data.

When realizing that you will always just be able to record snapshots of real time actions and interactions, you can then make your research inquiry clearer: Which snapshots are you actually most interested in and where/how do you find them?

Task 16
Think about the limitations of video recording and produce a list of the limitations.

Task 17
Think of ways to counteract some of the limitations of video recording. What other kinds of data might be useful for you to gain more holistic insight into what you intend to study?

How Much Data Is Enough?

When video recording, more is not always better. Let us go back in time and just imagine for a moment: we are now in the 1970s in North America when the audio recorder became widely accessible. Qualitative discourse analysts become more and more interested in spoken language. These researchers are interested not so much in the recording of speech as in the analysis of speech. Audio recorders are useful tools for qualitative analysts to collect spoken language data that then can undergo detailed analysis. These discourse analysts are interested in analyzing specifics; recorders are tools to allow the analyses because the recordings can be played and re-played. The researchers' focus, however, is *analysis*. When collecting video records of actions and interaction, we, as qualitative multimodal discourse analysts, will never want to lose that focus: Our focus is *analysis*. Recording makes the process of analysis possible.

The exact amount of data that needs to be collected and the amount of data that can be analyzed depends upon the researcher and/or team and the type of project. For a class project, for example, a 5–10 minute YouTube video will be sufficient. The bigger the project the more data will be collected and analyzed. But there is no clear right or wrong. Since we are interested in understanding *how* people act and interact, it is *this focus* that determines the amount of data needed as well as our camera placement.

Since there is no hard and fast rule about how much data you need to collect, you will want to stay as open as possible. It may be that you have over-collected and find it impossible to make sense of the vast amount of data. This is not a real problem, as you will see in the next chapter. There are good ways to determine what you will want to analyze from the vast amount collected. Or, you may find yourself in a position where you realize that you have not collected enough data to make any real sense of what you are looking at. Again, this is not a real problem as you will simply have to collect more data to get to a point where you feel comfortable with what you have in order to begin analysis. The next chapter will help you determine what kind of data you will want to collect more of.

Data collection is not a straightforward process. Especially if you are working with participants, you may find that timing is quite difficult so that your participants are ready to be video recorded while you are not ready to collect the data. Or you may find that you are ready to collect data and that you have spent much time preparing and then your participants back out at the last minute. Knowing this, you will give yourself enough time to collect data. Nothing is predictable when working with people and you will find that much also goes wrong. A camera may not be recording correctly. A battery may be faulty and not have charged. The lighting in the place you wish to record may be too low to give you good video footage, or numerous other little things can (and will) go wrong. You will lose some data at some point. You may record just those moments that you did not want to record and not be able to record those moments that occur every time when you have not yet turned the camera(s) on or have just turned them off. You thus may not be able to record what you had wanted to record at all. However, all of this is no downfall. Just be aware that this is normal and never the end of a project, but rather a natural beginning of a project. You will learn how to collect data by making many mistakes and you will learn just how limited video recording is and how important it is that you keep notes of those things that you could not record. You will also learn how important it is to speak to and/or interview participants about those aspects that you are interested in, but cannot get on camera, and in the end, you will get whatever you will get, as Ron Scollon used to tell his students. A good idea when working with participants is to let them know right after collecting your video data that you may want to contact them for follow-up questions or that you may wish to show them some video footage and ask questions about the video. Sometimes you will want to actually contact them at a later stage, while at other times this will not be necessary. However, having the possibility of going back and speaking with the participants can be invaluable.

Projects differ in size. Class projects are the smallest projects that allow students to get some hands-on experience. The next Section 3.1, gives an example of a class project in which we work through Phase I with a YouTube clip. Thesis and dissertation projects range in size depending upon their level of research needed to gain the qualification. Section 3.2 gives an example of a study, which in part can be a Research Masters project; and Section 3.3 illustrates Phase I of a project that is larger and which could – in part – be a PhD project. But the size of research projects also can depend upon the size of the research team.

Task 18

Think of a possible or real project that you will be working on and map out how much data you really need to collect in order to develop a project.

Recording and Camera Placement

Instead of simply recording what you can record, you may often want to make sure that you *record what you want and can analyze.* If you or your team cannot analyze the amount that you are recording, then you will want to ask whether there is a reason for recording it in the first place. Certainly, producing a corpus may be one of the reasons to record much more data than can be analyzed by the current research team. But for smaller projects such as class, thesis or dissertation projects, recording enormous amounts of data will make your life more difficult because you will later have to select which parts of the data you will want to focus on. However, as you will see in Phase II, having collected a great amount of data is also not a real problem. Still, video data is cumbersome and analysis of video data is very time consuming. Therefore, it is a good idea to be more realistic about data collection from the beginning. Being realistic also brings us to a discussion of how many cameras you will want to use when collecting your data.

Number of Cameras Needed

How many camera angles do you really need? This answer will be different for different projects. But generally, for smaller projects (such as class projects, BA, and Masters theses), you will want to use as few cameras as possible. In order to determine how many camera angles you really do need, you will have to work out the project details. These project details will allow you to assess important aspects such as your focus of study, your amount of data needed for analysis and the kind of data that you will need to collect in order to achieve your goal. You also need to consider your camera angle.

Task 19

Try to determine the focus of your research project in as much detail as possible.

Task 20

Think about what kind of data you will need in order to achieve your goal.

Camera Angle

Camera angles are important to consider before you begin to collect your data since the right camera angle will prove to be of great importance once you begin to analyze your data. Here too, there is no hard and fast rule. Many different camera angles can be used in research projects and sometimes you will be bound by circumstance to use not necessarily the most favorable camera angles for a study. However, thinking through the camera angle before you enter the field site, you will be sure to set up your camera(s) in the best place for the study that you are conducting. Sometimes, it is also good to consider the least favorable camera angles in order to determine exactly where to place a camera. For example, if you want to analyze how people act and interact together, you most likely do not want to mount a camera on the ceiling. A bird's eye view is a completely unnatural view for humans and thus, as researchers, we would see the world from a perspective that we do not usually see. Because of this unnatural (usually non-human) view, we would see participant's actions and interactions in quite a distorted way. Instead, you would want to place your cameras in a way as if you, the researcher, were watching the participants. This camera placement gives you a participatory view that will later allow you to easily analyze your data in interactive terms. Let us say you are filming two people working at a table together. Here, you may want to place a camera at a fair distance to best see the participants working together and you may not actually need more than this one camera. Or let us say you are filming a classroom. Here, you would want to place cameras at human height and work with as many cameras as it will take to have an often overlapping view of the entire classroom. During one of our recent classroom projects for example, we used three stationary cameras to video record the entire classroom and then used a mobile phone to hone in on specific groups or individual students. But here, a 360° view can also be very useful.

Certainly, there are projects that do warrant a bird's eye view for cameras. One such project would be a video recording in medical surgeries, which are usually recorded that way for teaching purposes, allowing the viewer to see doctors' hands. Another kind of project that would benefit from a bird's eye view of cameras would be a research project in which the focus of study is on general movements of people, for example in railway stations, in parks or the like.

Task 21

Think about your project and decide which camera angle(s) will be best.

Task 22

Now that you have decided upon the camera angle(s) needed, determine the number of cameras that you will absolutely need, minimizing the number of cameras particularly for small projects.

Corpora

Of course, there are researchers, centers, and labs dedicated to collecting and storing large corpora of video recordings. In case you have access to some of these corpora, you can select your data from a corpus as well, rather than video recording your own participants. When selecting data from a corpus, you will make similar decisions to the ones discussed above. For example, you will want to choose recordings that do not give you a bird's eye view if this is not preferable for what you intend to study. Or, select videos that do give you a bird's eye view if you are interested in studying general movements or if you are interested in actions and interactions that allow for no better camera placement such as the analysis of medical surgeries.

Even in cases where you have access to a video corpus which has been coded in ways that are not useful to you, you can still use the systematic analysis outlined in the next chapters. When using such a corpus, you just need to be careful in your selection of what it is you are studying.

A Common Reaction to Being Recorded

The more common it is to take videos of the self and of others around, the more likely it also is that participants react to the camera. We found that children in our school project engaged with the cameras by waving, smiling, and acting out seemingly pre-fabricated camera faces. However, after a while, even the most camera-reactive children began to ignore the cameras for large stretches at a time. Thus, there is little reason to be alarmed when participants react in these obvious ways to cameras. In fact, we can also use these ready ways of being when on camera as one of our research aims and actually study this phenomenon. Or, we can simply wait for these moments to be over and wait for times when participants behave in a more natural manner and begin our study at this point. Camera engagement may come up again and again, but it will also drop off again and again. But, since we see this quite frequently, especially in school-aged children, these ways of acting in front of and for the camera, in fact, may become quite natural and would therefore be well worth studying.

The Observer's Paradox: Does It Matter?

Labov (2006 [1966]) had been concerned with what he called the observer's paradox: the fact that a researcher could not collect data without being present and that the mere presence of the researcher meant that the participants altered their ways of speaking. When collecting video data, researchers are often also present and participants likely also alter their speech. However, speakers, Labov found, can only alter their speech for a short period of time. If "natural" speech production is a concern in your study, length of recording (maybe more than 10 minutes) will work against the observer's paradox. Besides speech, we do not usually see much alteration of actions in our participants. Nonverbal actions are more difficult to alter. But more importantly, actions that are being performed by participants can only be performed by them in a manner that is usual for them, because each individual has a particular repertoire of how to act. Thus, even when a participant puts on their best way of moving, sitting, walking, etc., it still is *their* way of acting.

Task 23
Think about the actions that actors perform. Are they natural for the actors? How are they different from naturally occurring actions of people in their everyday lives?

Using Readily Available Video as Data: YouTube, TV, and Movies

When using readily available video data from YouTube, TV, or movies, we always want to be clear that this kind of video data differs from researcher collected video data of participants acting and interacting. Of course, we all know that pre-recorded content is often performed, we also know that not all YouTube videos or all TV programs are performed in the same sense as produced movies. However, we do want to make a distinction between pre-recorded data and naturally occurring researcher collected video. Such recordings often have a different temporal aspect in the performance of motions. For example, a movie star may blink in a deliberately slow fashion in order for the viewer to notice this blinking of the eyes. In naturally occurring data, such deliberate blinking can also be found, but the meaning of such blinking may be different than it may be in a movie.

Such examples most certainly are worth studying, both in naturally occurring and maybe particularly in filmic data where such blinking is more readily found. But besides enhanced actions, we find that readily available content is usually especially edited for the viewer.

Video-Editing in Readily Available Content

There is no problem with the fact that readily available video data such as movies or TV shows are commonly edited to enhance the viewer experience. In fact, we can study such editing in interactional terms and discover what the viewer experiences due to the editorial effects.

When a researcher studies such video data, the researcher is the person interacting with the program and thus studies the edits from their own perspective. In case researchers do not wish to study their own experience in watching a show or film, other people can be studied watching the content. What is important is to realize that video data is by no means a source of meaning in and by itself. It is a source that is made, watched, and experienced by human beings and only makes sense when this is the case. As discourse analysts, we want to be sure never to forget the person in our endeavor to study video: the person that performs the actions as well as the person that views or experiences the actions. Meaning is made when these two facets, people *and* recording, come together. This point is easily recognized when thinking about the fact that, if you were trying to examine a film that you have never watched, you would have little to say about its meaning. Only when you have watched the film, will you be able to make sense of the film. Certainly, it can be argued that meaning is embedded within the film itself, but this meaning cannot be seen as a stand-alone source. Only by a social actor interacting *with* the content can meaning be understood, even that meaning which has been embedded previously by other human beings. As discourse analysts, we are aware that meaning making is always an interactive process by people with the content and therefore, we always have to include the people making sense of the artifact. We will get into more detail in regard to this very important point in the next chapter. For now, the most important thing to understand is that when you are analyzing a film, you are analyzing it through *your eyes*. Just as a text only has meaning for a person when they read or write it, a film only has meaning for an individual when they watch it, produce it, or when they play some kind of role in the making of the movie itself.

The Place of the Researcher

Before collecting data, it is important to consider the role of the researcher during recordings (Norris et al. 2014). Since the video camera(s) only capture certain aspects of a much larger whole, it is useful if the researchers conducting the study can be present during data collection. This, of course, also means that researchers need to be considered in the analysis (as shown in Phase II), even if only so far as to acknowledge researcher presence. Quite often, researcher involvement when recording participants can also be an interesting area of study. Researchers interact with the participants and at least some of these interactions are caught on camera. Pirini (2017), for example, examined how the researcher interacted with the participants and used this as part of his analysis when he investigated agency.

Besides the possibility of analyzing interactions that involve the researcher, researcher presence cannot be emphasized enough when video recording actions and interactions that participants perform. As mentioned above, there are always things that happen before the cameras are turned on, when they are already turned off, or outside of the cameras' view, which might very well inform your analysis of the recordings.

Step 7: Collecting Video Data, Taking Field Notes and Interviewing Participants

Data collection is often not easily divisible. We often video record participants at the same time as we are taking notes – either in field note books, on our computer, or in our heads – and we speak with participants, possibly interviewing them right then and there. Or, we set up specific times before and/or after video recording and take observational notes of naturally occurring (inter)actions. In either case, working with participants brings with it many challenges and on-the-spot decision making. No matter how well you have developed your ideas about data collection, surprises are bound to happen. The more participants you are working with, the more complex your data collection will be. Therefore, it is a good idea to keep your data organized as you collect.

Taking field notes during and after video recording and interviewing participants before, during, or after video recording their actions and interactions are helpful ways to gain a better understanding of what the participants do in and around your video recorded data. Most important, however, is to never lose sight of the one and only point that is driving your data collection: *you want to gain as holistical an understanding as possible of what your participants do in connection to your topic/theme.* Therefore, working closely with the participants is highly valuable.

Step 8: Producing a Data Collection Table

As you are collecting your data, you may want to keep track of the data that you have collected. A good way of doing this is by producing a data collection table. Certainly, you can collect any kind of data and adjust the data collection table accordingly, but some standard columns will be useful. Of course, smaller projects may only need one row instead to outline the data that has been collected (Table 3.1).

Table 3.1 Data collection table.

Data collected	Date	Place	Participants
Data session 1	Date collected	Place data was collected	× # participants
Data session 2	Date collected	Place data was collected	× # participants
Data session 3	Date collected	Place data was collected	× # participants

Step 9: Identifying the Recording Equipment, the Researcher(s), Video Recorded (Inter)Action and Animals Recorded or Not Recorded

Researchers are very important in studies where they are observing and recording (inter)actions. Without the researcher(s), there is no study. This is true also in research, where the researchers do not observe the (inter)actions, but rather just place the recording equipment into a setting. The mere placement of recording equipment means that

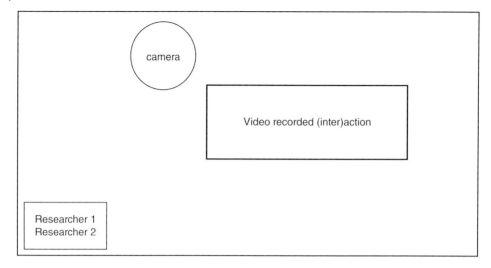

Figure 3.4 Position of researchers and camera in relation to the video recorded (inter)action.

there is researcher involvement. This involvement needs to be thought about carefully on the one hand and clearly shown in your data collection steps on the other hand.

A good way to do this is to draw a map of the place where recording took place. Here, you may want to illustrate the (inter)action studied, the placement of the recording equipment and the areas in which the researcher(s) are situated during data recording. You will also want to add animals that may be relevant to the recorded (inter)action, but which may not show up in a video. Such a picture will come in handy again, later, when or if one of the participants reacts to a researcher, another person not shown in the video, or a pet in the room. How many such graphs are needed will depend upon your study. In case you are recording in different locations and you are positioning the cameras differently because of the available space or the researcher is positioned in different places, you will want to indicate that for each one of your recorded data sessions. Often, we cannot easily illustrate the correct dimensions, but that is also often less relevant. Here, we really just want to acknowledge what else is going on around the (inter)action captured in our video data. Here, you will want to be creative in order to best illustrate your particular layout. The importance here is to show what is actually going on when you are observing/recording your data as shown in Figure 3.4.

Task 24
Illustrate the researcher(s), the cameras and other recording equipment, other people and animals present in your data.

Certainly, not all studies allow for such researcher involvement. If data is recorded by someone else or if data is taken from a corpus, or we use readily available data from the Internet, we only have video data available and likely have no way of contacting the individual participants for follow-up interviews. When this is the case, we want to be sure to understand and point out this limitation.

Step 10: Collating and Time Stamping

Once you have collected your data, you are now ready to collate various camera angles (if you have used more than one camera for recording) and you are ready to time stamp your videos.

But first, open a folder and *keep a copy of all of your raw data and back it up*. Keep this raw data folder and never do anything with it to change these files. These files are the ones that you will then be able to go back to when you have made mistakes or when you later have lost a file that you are working on.

Task 25

Open a raw data folder and organize all of your collected un-changed video files in here. Then back up this data folder.

Collating and Synchronizing Videos

There are many different programs on the market that allow you to collate and synchronize the various camera angles that you may have used. It really does not matter which program you are using. What does matter, however, is how you collate your videos. There is not necessarily a straightforward and easy way to collate the camera views, since data differs widely. However, adhering to a Western reading path of left-to-right and top-to-bottom is a good way of thinking through clear positioning of camera angles. Since we read left-to-right, it is usually a good idea to place the most complete angle to the left and then arrange close ups further to the right. This gives the viewer (and the researchers) a first view (on the left) of the larger picture of what is going on, then a more detailed one, etc. This helps us see, and helps others read the multiple camera angles more easily, and thus is one of the best ways to illustrate the camera views in one synchronized video. Depending upon the complexity of your collated data, you may also want to add a descriptor for each view to make it easier for the viewer to understand what it is they are looking at.

Since programs for synchronization and collation of video often allow you to either show all, or to only show some of the camera views, you will continue to be flexible during analysis. This means you do not necessarily have to (or always want to) work with a fully collated video when you analyze particular parts.

Task 26

Work in small groups and collate and synchronize some video files.

Task 27

Add descriptors for each camera view.

Task 28

Show your work to a larger group and explain your decision of where to place the individual camera views and the naming of your descriptors. Discuss whether or not the placement and descriptors are understandable to others unfamiliar with the data.

Time Stamping Your Video Files

Once you have synchronized all of the camera angles that you have used, or, if you are using just one camera angle, you are ready to time stamp your files. Again, it does not matter which program you choose to time stamp the data. What does matter is first, what you time stamp, and second, where you position the stamp.

What to Time Stamp

First, you will want to time stamp each collated video as it has been *recorded by you*, i.e. if you recorded a video of participants (inter)acting for a stretch of time, you time stamp the entire *uninterrupted recording*. With *uninterrupted recording*, I mean the time that *you recorded the participants without stopping the camera*. Here, you need to be wary of your camera. Depending upon what kind of recording device you are using, the camera may cut long recordings into shorter segments. When this happens, you will first have to reassemble all of the segments in order to reflect *your uninterrupted recording* and then you will need to time stamp the entire (collated) video of *uninterrupted* recorded (inter)action.

Task 29

Discuss why it is important to time stamp *your uninterrupted recording.*

Where to Time Stamp

A time stamp is usually placed in the top left corner of a video. Once a time stamp has been added to collated and/or reassembled video files, your data is ready for analysis. Some programs allow you to show various camera views and mute others. This is often a very good thing because, especially if you have recorded many different camera angles, you can choose to analyze specific angles only. However, if you are using a program that does not have this function, you can still synchronize and collate specific video files in order for you to focus your study. *The importance here is that your entire uninterrupted recording of an (inter)action is time stamped as one video file.*

Phase I: Summary

In Phase I of systematically working with multimodal data, we gain a deep understanding of data collection. Phase I consists of 10 steps:

1) Identifying a theme or topic
2) Developing research questions
3) Considerations before setting out on data collection: What is data?
4) Considerations before setting out on data collection: What are naturally occurring data?
5) Considerations before setting out on data collection: Ethics

6) Video recording and camera placement
7) Recording video data, taking field notes, and interviewing participants
8) Producing a data collection table
9) Identifying the recording equipment, the researcher(s), video recorded (inter)action and animals recorded or not recorded
10) Collating and time stamping

Now that you have learned this analysis phase and the individual steps, you will find an illustration of the Step-by-Step analysis in the next sections. First, in Section 3.1, I demonstrate Phase I of the Step-by-Step process with a YouTube video. Then, in Section 3.2, I illustrate how the 10 steps of Phase I are utilized in an experimental study, for which we collected data of 12 dyads (inter)acting via Skype to each perform two tasks together. In Section 3.3, I then show how the Step-by-Step process of Phase I works in an even larger study. Here, the examples come from a study that was conducted by a group of researchers in New Zealand to examine family (inter)action via video conferencing technology.

The Step-by-Step analysis of the YouTube clip demonstrates how the analytical steps of Phase I can be used for smaller data pieces; the Step-by-Step analysis of the dyadic teamwork illustrates how the steps are utilized for medium-size projects; and the Step-by-Step analysis of the family video conferencing (inter)actions shows how researchers can use the steps in Phase I to systematically make sense of the collection of larger data sets.

Phase I: Data Collection – Things to Remember

Things to Remember 1
Our interest in making sense of people acting and interacting drives our research theme, topic, and our research questions. The theme, topic, and research question(s) thus determine the *direction* for data collection. • Make a list of three themes or topics that you are most interested in.

Things to Remember 2
The size of the research project, dependent upon the academic requirements or the size of the research team, drives the amount of data to be collected. • Develop one general and three specific research questions for each theme/topic. • Based on your research questions for each theme/topic, decide how much data you will have to/want to collect.

Things to Remember 3
Before Data Collection Can Begin
Participant consent, permissions, or fair use are contemplated and/or sought. • Develop a consent form for your participants • Discuss whether you need to gain permissions or if your working with ready content falls under fair use

---

Things to Remember 4

Best (and worst) camera angles are discussed and the number of cameras needed to record for the purpose of your project is decided
- Make a drawing of the best camera position for your project

Limitations of video recording are discussed and the need for the inclusion of other data such as field notes, brief surveys or interviews is determined
- Develop some interview questions that will be helpful for you to understand the video data that you will record

Readily available data sources (corpora, YouTube, TV, or movies) are contemplated
- Make a list of the readily available data sources that you use to collect data

The place of the researcher in any particular research project is considered
- Where do you as researcher come into the data? Contemplate/discuss

---

Things to Remember 5

When Collecting Video Data Yourself

First, gain participant consent:
- Inform your participants about your project and let them fill out your consent form

Second, set up the camera(s)
- Follow your drawing for best placement (but be as flexible as you need to be in the given environment)

Before, during, or after video recording your participants (or depending upon your project):
- Collect interview data from your participants
- Take field notes about anything the cameras do not record and of your initial thoughts regarding the data

When Collecting Already Recorded Video Data

Generally survey the possible data
- Find the YouTube, TV series, or movie that you wish to work with
- Note down the URL(s)
- Take field notes on initial thoughts regarding the data

Things to Remember 6

As you are collecting data, you want to produce a data table that includes some information regarding your data:
- Include the session, date collected, place, and information about your participants.

Things to Remember 7

Since often your initially thought best camera placement will not actually be the one you have used in the field, make a new drawing:
- Include here not only the camera positioning, but also the researcher positioning during data collection and any animal present that may become relevant during data analysis

---

Research Projects

Researchers, just as participants, only have a certain repertoire of acting and understanding available to them. Because of our own limitations as people, we do not necessarily understand *why* participants are doing what they do in video recordings. We can only see the world from our perspective and may interpret other people's actions quite incorrectly. Therefore, researchers will want to be careful in their analysis and make sure that they do not fall into wild speculations about what *they think* is happening. Rather, as researchers we use theoretical notions and analytical tools that allow us to analyze *what is actually happening* in the data available to us. This is the reason for a strong theoretical/analytical framework. Multimodal (Inter)action Analysis is not a wild task of interpretation. In fact, if used correctly, the analyses are replicable, i.e. another researcher examining the same data pieces with the same focus, using the same transcription conventions and analytical tools will arrive at the very same analysis. Such replicability brings with it a strong facet of reliability.

Best research projects, no matter how small or large, are those where the collected data is interesting and relevant in today's world *and* in which data analysis is based on strong theoretical and analytical frameworks that tightly fit together, and which are reliable, resulting in new and exciting findings. When research projects include these facets, however, they not only result in new knowledge, but, and this is particularly important for researchers of all levels, result in replicability. As this chapter discussed in detail how to collect interesting data, the next sections illustrate how the steps offered here can be utilized for different kinds of projects and the next chapter offers Phase II, which demonstrates how to begin working with the collected multimodal data.

3.1

Systematically Working with Small Data Sets/Data Pieces

Phase I Data Collection

In order to systematically work with even small data sets/data pieces of video, it is paramount to go through analysis phases and steps in order to make data analysis most reliable.

In this section, I exemplify the steps of Phase I outlined at the beginning of this chapter with a YouTube video (a deliberately filmed and enacted event). This part may be particularly useful for classroom use. Here, the tasks guide the student to first think through data collection (Steps 1–6), and second to collect and systematically begin working with actual data (Steps 7–9).

A Step-by-Step Guide to Analyze a YouTube Video

Phase I: Data Collection

Your interest guides your choice in data collection. First, you want to identify a theme or topic that you can easily find on YouTube and develop one to three research questions (Steps 1 and 2) that will guide you in either finding the right clip or guide you in your ways of thinking about a clip that you already have found. Then, you want to discuss in groups whether the videos on the Internet are data and if some or any of the videos can be seen as naturally occurring data (Steps 3 and 4). Next, you want to find out about ethics and fair-use policies. The Internet is a handy tool for this (Step 5).

When examining YouTube videos, think about the limitations of video and think about the question: Can you say something about camera placement (Step 6)? While you are less likely to be able to interview the participants shown in a YouTube video, you are still able to take notes about the clip (Step 7). Of course, working with one YouTube video does not make for a large data collection table. However, you can still use the columns to illustrate your data (Step 8). Next, you want to think about the position of the researcher. Where are you in relation to your data (Step 9)? Since YouTube videos have a running time stamp at the bottom, there is no need to worry about time stamping your data (Step 10). Thus, for a YouTube video you only follow 9 out of the 10 steps of Phase I. First, let us begin with Step 1 of Phase I.

Systematically Working with Multimodal Data: Research Methods in Multimodal Discourse Analysis, First Edition. Sigrid Norris.
© 2019 John Wiley & Sons, Inc. Published 2019 by John Wiley & Sons, Inc.
Companion website: www.wiley.com/go/Norris/multimodal-data

Step 1: Identifying a Theme or Topic

I googled YouTube, and began to click on videos randomly. What caught my interest was the talk show genre. But it really does not matter what your data entails. You, in fact, can explore any theme or topic or genre that catches your interest. As long as there is some kind of (inter)action shown in the video, you can always use this analytical framework and the phases and steps presented in this book to make sense of the complexity of the video.

Task 1: YouTube

Refer to Step 1 in Section 3.0 of this chapter. In small groups, think about the themes or topics that interest you. Then find a few examples to show to the class.

A YouTube clip appears to be a simple data piece. However, as you will see in the phases of analysis, even a YouTube clip has its own complexity that needs to be taken into account.

Step 2: Developing Research Questions

After watching some YouTube clips of talk shows, I developed the following research questions:

1) How do the show host and the guest (inter)act in a talk show?
2) How do the show host and the guest (inter)act with the audience (present)?
3) How do the show host and the guest (inter)act with the camera (external audience)?
4) How is the clip structured to appear as if it was a naturally occurring (inter)action/ what enhances this perception?
5) Which aspects of the clip demonstrate that it is not a naturally occurring (inter) action/what makes this fact obvious?

Task 2: YouTube

Refer to Step 2 in Section 3.0 of this chapter. In small groups, think about some research questions that come to mind. Then discuss these with the class.

Step 3: Considerations Before Setting Out on Data Collection: What Is Data?

Before collecting your *data*, you need to be sure that you know what data is.

Task 3: YouTube

Refer to Step 3 in Section 3.0 of this chapter. Think through the meaning of data collection versus watching YouTube videos for fun. Discuss in groups and sum up in class.

Step 4: Considerations Before Setting Out on Data Collection: What Are Naturally Occurring Data?

When working with YouTube as our data, are we working with naturally occurring data?

Task 4: YouTube

Refer to Step 4 in Section 3.0 of this chapter. How would you define naturally occurring data? Can YouTube videos be naturally occurring data? Discuss in groups and sum up in class.

Step 5: Considerations Before Setting Out on Data Collection: Ethics

When conducting a multimodal analysis of a YouTube video, do you have to worry about ethics?

Task 5: YouTube

Refer to Step 5 in Section 3.0 of this chapter. What do you know about fair-use policies? Find out online, discuss in groups, and sum up in class.

Step 6: Video Recording and Camera Placement

While you are not recording the data yourself when working with online YouTube clips, you will want to have a close look at the camera placement. At this point, just think about the various possibilities that may come into effect.

Task 6: YouTube

Refer to Step 6 in Section 3.0 of this chapter. Working in groups, make a list of some possible numbers of cameras, camera angles, and camera shots that you may find in a YouTube video. Discuss in class.

Task 7: YouTube

Refer to Step 6 in Section 3.0 of this chapter. Working in groups, think about people performing for the camera. What can you say about this aspect? Then, think about the observers' paradox. Is this notion relevant for YouTube videos? Discuss in class.

Task 8: YouTube

Refer to Step 6 in Section 3.0 of this chapter. Working in groups, think about where you, the researcher, come into play when analyzing a YouTube video. Discuss in class.

Step 7: Collecting Video Data, Taking Field Notes and Interviewing Participants

Now that you have thought through the notion of data from many different angles, it is time to collect your data. Then, you want to take some field notes. Unless you know the person/people who made the YouTube video that you are analyzing, you will likely not be able to interview the participants in your data. However, you can take initial field notes about the video that you have chosen. Write down what jumps out at you. For example, if you are interested in camera shots such as close ups and they come up often in your video, make a note of that. However, you do not want to become too detailed at this time. Field notes are notes to get you thinking about your data. They are not a reflection of your data, i.e. these are not transcripts of what is going on. In fact, some of your field notes will later turn out to be irrelevant for your analysis. That is fine. At other times, you will want to add to your initial field notes or make changes to your list of notes, because you no longer think that a point is relevant. That, too, is fine. *The notes are for you to make sense of your data.* Also, do not go overboard. For a 5–10-minute clip, you will not want to make more than 5–10 notes. Also, you will want to name your initial feeling towards the video. As you will see below, I noted that I think it is a "very cute video." This is my subjective feeling when watching the clip. But this may later become a research interest, so that later, I may ask "Why is it that I think this is a very cute video?"

Example: Ellentube
Collecting Video Data
When working with a YouTube clip such as Ellentube, the data set is the entire screen layout on the day that you have first chosen to work with your clip. I first located the Ellentube clip on 2 July 2016, and thus took a snapshot of the screen on that day (as illustrated in Figure 3.5).

Because of my initial interest in the talk show genre, I decided to work with Ellentube. I chose the YouTube video *Kai Sings "Cake by the Ocean"* particularly, because there we have an adult show host and a child guest. Thus, you find my general interest in adult-child (inter)action as well as my specific interest in the talk show genre embedded in this clip.

Task 9: YouTube

Refer to Step 7 in Section 3.0 of this chapter. Find a YouTube video that interests you. Discuss your choice in groups, and show a one-minute segment of your video to the class.

Task 10: YouTube

Go back to Step 2 above and discuss how your research questions are relevant for your chosen video.

Figure 3.5 Snapshot of screen on the day the YouTube clip was selected as data piece.

Example: Ellentube
Taking Field Notes
When I first watched *Kai Sings "Cake by the Ocean"* on Ellentube, I noted the following:

- Lots of camera work
- Kai seems very focused on the (inter)action
- Very cute video
- Some extra laughing of ephemeral audience could be interesting to look at
- Ellen: facial expression, head movement, and gaze seem particularly interesting

Task 11: YouTube
Watch your chosen YouTube video and make a list of 5–10 field notes.

Step 8: Producing a Data Collection Table

Once you have chosen your YouTube data, you will want to produce a data collection table (albeit ever so small) in order to keep track of your data.

Example: Ellentube
Producing a Data Collection Table

Table 3.2 Sample of a data collection table for our YouTube example.

Data collected	Date	Place	Participants, (possibly ages, etc.)
Kai Sings "Cake by the Ocean"	2 July 2016	https://www.youtube.com/watch?v=h9fZY0KFNQM	Ellen (show host) Kai (eight-year old guest) Football team Present audience Camera team External audience (researcher)

Task 12: YouTube
Produce a data collection table of your chosen YouTube video.

Step 9: Identifying the Researcher in Relation to the YouTube Video

Now you want to show yourself, the researcher in relation to your chosen YouTube video. For this, you can have a friend take a picture of you as you are watching the video. The only important thing here is that you, the device that you are watching the clip on, and a picture of the YouTube video are visible. But you can also draw something that shows the researcher as illustrated in Figure 3.6.

Figure 3.6 The researcher as viewer and multimodal analyst of the video.

Task 13: YouTube
Illustrate yourself as researcher in relation to your data.

Phase I: Summary

In Phase I of systematically working with multimodal data, we gain a deep understanding of YouTube data collection. Phase I consists of nine steps:

1) Identifying a theme or topic that can be studied in a YouTube video.

2) Developing research questions relevant for the YouTube video.
3) Considerations before setting out on data collection: Is it data when you examine a YouTube video?
4) Considerations before setting out on data collection: What are naturally occurring data? Especially since you are working with a YouTube clip, think about how naturally occurring the data is and place the data on a continuum from naturally occurring on the left to entirely not naturally occurring to the right. Then discuss.
5) Considerations before setting out on data collection: ethics. Think about fair-use policies.
6) Video recording and camera placement. Draw a graph to illustrate the positioning of cameras when data was collected (decided upon) and take a snapshot of the entire screen.
7) Taking field notes: take notes when watching the YouTube clip.
8) Producing a data collection table.
9) Identifying the researcher in relation to the YouTube clip.

Task 14: YouTube
Follow the 9 Steps of Phase I before moving on to Phase II.

3.2

Systematically Working with Medium-Sized Data Sets

Phase I Data Collection

When working with medium-sized data sets, it is important to work systematically in order to make your study replicable; by working in a systematic manner, that makes your study replicable, you also make your findings reliable.

In this section, I exemplify the steps of Phase I outlined at the beginning of this chapter (3.0) with an experimental study that we conducted in the Multimodal Research Center. The study that I exemplify here, in fact, is part of a larger study, but this part will work well as an example of a stand-alone medium scale study. This kind of study may be particularly useful for small research teams with upper-level students working in liaison, so that BA and MA theses result from various aspects of the data as well as published articles.

Here, the hands-on examples and the tasks guide the researchers to first engage in thinking through data *and* the collection process for an experimental study (Steps 1–6); and second, this section guides the researchers to set out on data collection and the systematic tracking of the data when beginning to work with the multimodal material (Steps 7–10).

A Step-by-Step Guide to Analyze Experimental Data

Phase I: Data Collection

What is meant here by an experimental study is the fact that in this kind of study the researchers collect data, in which they are keeping some aspects of the study constant. As you will see below, in our study, we kept two aspects constant: first, we kept the place of data collection (with its camera positions) constant; and second, we kept the tasks constant (at least to a degree as you will see below).

An experimental study, gives researchers control over examining particular parts of (inter)action by being able to induce a certain aspect of (inter)action that the researchers are interested in. Besides the ability to induce a relatively narrow theme or topic to study, an experimental study also has the advantage that it is relatively easy for researchers to conduct. But where do you start?

First, you want to identify a theme or topic that interests you and begin to develop research questions (Steps 1 and 2) that will guide you in thinking further about a possible

Systematically Working with Multimodal Data: Research Methods in Multimodal Discourse Analysis,
First Edition. Sigrid Norris.
© 2019 John Wiley & Sons, Inc. Published 2019 by John Wiley & Sons, Inc.
Companion website: www.wiley.com/go/Norris/multimodal-data

study. Then, you want to discuss in a group whether video recordings of experiments can be seen as naturally occurring data (Step 3 and 4). Next, you want to give ethics some thought. How do you find participants for your study? What do you need to list on your consent forms? Do you have to apply for ethics at an ethics board at your university? What kinds of questions are you required to address (Step 5)?

When developing an experimental study, think about the limitations of video recording and discuss the number of cameras and their possible placement (Step 6). Then think about some questions that you will want to ask your participants, and discuss your way of taking field notes of things that are not recorded (such as the *feel* of the (inter) action (Step 7)). Now that you are recording (inter)actions, you will want to keep track of your collected data and produce a data collection table (Step 8). Then, you want to think about the position of the researcher. Where are researchers positioned in relation to the data (Step 9)? Finally, you will want to collate and synchronize your data if you have used more than one camera; then time stamp the collated video in the top left corner (Step 10). But first, let us begin with Step 1 of Phase I.

Step 1: Identifying a Theme or Topic

We had conducted the family video conferencing study discussed in the next section and had been puzzled about a few things in regards to people (inter)acting via video conferencing technology. In particular, we became interested in the topic of teamwork, i.e. people doing things or solving problems together. Thus, we identified our theme as dyadic team (inter)actions via video conferencing technology.

In order to best study this topic, in other words, the easiest and most efficient way that entailed the fewest hoops to jump through, seemed to be an experimental study in which we could recruit participants, bring them into the research center, record them, and finish the recording of quite a few people in a relatively short time. This was our thinking as we developed this experimental study.

Of course, it really does not matter what your study is about. You, in fact, can explore any theme or topic that catches your interest and that can be studied by setting up an experiment. You can always use this analytical framework and the phases and steps presented in this book to systematically make sense of the complexity of the multimodal data that you collect.

Task 1: Experimental Study

Refer to Step 1 in Section 3.0 of this chapter. In your group, think about the themes or topics that interest you. Your interest may be a result of a previous study, literature on a specific topic that you have read, or simply a result of your curiosity. Discuss your ideas.

Note 1: Experimental Study

Since you wish to study a particular facet of (inter)action, a review of literature is in order here, so that you know what has been done before and how you can develop a study that moves us beyond that which has been studied before.

Step 2: Developing Research Questions

Thinking through our developing study, we began by asking a broad research question: *How do people multimodally produce action together via video conferencing technology?* We particularly asked a broad research question because we intended to collect an amount of data that would result in various articles, BA and MA theses, which in turn would ask more specific questions. The example here is based on one part of the data collected – but, as mentioned above, this part can also be viewed as a stand-alone study.

Task 2: Experimental Study

Refer to Step 2 in Section 3.0 of this chapter. Within your group, think about one or two broad research questions that come to mind. Then discuss.

Step 3: Considerations Before Setting Out on Data Collection: What Is Data?

The way we look at data is as follows: when recording videos of people (inter)acting, the videos themselves (even when downloaded) are just raw footage until one or more of our researchers begin to work with the videos. Hours of video themselves are not really much of anything. They only become research data when they are being analyzed. When looking at data in this way, we concentrate our data collection *with a view towards analysis.*

This also means that we want to analyze all of the data that we collect, not just snippets of it. The reason is that we like to see what *really is* in the video data, and not to focus on what we *think* is interesting. In other words, we work data driven. When working data driven, we do not look for something specific in our data first. Rather, we examine our data and see what we find. Thus, we move from a bigger picture to a smaller one and do not limit our point of view before beginning to analyze the data. By working in this way, we do not simply find those specific actions that we already know are (probably) in the data; but rather, we (also) find that people act in ways that we had not previously anticipated. It is the latter that is particularly interesting to us because there is much that we do not yet know about the multimodal production of actions. Multimodal discourse analysis is still a very young area of inquiry and thus, it is an exciting area, which allows for new discoveries.

Task 3: Experimental Study

Refer to Step 3 in Section 3.0 of this chapter. Think about how defining data in the way defined in this book focuses the researchers towards data analysis.

Task 4: Experimental Study

Discuss the collection of corpora. What are corpora when you work data driven and how can we use corpora collected by people other than the researchers themselves in a data driven way?

Step 4: Considerations Before Setting Out on Data Collection: What Are Naturally Occurring Data?

Intending to work with experimental data, we discussed whether or not the (inter) actions would be naturally occurring. Our view on the matter is the following: the place (pre-determined by us), technology (provided by us), and the tasks (given by us) move our data away from naturally occurring. However, because we are not telling people *how* to act, react, or (inter)act, in any specific way, our data really are in some sense still quite natural. Thus, when investigating the *actions* that participants perform, these actions are still naturally occurring in the moment, even though the overall tasks and the setting have been pre-set. Therefore, we can speak of this kind of data as both, experimental *and simultaneously* naturally occurring. Both of these ways of looking at experimental data are true, placing this kind of data somewhere on the continuum between naturally occurring and experimental, but certainly closer to the experimental side. Therefore, we called it experimental. Being clear about where our data sits on the naturally occurring – experimental continuum was particularly important for our student researchers who are working on theses based on parts of the data.

Task 5: Experimental Study

Refer to Step 4 in Section 3.0 of this chapter. Think about different kinds of experimental studies, which would be positioned on various places on the naturally occurring – experimental continuum.

Note 2: Experimental Study

The more constancy you introduce into an experimental project, the closer the study will be towards the experimental side of the continuum.

Step 5: Considerations Before Setting Out on Data Collection: Ethics

When conducting an experimental study with participants, we need to be clear about our ethical considerations. Our university requires long documentation for *human subject research*. Some of the very important points to consider when conducting the kind of study that we intended to conduct is the way we see the participant. For us, participants are the ones who know. They know how they do things and we are the ones who wish to study what they do and, particularly, how they do it. There is no right or wrong way for our participants to perform a task and we are not interested in evaluating them in any way. Of course, our participants are free to engage in the study or not. Taking part in our study is completely voluntary.

Besides the voluntary aspect, we also considered who could and who could not participate. We only excluded a few kinds of people: first, our own students were excluded from this study, because we intended to study participants who had no previous detailed knowledge of the research project; second, we excluded minors, since our focus of the study was on adults only.

When we discussed how to recruit participants, we decided to go about it in two ways: we would recruit people from our own closer networks by telling them about the study and seeing who was interested in participating in snowball fashion, and we would recruit people from our larger networks through social networking sites.

We then formulated an information sheet and a consent form, both of which, once approved by the ethics board, we gave or sent to potential participants before the study.[1] Only once the consent forms had been signed, were participants able to take part in the study.

Task 6: Experimental Study

Refer to Step 5 in Section 3.0 of this chapter. What does your university require you to do in regard to ethics? If you are required to fill out an ethics application form, use the form to think through your group's ethical considerations. While the forms can be quite lengthy, they can be a good way to think through and discuss research ethics.

Note 3: Experimental Study

Particularly research students will benefit from a discussion about ethical considerations, since they will have to write a section on ethics in their theses.

Step 6: Video Recording and Camera Placement

Before setting out on conducting our study, we contemplated how video recording would work in an experimental study. There were many aspects such as numbers of participants, numbers and kinds of tasks, and aspects of video recording as well as camera placement to consider before we were ready to collect data. While video recording gives us much more insight into (inter)action than audio recording, we nevertheless want to never forget the limitations that video cameras bring with them.

Limitations of Video Recording

Video recording in an experimental study brings with it limitations. Most of the limitations we found positive, yet video recording also has negative limitations. In order to be clear about the limitations of video recording, we needed to contemplate both (positive and negative) ways in which video recordings introduced limitations into our experimental study. The negative effect was primarily that our data collection was going to be very focused and thus limited. This means that we would not be able to say much about how particular people (inter)acted beyond the recorded time. But, since our idea had been to focus our study upon particular tasks that participants would perform, we noted the limitation as negative on the one hand, but also noted the limitation as a positive limitation on the other hand. Thus, the positive effect of video recording in an experimental study was that we could record specific instances of different people (inter)acting, working together on the same or similar tasks. However, since our research

---

1 Since we are working in New Zealand, all information sheets and consent forms naturally had to be reviewed and accepted by our ethics board along with a detailed ethics proposal of the study before we could proceed and actually hand them out to potential participants.

question *How do people multimodally produce action together via video conferencing technology?* was quite broad, we needed to delve into the nitty-gritty of numbers of participants at this time, and decide how many we would record in all. We also needed to discuss the number of tasks and their anticipated length, and develop the tasks that participants were to perform.

Yet, there was one other negative point that we raised in regard to video data: The video equipment cannot record the feel of a room, the level of ease, happiness or unhappiness, that people can recognize. But we decided to leave this limitation as a point to discuss further in connection with the place of the researcher (see below).

How Much Data Is Enough?
When thinking about video recorded data as analyzable data, we quickly discussed the number of tasks with approximate recording times and the number of participants.

How Many Participants at a Time and How Many Tasks?
We decided to study dyads in order to make data collection and analysis manageable for student researchers in particular. In a previous study (Norris and Pirini 2017), we had found that participants really liked performing tasks, and that they often took longer to finish the tasks than we had anticipated. In that project, we had studied dyads performing four tasks together without giving them a strict time limit. In this new study, therefore, we decided that we wanted to ask dyads to work on only two tasks and limit the time for each task to about 15 minutes. This meant recording no more than about 30 minutes of data per dyad. The reason for this change in the number of tasks (from the previous four tasks) was that we decided to collect data of a good number of dyads, rather than collecting data on a small number of dyads working on more tasks together.

Number of People at a Time and Tasks to Record
Two people working on two tasks of approximately 15 minutes each would give us a maximum of 30 minutes of data per dyad.

What Kinds of Tasks?
Now it was time to decide what kinds of tasks we wanted to ask the participants to perform. We knew that we wanted to collect data on tasks that participants could finish in about 15 minutes or less. Here our general research question guided our direction: *How do people multimodally produce action together via video conferencing technology?*

In a brainstorming session, we discussed possible tasks, but soon veered into the direction of particular interest to all of us: while in previous studies, we had focused our data collection on participants (inter)acting via video conferencing technology, here, we wanted to add a facet in complexity and wanted to see not only how they (inter)acted with each other, but how they also (inter)acted with the technology available to them. We thus decided that we wanted participants to use online search functions in order to complete the tasks. Since the tasks were not supposed to be too difficult, thus making sure the participants could finish a task in less than 15 minutes, we soon settled on the first task: find a place to have dinner in a given foreign city. This task would ensure that participants had to search online for places to go and they would have to discuss among themselves and arrive at a decision (we surmised that a few BA or MA theses could be developed from this first task).

Next, we decided to develop a task that was quite different from the first. Here, we determined that we wanted to introduce a choice. This meant giving participants two possible tasks to work on and having to choose one of them. The reason we decided to introduce a choice was that we wanted to see how choosing a task would proceed (and we surmised that a possible BA thesis could result from this data). Then, while the first task would most definitely entail searching online, we wanted to develop a second task, where searching was a possibility, but not a necessity. For these reasons, we decided to focus the second tasks on current issues. We found current issues in the news, chose two at a time, and asked the participants to select one of the issues and find a solution (a few more possible BA or MA thesis could be developed from this second task).

In order to stay with our time limit, the participants would be asked to complete each task within no more than 15 minutes. Since we did not want to put too much pressure on our participants, we decided not to force the time, unless a dyad were to show no sign of finishing close to the time.

The Kinds of Tasks

Task 1: The participants were given a particular city in some foreign country (the city/country differed for each dyad) and a name/place of a hotel that the participants were ostensibly staying at. They were asked to find a place to have dinner together.

Task 2: The participants were given two current issues, asked to choose one of them, and asked to find a solution.

How Many Dyads?

Then, we thought about the kinds of questions that our student researchers might have. Student research questions for BA and MA theses, of course, would have to be much more focused than our general research question introduced above. So, for example, if a student researcher was interested in examining a specific lower-level action in a specific moment of (inter)action (say a gaze shift during a disagreement in dyadic teamwork) then the student would have to look at about 6–12 dyads depending upon the number of occurrences of a disagreement including such a shift in order to write a good BA or MA thesis. In order to quickly facilitate students working on the data for their BA or MA theses, we therefore decided that we would begin by collecting data of 12 dyads.

Number of Dyads to Study

Twelve dyads working on two tasks each with no more than 30 minutes of video, would result in about 4–7 hours of video data.

Camera Angle(s), Number of Cameras, and Camera Placement

Next, we had to decide on the camera angles, which would also help us in deciding the number of cameras and the camera placement needed. Since our primary interest was video conferencing, we certainly needed to record the screens of the participants. From previous studies, we had already installed the program Screenflow on both a research laptop and a research work station. Also, in our previous teamwork study, we had been working with one stationary camera that recorded the entire body of the participant, and a second stationary camera that recorded the upper body of the participant. We discussed the camera angles and numbers of cameras from the other study, and decided to repeat what we had done there.

Next, we set up the computers, cameras, and checked the camera angles that would work best. Once we had set up the cameras to our satisfaction, we drew a diagram (Figure 3.7)[2] for camera placement. A detailed diagram as the one shown here, allowed us to keep camera angle and position constant on different days of data collection.

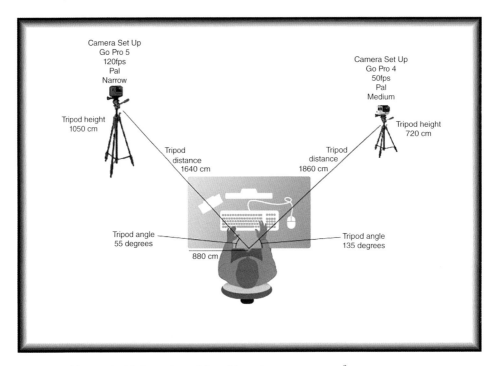

Figure 3.7 Diagram 1 – birdseye view of the table and computer set up.[2]

Thus (when all cameras worked), we collected four different views for each participant, giving us two webcam views, two Screenflow views, two full-body views, and two upper-body views for each dyad. This is a lot of data collected, but as you will see in later chapters, not all views are always needed when it comes to analysis. For example, a BA or MA student could choose to study only the upper-body views in connection with the webcam; or a student could focus a study only on the Screenflow and webcam data. But different camera views may also be used in order to transcribe different modes (as we will see in Chapter 6).

Number of Cameras to Use

2 × Camera 1:   Webcam
2 × Camera 2:   Screen recording
2 × Camera 3:   Full-body view
2 × Camera 4:   Upper-body view

---

2 This graph was produced by Ivana Rajic, who was working on the project as a research assistant and is basing her MPhil thesis on parts of this data.

The Place of the Researcher

Before moving on to actually collecting data, we still needed to discuss where we wanted to position ourselves, the researchers. Since we had brought up the limitation of video equipment and the inability to record general feelings that people can detect, we all agreed that we wanted to be present during data collection. This presence does two things: one, it allows you, the researcher, to gain a deeper understanding of what the participants are doing; and two, it allows you to note those aspects as the general feel of a room, that cameras do not capture.

Task 7: Experimental Study

Refer to Step 6 in Section 3.0 of this chapter. Working in your group, begin to develop an experimental study: think through how many participants you wish to record at a time; how many tasks (and what kinds of tasks) you want them to finish in how much time; and how many sets of participants you intend to record. Discuss.

Task 8: Experimental Study

Refer to Step 6 in Section 3.0 of this chapter. Working in your group, think about people performing for the camera. What can you say about this aspect? Then, think about the observers' paradox. How is the notion relevant for your experimental study? Discuss.

Task 9: Experimental Study

Refer to Step 6 in Section 3.0 of this chapter. Working in your group, think about where you, the researchers, come into play when recording video data in your experimental study. Discuss.

Note 4: Experimental Study

Discussing performing for the camera and the observer's paradox is particularly important for student researchers, since they will have to address these aspects in their theses.

Step 7: Collecting Video Data, Taking Field Notes and Interviewing Participants

Now, we were ready to begin recruitment and data collection. Recording sessions were restricted by participant and researcher schedules. Because most of our participants worked during the day, early evening hours were convenient and this time was also good for us in regard to room availability. We had decided to place one participant in the research center and the other participant in a different room located on the same floor as the center. During data collection, one researcher was present in each room. Because the rooms were not too far apart, the researchers could step into the hallway and one of them could clap loudly to indicate the beginning of the recording session. This clap was then recorded in both rooms, which later made synchronization of the videos easier.

Since we collected no more than 30 minutes of data per dyad, we could easily schedule two to three dyads in one evening, allowing us to collect our data relatively quickly.

The researcher in each room could observe and take some notes about aspects not recorded by the cameras. Further, the researchers had a list of questions that they asked the participants after the second task was completed and they had signed off from the video conferencing program.

Some Interview Questions

1) Do you think it is harder, easier, or about the same to tell how the other person feels via video conferencing technology or face-to-face?
2) Do you work with tasks like these in your day-to-day life?
3) Do you use video conferencing in your day-to-day life?

Step 8: Producing a Data Collection Table

Collecting our data, we kept track of the recordings by producing a data collection table. Here, we consistently called the research center (with the stationary computer) room A and the participant working there, participant A. We always referred to the other room as room B and the participant working there as participant B (Table 3.3).

Table 3.3 Sample of a data collection table for our experimental study. Reproduced with permission of the participants.

Data collected	Date	Place	Participants
Dyadic Teamwork 1	June 2017	Room A: MRC Room B: WT 604	Participant A: Alisa Participant B: Milena
Dyadic Teamwork 2	July 2017	Room A: MRC Room B: WT604	Participant A: Brownie Participant B: Ivana
Dyadic Teamwork 3	July 2017	Room A: MRC Room B: WT 604	Participant A: Dunja Participant B: Sara

Step 9: Identifying the Recording Equipment, the Researcher(s), and the Video Recorded (Inter)Action

Since our set-up was constant, we only had to add the researcher to Figure 3.7 for each of the rooms as illustrated in Figures 3.8 and 3.9.

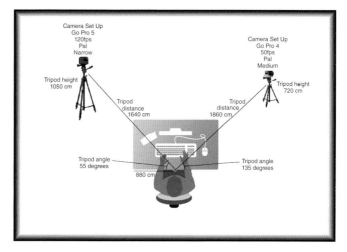

Figure 3.8 Position of the researcher in room A.[2]

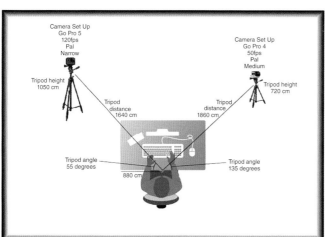

Figure 3.9 Position of the researcher in room B.[2]

Step 10: Collating and Time Stamping

Once data for a dyad was collected and all files were downloaded, the files were ready to be synchronized and time stamped (Figure 3.10).

Figure 3.10 A view of all collected data of one dyadic team working via video conferencing technology, collated, synchronized, and time stamped. Reproduced with permission of the participants.

In the collated view, we see all collected data files from broadest (full body of the individuals) to medium-sized (upper-body shot) and most detailed view (webcam image of the individuals) and the screens of the individuals. Each time, the face of an individual is arranged at (about) the same height to make it easier for the viewer to make sense of the collated videos. The top row consists of the views generated about participant A and the bottom row shows the views generated about participant B. The time for the video is positioned in the top left corner.

Since this is an experimental study, we kept the rooms in which we collected the data consistent and could then be consistent in always showing the top row of participant A in room A (MRC) and the bottom row always showing the videos recorded of participant B in room B (WT604). We thus see three images of the same person from different points of view as well as their screen view in the same row.

We read the image from left to right and top to bottom. However, showing all collected data pieces in one video is also incredibly complex, and not necessarily the best way for all analysis purposes. Yet, when keeping *time stamping* and *data collation* consistent, we allow for easier comparison among data pieces. The various views in such a collated video show us the detail in the (inter)action and, as we will see in later chapters, allow us to discern which views are best for transcription and deep analysis.

Phase I: Summary

In Phase I of systematically working with multimodal data, we gain a deep understanding of experimental data collection. Phase I consists of 10 steps:

1) Identifying a theme or topic that can be studied in an experimental setting or by utilizing an existing corpus of an experimental study.

2) Developing research questions relevant for the experimental study or corpus.
3) Considerations before setting out on data collection (or selection from a corpus): is it data from when you are collecting footage or when you are selecting videos from an existing corpus? Why or why not?
4) Considerations before setting out on data collection (or selection from a corpus), what are naturally occurring data? Especially since you are working with experiments, think about how naturally occurring the data is and place the data on a continuum from naturally occurring on the left to entirely experimental to the right. Then discuss.
5) Considerations before setting out on data collection (or selection from a corpus): ethics. Think about what is essential when working with people. What kind of ethics was required and has been gained?
6) Video recording and camera placement. Draw a graph or multiple graphs to illustrate the positioning of cameras when data will be (or for corpora-use, when data was) collected.
7) Recording video data, taking field notes and interviewing participants or selecting this kind of data from a corpus.
8) Producing a data collection table.
9) Identifying the recording equipment, the researcher(s), video recorded (inter) action and animals recorded or not recorded.
10) Collating and time stamping the data.

Task 10: Experimental Study
Follow the 10 steps of Phase I before moving on to Phase II.

3.3

Systematically Working with Large Data Sets

Phase I Data Collection

When working with large data sets, a systematic way of working ensures replicability of your study and reliability of your findings.

In this section, I demonstrate the steps of Phase I outlined at the beginning of this chapter (Section 3.0) for working with large data sets. Here, I illustrate the steps with an example of a relatively large study on family video conferencing (inter)actions conducted at the Multimodal Research Centre. A study of this kind is doable for a research team, including upper-level students, and BA, MA, or PhD theses may result from a study like this.

In this section, hands-on examples and tasks guide the researchers to think through data and the collection process of a relatively large scale video ethnographic project (Steps 1–6). Following this, the sections guide the researchers in data collection and systematically tracking the multimodal data (Steps 7–10).

A Step-By-Step Guide to Analyze Video Ethnographic Data

Phase I: Data Collection

This project is a video ethnographic study. The reason for calling it video ethnographic is that ethnographers may study the same participants using video cameras as tools to record (some of) the data over a long period of time (Norris 2011a). Or video ethnographers may study the same interactions by different people over a period of time (Barton 1998; Iedema 2003). In the study described below, we studied different people, but the same (or similar) (inter)action over a period of about one year. A video ethnography gives researchers the ability to engage in-depth with the type of (inter)action that they study. Because data is collected over the course of time, the researchers gain their understanding of what is going on gradually, being able to make sense of the data that they have collected and are collecting in light of their overall understanding of the situation that they are studying. But where do you start?

You begin by identifying a theme or topic that you are interested in and develop one to three broad research questions (Steps 1 and 2), which will guide you in framing a possible video ethnographic study. Because you will be studying a particular (inter) action, you will want to think about the naturalness of such an (inter)action for your participants (Steps 3 and 4).

Systematically Working with Multimodal Data: Research Methods in Multimodal Discourse Analysis,
First Edition. Sigrid Norris.
© 2019 John Wiley & Sons, Inc. Published 2019 by John Wiley & Sons, Inc.
Companion website: www.wiley.com/go/Norris/multimodal-data

A video ethnography will entail much thought in regard to ethics. Who can and who will not be able to participate in your study? What is essential on your consent form and what will you tell your participants about your study? What age groups are you studying and how will you make sure that you will work ethically with all involved (Step 5)?

When conducting a video ethnography, you will need to think about the number and placement of your cameras, considering that more video footage is not always better (Step 6). After that, you will want to think of questions that you want to ask your participants. What can you ask your participants to help you make sense of the (inter)action that you are studying? Then think through the notion of taking field notes to jot down those aspects of the (inter)action that will not be video recorded (Step 7).

As soon as you begin to collect data, you will want to keep track of all data that you are collecting and produce a data collection table (Step 8). Now that you are recording data, you will want to keep track of where the researchers are positioned during data collection (Step 9). Finally, you will want to collate and synchronize your data if you are using more than one camera to record the (inter)action and time stamp your data in the top left corner of the video. But now, let us begin with Step 1 of Phase I and go through all of these steps in detail.

Step 1: Identifying a Theme or Topic

Video conferencing (inter)actions were becoming more frequent in our lives and we began to speak with other researchers[1] and read about the research that was published on the topic. Finding not one video ethnographic study on family (inter)actions via this technology, we began to develop our project. Thus, we became interested in the topic of family (inter)action via video conferencing technology out of pure curiosity.

We decided that family (inter)actions are best studied in the homes of our participants. Further, we decided that we wanted to be able to speak with our participants about their experiences on the topic and we wanted to have a range of participants, not controlling for much of anything other than the fact that we said that there had to be one young child in the family. Thus, we did not control the size of the family involved, the age or gender of participants, or even the time when recording would take place. As in any ethnographic study, we recorded when we found interested participants and we recorded when participants and researchers found a suitable time.

But of course, a study like this one is only one possibility. There are many themes and topics that can be explored setting up a video ethnographic study. No matter what your study is about, you can always use the phases and steps presented in this book to systematically make sense of your video ethnographically collected material.

Task 1: Video ethnographic Study

Refer to Step 1 in Section 3.0 of this chapter. In your research team, think about the themes or topics that interest you. Your interest may be a result of your own experience, previous research that you have conducted, literature on a specific topic that you have read, or simply a result of your curiosity. Discuss your ideas.

---

1 In particular, I would like to thank Theo Van Leeuwen for his insightful ideas that sparked my interest in this area of research.

Note 1: Video ethnographic Study

Since you wish to study a particular facet of (inter)action, a review of literature is in order here, so that you know what kind of research in the area has been conducted before and how you can develop a study that moves us beyond that which has already been studied.

Step 2: Developing Research Questions

As we began to develop this research project, we thought of a question that most pertinently reflected what we were after. Thus, we first asked *How does video conferencing affect interaction in families?* But, since we clarified what we meant by a family (there has to be at least one young child) we added *with young children* to our original question so that it now read *How does video conferencing affect interaction in families with young children?* We had two reasons why we wanted to recruit families with young children in our study: first, we wanted to have as much of an age- and generation spread as possible, and second, we were all interested in children using technology. With a question as this one, we could, but did not have to look at the (inter)actions with children. We also asked a broad research question because we wanted to allow for more detailed research questions to be asked later, when students and researchers were working with the data.

Task 2: Video ethnographic Study

Refer to Step 2 in Section 3.0 of this chapter. Within your group, think about one or two broad research questions that come to mind. Then discuss.

Step 3: Considerations Before Setting Out on Data Collection: What Is Data?

When conducting a video ethnographic study, all video footage and all recorded interviews are raw footage until one or more of our researchers begin to work with the videos. By researchers working with the footage in systematic ways, this footage becomes research data. Because of this point of view taken, we collect data with an eye towards analysis. Our intent here is to analyze all of the data that we collect. We work in this way because we are truly interested in what our data tells us. Working in a data driven way helps us to see what *really is* in the video data and not to focus on what we *think is interesting*. When working data driven we do not examine specifics in our data first. Rather, we systematically work through our data and see what we find. Thus, we begin by examining the bigger picture and then systematically look at the details after that. This kind of working allows us to be open to new findings and disallows us from limiting our point of view before we have actually analyzed the actual data that we have collected. Therefore, we do not simply discover those specific actions that we already know are (probably) in the data; but rather, we (also) discover that people act in ways, that we had not previously anticipated. In fact, the less preconceived notions one has when looking at the data, the more likely one is to find something new. Since multimodal discourse analysis is still in its infancy, there is much that we do not know about the multimodal production of actions. This ability to make new discoveries about multimodal (inter)action, makes this area of inquiry very exciting.

Task 3: Video ethnographic Study

Refer to Step 3 in Section 3.0 of this chapter. Think about how defining data in the way defined in this book focuses the researchers towards data analysis.

Task 4: Video ethnographic Study

Discuss the collection of corpora. What are corpora when you work data driven and how can we use corpora collected by people other than the researchers themselves in a data driven way?

Step 4: Considerations Before Setting Out on Data Collection: What Are Naturally Occurring Data?

Ethnographic studies in general intend to collect naturally occurring data. We intended to do just that. However, because we intended to collect data on a computer screen, we needed to use screen-recording software. We quickly found a software that was not too expensive. However, it had to be installed and could not easily be moved. We also did not find it feasible to ask participants to allow us to download screen-recording software on their home computers. Therefore, we decided that it would be best to ask participants to use a research laptop with the screen-recording software installed. This, of course, brought us to discuss the fact that this way of collecting data would move us a bit away from collecting naturally occurring data. Nevertheless, we were collecting data in the homes of the participants and at a time determined by them, when they could (inter)act via video conferencing technology with family members of their choice. Thus, we still were going to record relatively naturally occurring data. Further, we discussed that the participants would (inter)act in their natural ways, even when using a research laptop, because they were not told how to act or with whom to (inter)act. Therefore, this study would be placed further to naturally occurring on a naturally occurring – experimental continuum.

Task 5: Video ethnographic Study

Refer to Step 4 in Section 3.0 of this chapter. Think about different kinds of video-ethnographic studies, which would be positioned on various places on the naturally occurring – experimental continuum.

Note 2: Video ethnographic Study

The more constancy you introduce into a video ethnographic study, the closer the study will be towards the experimental side of the continuum.

Step 5: Considerations Before Setting Out on Data Collection: Ethics

Before conducting a video ethnography, we need to think through the ethical side of our research. Since the Multimodal Research Centre is located in a country where formal human subject research ethics applies, we are always required to work through a lengthy document that invites us to think through our research ethics. However, no matter if you have to formally apply to an ethics board, or if you if you are not required to go through such a formal process, you will need to consider ethics.

One important point in the study that I am outlining here was that we were not setting out to evaluate our participants. Rather, we wanted to learn from them. Participants were thus put in the position of the knower and we were placed in the position of the learner. This kind of positioning minimizes the possible power difference between researcher and participants.

Participation was also completely voluntary. We talked to people in our wider networks about the study, and often found people inquiring if they could take part in our research project. Since we had defined the participants for this study as families with at least one young child, not all families could participate. However, when a family who would have liked to participate did not fit our definition, they often referred a family to us that did fit the definition.

Besides the fact that participation in the project was entirely voluntary, participants also had the option to withdraw from the study at any time they wished. This became important at a later stage after data collection had been completed and data analysis was already underway, since two people decided that they actually did not wish to participate. Thus, at the beginning of data analysis, we had 84 participants and later, this was reduced to 82.

Task 6: Video ethnographic Study

Refer to Step 5 in Section 3.0 of this chapter. What does your university require you to do in regards to ethics? If you are required to fill out an ethics application form, use the application form to think through your group's ethical considerations. While the forms can be quite lengthy, they can be a good way to think through and discuss research ethics.

Note 3: Video ethnographic Study

Particularly thesis students will benefit from a discussion about ethical considerations, since they will have to write a section on ethics in their theses.

Step 6: Video Recording and Camera Placement

Video ethnographic data collection is very much dependent upon the participants, on their time, their willingness to spend time on a research project, and their interest.

How Much Data Is Enough?

Knowing that all data collection is dependent upon our participants, we built this uncertainty directly into the project, deciding that we would collect data over a period of about one year and then stop.

Knowing when to stop data collection is a very important aspect in conducting the kinds of studies that we conduct. In many ways, you can never get enough data: There is always more that you could be collecting. However, we do not collect data because we can collect data: we collect data because we want to analyze it and arrive at novel findings.

Camera Angle(s), Number of Cameras, and Camera Placement

Since we had no way of knowing how many family members were participating at any one time, we needed to carefully consider what to video record. Most likely, there was much of interest going on in the families and researchers could easily get side-tracked. Since we decided to work in a research team in different parts of New Zealand (Auckland and Wellington), we needed to make sure that all researchers knew the actual focus of video recording. However, we also wanted to give researchers the freedom to decide what exactly they needed to record in order to best represent the video conferencing interactions. Family interactions, no doubt, would vary widely.

We used a video recording software which was installed on two research laptops (one was used in Auckland and the other one in Wellington). This gave us the view of what New Zealand participants saw (including their own webcam images). Further, we decided to record the New Zealand family (inter)acting via video conferencing technology with either one or two tripod mounted cameras. The second camera could be used if, for example, a young child was involved, who was moving across the room while an adult was (usually) sitting and looking at the screen. The decision to use one or two cameras had to be made on the spot and the decision was left to researchers recording the (inter)action.

The camera angles depended upon the layout of the room(s) and where the participants positioned the laptop. The aim, however, was to record a full-body view of the New Zealand participants (inter)acting via the technology. Because it was important to work in very different spaces, with different numbers of people and their laptop positioning, we did not draw a diagram. Rather, we felt that such a diagram might limit researcher decision making in regards to camera placement.

Number of Cameras Used

Camera 1: Webcam (of New Zealand participants)
Camera 2: Screen recording (of New Zealand laptop)
Camera 3: Full-body view of those New Zealand participants engaged in the video conferencing (inter)action
Camera 4: View of child/children's movements in the area of the video conferencing (inter)action

The Place of the Researcher

As in other ethnographies, our researchers all took an active part in the field during data collection. In a video ethnography, we value (inter)actions among participants and researchers. Participants are more viewed as co-researchers and researchers become co-participants in such a study. In much of our collected footage, one or more researchers are clearly visible and clearly (inter)acting with the New Zealand as well as with distant participants. There is no effort made to become invisible as researchers, because we believe that we learn most of what we are trying to study by experiencing it in as much detail as possible. Quite frequently, researchers were addressed by participants during technology breakdown. They were (inter)acted with before and after data collection, and researchers could call upon (those willing) participants for playback sessions and/or queries resulting during data analysis.

Task 7: Video ethnographic Study

Refer to Step 6 in Section 3.0 of this chapter. Working in your group, begin to develop a video ethnographic study: think through what kind of (inter)actions you are interested in; how long you intend to collect data (or how many participants you would want to work with). Discuss.

Task 8: Video ethnographic Study

Refer to Step 6 in Section 3.0 of this chapter. Working in your group, think about people being recorded and thus possibly performing for the camera. What can you say about this aspect? Then, think about the observers' paradox. How is the notion relevant for your video ethnographic study? Discuss.

Task 9: Video ethnographic Study

Refer to Step 6 in Section 3.0 of this chapter. Working in your group, think about where you, the researchers, come into play when recording video data in your video ethnographic study. Discuss.

Note 4: Video ethnographic Study

Discussing performing for the camera and the observer's paradox is particularly important for student researchers, since they will have to address these aspects in their theses.

Step 7: Collecting Video Data, Taking Field Notes, and Interviewing Participants

Once we had determined how and for how long to record data, we were ready to begin recruitment of participants. Putting participants in charge of times and days meant that we had to be most flexible. We frequently visited the New Zealand participants' homes on weekends or evenings. Each family was visited by one to three researchers. Researcher numbers varied, first, because of availability and second, because all wished to take part in data collection. We all wanted to get a feel for the participants and the way video conferencing technology was used by them. Data collection proceeded in spurts. Sometimes, we would have three families who all wanted to be recorded in the same week, and sometimes, we would have none for a stretch of time. In between, data collection simply proceeded at an average pace. After about one year, and after having collected data of 17 families with 84 (82) participants from under one year to a woman in her mid-80s, we decided that we had collected enough data.

During data collection, researchers engaged with the participants and either took notes in the homes during data collection or later. Initially, we had wanted to do a follow-up filming of each family and interview the participants during video conferencing, but this in fact only happened once. It was simply too difficult for most participants to set up another time for filming, and we quickly decided to conduct our brief interviews with one participant over the phone. Since the interviews were not a major data set, but rather a way for us to follow up, the phone interviews worked out well.

Some Interview Questions

For our video ethnography, we used an open-ended interview with indicative questions. This means that we used these types of questions to dig deeper into what our participants thought of video conferencing. Some questions that we asked were the following:

1) How often do you use video conferencing technology?
2) Is video conferencing technology better than calling?
3) When would you use video conferencing technology and when would you use the phone?

Step 8: Producing a Data Collection Table

Collecting our data, I began to develop the systematic way of working with multimodal data presented in this book. With this many participants, six researchers working on data collection and later analysis, it became evident that a systematic way of working became necessary (Table 3.4).

Table 3.4 Sample of a data collection table for our video ethnographic study. Reproduced with permission of the participants.

Data collected	Date	Place	Participants
Family 1	December 2013	Auckland, NZ and Melbourne, AU	Uncle: Mic Aunt: Abbie Mother: Jo Sophie (3) Aila (6) Jake (8)
Family 2	December 2013	Auckland, NZ and Toronto, Canada	Mother: Rachel Chris (4) Larry (9) Grandmother: Mel
Family 3	November 2014	Auckland and Canada	Mother: Clara Morgan (nine months) Isabel (nine months) Madeline (nine months) Uncle: Doug Eddie (11) Steve (12)

Step 9: Identifying the Recording Equipment, the Researcher(s), and the Video Recorded (Inter)action

Since the positions of recording equipment and the researchers differed for each recorded family, we drew diagrams of their positioning during or after data collection. An example of the position of researchers and the static camera is shown in Figure 3.11.

Caterpillar on side table

Researcher 1 on easy chair

camera on tripod

Researchers 2 & 3 on sofa

Figure 3.11 Position of the researchers while recording Family 2. Reproduced with permission of the participants.

Step 10: Collating and Time Stamping

Once the data for one family video conferencing (inter)action had been collected, the data needed to be synchronized and time stamped (Figure 3.12).

In the first row of the collated view, we see the grandmother (in Canada) as the New Zealand family sees her on screen. We see the New Zealand mother and son (on webcam) as the grandmother in Canada sees them on her screen. In the bottom row, we

Figure 3.12 A view of all collected data of Family 2's video conferencing (inter)action, collated, synchronized, and time stamped. Reproduced with permission of the participants.

see the external camera view of the New Zealand family (inter)acting in front of and with the camera in their home.

Because data collection varied depending upon the researchers' perceived need for either one or two external cameras, the collated data of various families differs. For this study, such difference is welcome. Here, we wanted to find out how families use video conferencing technology and what else they do as they are engaged in a video conferencing (inter)action. No family is alike, and therefore, a variety of recording possibilities was useful.

Certainly, a collated view is always quite complex, and often, especially for transcription or analysis purposes, not all views are always needed. But views available allow us to choose to focus on any particular views when transcribing, as we will see in Chapter 6. At this point, in order to systematically work, it is necessary to actually collate what it is you have collected in order to gain a very good idea of what kind of data you have to work with.

Phase I: Summary

In Phase I of systematically working with multimodal data, we gain a deep understanding of video ethnographic data collection. Phase I consists of 10 steps:

1) Identifying a theme or topic, that can be studied in a video ethnography.
2) Developing research questions relevant for the video ethnography.
3) Considerations before setting out on data collection: What is data?
4) Considerations before setting out on data collection: What are naturally occurring data?
5) Considerations before setting out on data collection: ethics. Think about what is essential when working with people. What kind of ethics was required and has been gained?
6) Video recording and camera placement. Discuss why camera placement in video ethnographies can usually not be predetermined.
7) Recording video data, taking field notes, and interviewing participants.
8) Producing a data collection table.
9) Identifying the recording equipment, the researcher(s), video recorded (inter) action and animals recorded or not recorded.
10) Collating and time stamping the data.

Task 10: Video ethnographic Study

Follow the 10 steps of Phase I and move on to Phase II as you see fit. Sometimes, data collection proceeds quickly and you will not have time to worry about the next Phase before all of your data has been collected. In other studies, data collection proceeds slowly and it may be a good use of your time to begin Phase II for the collected data pieces as data collection is still ongoing.

Chapter 4

Systematically Working with Multimodal Data Phase II

4.0

Phase II: Delineating the Data

As we learned in Chapter 2, we theorize that all modes together build one system of communication. In order to study the multimodality of social action, therefore, we are not well advised to prioritize one mode such as language, just as we would not be well advised to *only* study verbs if we wanted to study how people speak. For this reason, I would advise you not to transcribe all of your verbal data in the hope of getting the gist of what is going on before coming back to your much more complex video data – at least not if you truly want to understand your data multimodally. Why not? If you transcribe all of your audio data first before really looking at your video data, you will be tempted to analyze the spoken language and add some of the other modes as you see fit. However, in order to truly understand actions and interactions multimodally, we need to proceed by investigating the (inter)actions holistically from the very beginning.

Note 1
The objective of Phase II is to guide us to deeply understand our data.

So, Where Do We Begin?

By now, you have downloaded or recorded videos of people acting and interacting. You collected your data sets either based upon particular research questions or have developed some interesting questions after having found your data as discussed in Chapter 3. Your interest will have something to do with people (inter)acting. But what do you do now that you have your downloaded video, or collected your many hours of video data filled with many (inter)actions – no matter if one person (inter)acting alone or multiple people (inter)acting together – some of which you had set out to collect, and some of which (and possibly many hours of which) you never anticipated to collect?

Video data is cumbersome, no matter if you are working with a YouTube clip or your own recorded data. Either way, you cannot simply transcribe all of it multimodally. Why not? The answer is quite simple. It takes much too long to produce good multimodal transcripts, no matter if you use a computer program such as ELAN (https://tla.mpi.nl/

Systematically Working with Multimodal Data: Research Methods in Multimodal Discourse Analysis,
First Edition. Sigrid Norris.
© 2019 John Wiley & Sons, Inc. Published 2019 by John Wiley & Sons, Inc.
Companion website: www.wiley.com/go/Norris/multimodal-data

tools/tla-tools/elan;[1] Sloetjes and Wittenburg 2008) or if you use any kind of video software and take snapshots manually. The amount of work, in fact, is the same for either transcription method and transcribing multimodal data takes many hours, sometimes, for as little as a minute of data. Therefore, we do not begin by transcribing video data. Yet, your focus is multimodality and the complexity of multimodal (inter) action. In order to gain clarity and truly understand what we have collected, we begin by delineating our data.

Phase II: Delineating the Data

When beginning to analyze data, you need to worry about only one thing: How do *you* best understand *what* you are working with? In other words: *What exactly is your data*?

I often see students and researchers who have already collected a great amount of interesting data, but they are not clear what exactly it is that they have collected. Usually, data collection is driven by some research question or research interest. The data is then downloaded in folders or databases, sometimes it is sorted by dates, people, or by places. Yet, many times, whichever way the naming of videos occurs during data collection, naming of videos is difficult to remember and to make sense of at a much later point in time. Since data collection precedes data analysis, the amount of data collected and the ambiguous names of the files can result in a feeling of being overwhelmed and not knowing just where to start to make sense of the data.

First of all, you want to realize that this is *normal*. There is no magic way to name your files. No matter what you do during data collection, you will later not remember what is in a video simply by looking at the name of a file. Therefore, we need to work analytically when working with our, often very complex, data.

In order to make sense of our multimodal data, we want to work analytically, using analytical concepts from the very beginning. The first, and most helpful concept for the beginning of data analysis is the *site of engagement*. The site of engagement, as defined by Scollon (1998, 2001a), is the window opened up through practices that make concrete mediated actions possible. Here, we want to use this concept in order to understand that our own actions as researchers are also mediated actions. We analyze particular data and thus we become a part of the data analysis. Phase II allows us to make sense of the data that we have collected in analytical terms.

Phase II consists of five steps. Here, we want to gain a clear understanding of the data that we are working with. In Step 1, we want to produce a data set table. Then, in Step 2, we want to be clear that *we* are analyzing this data. Researchers thus show themselves as one social actor, who is working with the data. In order to do this, we want to draw a site of engagement that includes the researcher(s) and the data set that we are working with. After that, in Step 3, we want to illustrate a data piece. Then, in Step 4, we want draw a site of engagement that illustrates one particular data piece and the researcher. Once we have completed these four steps, we are ready to re-formulate our research question. Here, in Step 5, we produce a general research question, which now *embraces our data*, allowing us to work in a data driven way. At a later time, we may return to the

---

1 Max Planck Institute for Psycholinguistics, The Language Archive, Nijmegen, the Netherlands.

research questions that we asked before data collection. However, quite often, initial research questions, which you have formulated before you even collected data, are less useful for data analysis.

Step 1: Identifying Your *Data Set*

In order to understand the entirety of the data that you are working with, which we will from now on call your *data set*, you want to produce a *data set figure* or a *data set table*. The data set figure (shown in Section 4.1) can be a screenshot of your computer screen that shows where you have found your data piece, including all other information present. Thus, if you are working with online content, a data set is the place online where you have located your data piece(s).

If you have collected your own data, either by video recording the data yourself or by selecting videos from a corpus, you want to produce a data set table. A data set table needs to show your data in a way that is *useful to you*, since this table illustrates the first analysis of your data. There are some parts that are necessary in a data set table. We will call these the standard parts of a data set table. But there may also be columns in a data set table that are flexible. These flexible parts are those that each researcher has to develop in order to best make sense of their data set. A data set table is developed first and foremost for researchers' use. In written work, such as a thesis, a data set table can be included in the appendix or can be presented in a chapter. However, the primary use of the data set table is for the researcher(s) to gain clarity about the data that they are working with.

The name that you give your data pieces (column 1 in the data set table) will reflect what you are studying. As you will see in one of the sample projects in Section 4.2, a data piece is named Dyadic Teamwork 1 Task 1; another data piece is called Dyadic Teamwork 1 Task 2; a third data piece is called Dyadic Teamwork 1 Interview A; and a fourth data piece is called Dyadic Teamwork 1 Interview B. There, 1 reflects the group that we studied and, since we asked the groups to complete two tasks and then interviewed the participants individually afterwards, we delineated the data into four data pieces: Task 1, Task 2, Interview A, and Interview B. But please be aware, this does not mean that you need to cut the data into four snippets. Rather, we want to make sense of that which we have collected, dividing it in the table in a sensible way, without actually doing anything to our data. By delineating data in this way, we can easily focus our further analysis on either Task 1 or Task 2, Interview A or Interview B. But we can also just as easily focus on a particular dyad, performing both tasks, and comparing them with another dyad performing the same (or similar) tasks. Thus, how I divide the data in my data set table is already an initial analysis of the collected data.

Or, when you have a look at the example in Section 4.3, you will see that I numbered the data pieces by the family that we were studying. There, I called a data piece Family 1 video conferencing and another data piece Family 1 phone interview. The point is that your naming of your data in the data set table has to make sense to you, has to be consistent, and has to show the cohesion between the data pieces that belong together (coming from the same family, for example).

Thus, the first column shows the name of your data pieces. Here, it is not so important how you decided to name your data pieces. Rather, it is important from now on to be systematic in your naming of all data pieces that you have collected for this project. Also, it is very important to realize that a data piece can, but does not necessarily have to, consist of the data collected in one recording. If it makes sense for you to select a certain piece of your collected data for analysis, such as Task 1 or Task 2 exemplified in Section 4.2, then you want to delineate these parts now as (possible) separate data pieces (even if there is no break in recording of the pieces). However, you also want to be careful not to cut up your data into segments that are so small that you easily get lost (particularly if you have a lot of data), or that your minute detail will keep you from working in a data driven way. Here, we want to understand what kind of data we have collected. We do not want to go into a *deep* analysis at this point. The reason is that you can much too easily get lost in too much initial detail.

The second column in your data set table shows the length of the data piece named in column 1. This gives you a very clear understanding of the *amount* of data that you have collected and that you are analyzing. This is important, also, in case you will have to make changes because your project has become too large to deal with. But before you can decide what to leave in and what to leave out, you need to have a clear idea of the data that you actually have collected.

The third column lists the participants in the particular data piece and one to three mediational means/cultural tools that they used. The fourth column shows some important notes, such as relationships, pets or people seen in (or close to) the video that are not participating. In the last standard column of a data set table, we want to include observational notes for video data where we can list notes about the participants or the setting in which the video was recorded. Or, for interview data pieces, we will want to note a particular question or point discussed.

Most important when developing a data set table, is to be careful and realize that *too much detail is not helpful.* By producing a data set table, we want to *disambiguate* our data set. We do not want to show the high complexity that no doubt is embedded in the data set. *Less is therefore better.*

Now, if you realize that you have collected too much data once you have produced your complete data set table, you can make an informed decision about which data to focus on and which data to leave for later. For example, in Section 4.2, where I describe the experimental study, it is easy to focus on only one task. Similarly, it is easy to focus a study on a certain constellation of participants (shown in Section 4.3), where I outline an ethnographic study of families in New Zealand (inter)acting via video conferencing technology with family members at a distance. For example, there, we could focus on a participant constellation that embraces three generations (child, parent, grandparent); or, we could focus on children of particular age groups, i.e. focus on those family (inter)actions where at least one child is under 1; or focus on those families where at least one child is between 2 and 5, and so on. Without, however, knowing your data set, you are less likely to make an informed decision on what would be a good sub-study of a data set that is too large to focus on for one researcher or a small research team. Of course, you may have the demographic data (ages, places, etc.) on your consent forms or in a table together with your consent forms. But actual demographic data is often too detailed to make sense of when listed in a data set table. Thus, while such data can be handy at times, you can always refer to it if and when needed. However, if you are interested in a certain age group (such as young children as shown in Section 4.3), you can list this information in the notes-column.

As mentioned above, the data table below lists the standard columns needed in a data set table. At times, and depending upon your study, you will want to add other columns. The only important thing to remember is to keep the table as clear and simple as

Table 4.1 Data set table.

Name of data piece	Length of recording	Participants + 1–3 important mediational means/ cultural tools	Notes (relationship, pets, people not participating)	1–3 Observational Notes and/ or special points in interviews (brief generally relevant notes)
Data piece 1	Length	× # participants + Cultural tool 1, 2, 3	Notes	Observational notes
Data piece 2	Length	× # participants + Cultural tool 1, 2, 3	Notes	Interview notes
Data piece 3	Length	× # participants + Cultural tool 1, 2, 3	Notes	Observational notes

possible. Too much detail will obscure what you have collected and will add complexity and confusion rather than bringing you clarity (Table 4.1).

Once we have listed all data pieces in this data set table, we want to gain a deep understanding of an individual data piece in relation to ourselves, the researcher.

Step 2: Understanding the Site of Engagement That Includes the Researcher and the *Data Set*

In order to be clear about your own involvement in data analysis, you want to first draw the site of engagement that you as researcher are engaged in. Here, the researcher is the social actor and the data set is the mediational means or cultural tool that the researcher is analyzing. The mediated actions of analyzing the data are the concrete mediated actions at this site of engagement. These concrete mediated actions are made possible by the intersecting practices of watching and re-watching the videos, transcribing data, analyzing data, and writing up the findings (Figure 4.1).

When illustrating your engagement with a data set in the above analytical terms, we clearly see that researchers are always part of this site of engagement. Without researchers, there will be no data analysis; and without researchers having learned and developed the practice of watching and re-watching videos in order to analyze them; or without researchers having learned the practice of transcribing videos by using transcription conventions; or without researchers having learned the practice of analyzing data utilizing analytical tools; or without researchers having learned the practice of writing up findings, there is no research.

In other words, we can only speak of research taking place when researchers draw on understood practices in order to produce their concrete mediated actions. By drawing on commonly understood research practices, the researcher can then, through concrete mediated actions, use as well as develop these common research practices.

Important here is to realize that the researcher is not ambiguous. The researcher is just as important a part of the site of engagement as is the data set.[2]

---

2 For ease and clarity – particularly for the beginner of multimodal analysis – I have not incorporated the notion of discourses in the site of engagement. However, for those interested, please refer to Norris (2014b).

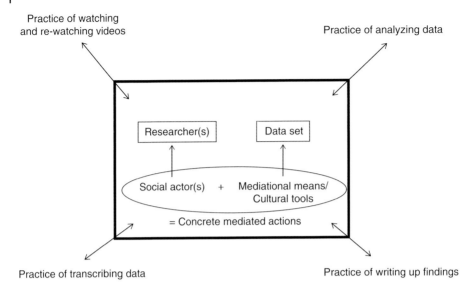

Practice of watching
and re-watching videos

Practice of analyzing data

Practice of transcribing data

Practice of writing up findings

Figure 4.1 The site of engagement that embraces the researcher(s) and the data set.

Task 1

Practices, according to Scollon (1998, 2001a) are mediated actions with a history. Think of other practices that come into play in the above site of engagement and discuss.

Task 2

Discourses, according to Norris (2014b), are practices of a larger order that usually have an institutional dimension. When thinking of discourses as larger order mediated actions with a history, how can we also show how discourses intersect at this site of engagement?

Step 3: Identifying a *Data Piece*

In Step 3, we want to illustrate a representative data piece that focuses us upon individual data pieces that we are about to analyze in detail. Usually, one snapshot of one of our videos listed in the data set table is all that is needed here (Figure 4.2).

Screenshot of
a representative
data sample

Figure 4.2 Screenshot of a representative data piece.

Task 3

What may be the purpose of this, rather obvious, step in our systematic analysis? Discuss.

Step 4: Understanding the Site of Engagement That Includes the Researcher and the *Data Piece*

When working with data, it is easy to forget that we, the researchers, are engaged in medi-ated action. In order to be clear about our own involvement in data analysis, we want to take an analytical view of the data analysis process and draw a site of engagement that includes one particular data piece *and* the researcher.

Here, the researcher is the social actor and the data set is the mediational means or cultural tool that the researcher is analyzing. The mediated actions of analyzing the data are the concrete mediated actions in this site of engagement, which are made pos-sible by the intersecting practices of closely watching and re-watching the video, and (as described in Phase III) the practice of listing higher-level mediated actions, or (as delin-eated in Phase IV) the practice of transcribing data utilizing transcription conventions, and (as exemplified in Phase V) the practice of utilizing analytical tools to analyze the data (Figure 4.3).

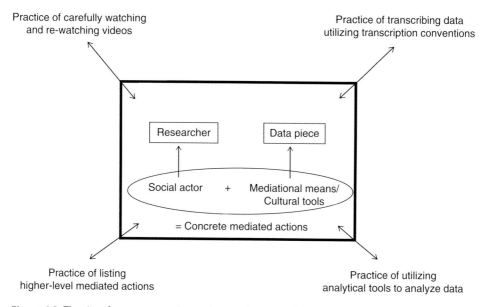

Figure 4.3 The site of engagement that embraces the researcher and a *data piece*.

Task 4

Why is it important to embed the researcher together with the data when we, for exam-ple, study a YouTube video? Discuss.

Task 5

How does the analytical tool *site of engagement* clearly help differentiate between people watching a video for entertainment and researchers watching a video for analysis?

Now that we have illustrated how the researcher is a part of this data analysis, we want to delve deeper into the individual data piece(s). After having completed these four steps, we are ready to re-formulate our research question.

Step 5: Phrasing a Research Question That Encircles Your Data

Here, in Step 5, we produce a general research question, which embraces our data, allowing us to work in a data driven way.

You may wonder why this is necessary since you, no doubt, have formulated research questions long before you began your data collection. The answer is quite simple. Research questions are a way of focusing our research. First, we develop research questions (see Chapter 3) that focus our data collection. Once data is collected, the research question needs to guide our data analysis. In order to let the data tell the story, we need to open our minds to other possibilities than those that we had developed before collecting data. Now, we want to phrase just one research question. This new research question shall encircle *all our data*. Thus, from this point you do not want to worry about what you had thought that you would find. A new research question that clearly encircles your data will allow you to really work with the data without obstructing your analysis of the data that you have collected. A good example of a new and widely open research question is:

How do social actors (inter)act during/via/in/at whatever it is that you are studying?

With this general research question, you have freed yourself of preconceived notions other than those theoretical ones that are embedded in the question. The theoretical notions embedded here are:

1) That you are interested in what social actors (usually humans, but sometimes also animals) *do*.
2) That you see social actors as always (inter)acting, i.e. *acting and interacting with other social actors, the environment, and objects.*

Rephrasing your research question concludes Phase II of systematically working with multimodal data.

Task 6

What is helpful when you think about research questions as first driving our data collection and now having to be rephrased in order to drive our data analysis? Discuss.

Task 7

Can you already foresee how the research questions that you formulated for data collection are either discarded completely or how they may be taken up again at a later time? Discuss.

Phase II: Summary

In Phase II of systematically working with multimodal data, we gain a deep understanding of our data. Phase II consists of five steps:

1) Identifying your *data set*
2) Understanding the site of engagement that includes the researcher and the *data set*
3) Identifying a *data piece*
4) Understanding the site of engagement that includes the researcher and a *data piece*
5) Phrasing a research question that *encircles your data*

Now that you have learned the individual analysis steps of Phase II, you will find an illustration of this Step-by-Step analysis in the next sections. First, in Section 4.1, I demonstrate Phase II of the Step-by-Step process with a YouTube video. Then, in Section 4.2, I illustrate how the five steps of Phase II are utilized in an experimental study, for which we collected data of 12 dyads (inter)acting via Skype each performing two tasks together. In Section 4.3, I then show how the Step-by-Step process of Phase II works in an even larger study. Here, the examples come from a study that was conducted by a group of researchers in New Zealand to examine family (inter)action via video conferencing technology.

Phase II: Delineating Your Data – Things to Remember

Things to Remember 1
Before delving into a deep analysis of data, we want to make sure that we actually know what kind and how much data we have collected. For this, we need to understand our data set. • Produce a data set table.

Things to Remember 2
Data sets do not become data sets without a researcher. In order to realize our research presence in relation to the data set, we want to utilize the analytical tool site of engagement (Scollon 1998, 2001a). Thinking about our presence in relation to the data through this analytical tool allows us to concretely and honestly position ourselves as researchers. • Produce a figure in which you use the site of engagement, positioning yourself as researcher and the data set that you are working with. • Add the practices that you engage with.

Things to Remember 3
While data sets position our data pieces in a larger frame, we will of course multimodally analyze data pieces. Therefore, illustrating a data piece is most important. • Identify a data piece.

Things to Remember 4

Data pieces can clearly not be analyzed without a researcher. In order to realize our research presence in relation to the data, we want to again utilize the analytical tool site of engagement (Scollon 1998, 2001a). Thinking about our presence in relation to the data piece through this analytical tool allows us to concretely and honestly position ourselves as researchers.

- Produce a figure in which you use the site of engagement, positioning yourself as researcher and the data piece that you have identified.
- Add the practices that you engage with to this graph.

Things to Remember 5

Now that you are clear about the data set and the data pieces that you are working with, it is time to begin working in a data driven manner.

- Look at your data set and your sample of a data piece and formulate one general research question that encircles your entire data, making use of the wording:
  How do social actors (inter)act during/via/in/at 'whatever it is that you are studying'?

4.1

Systematically Working with Small Data Sets/Data Pieces

Phase II Delineating the Data

In this section, I exemplify the five steps of Phase II outlined in the beginning of this chapter with the same YouTube video (a deliberately filmed and enacted event) that I introduced in Chapter 3.1. This part, a continuation of Chapter 3.1 may be particularly useful for classroom use. Here, the tasks guide the student to engage in preliminary data analysis.

A Step-by-Step Guide to Analyze a YouTube Video

Phase II: Delineating the Data

First, we want to understand our *data set* (Steps 1 and 2) in order to later make connections between the micro analyses, which you will no doubt arrive at, as well as being able to make connections between an intermediate and/or macro analysis of your data. But you also need to understand the actual data (Step 3 and 4) that you have collected and are focusing on. Then (Step 5) you want to re-formulate your initial research questions in order to encircle your data.

When working with data that we select, we first need to understand what our data set includes (Step 1) before we can place ourselves (the researcher) into the site of engagement that encircles the data set and the researcher (Step 2).

Step 1: Identifying Your *Data Set*

Here, you want to look at the bigger picture (the *data set*) that your chosen YouTube clip fits into. Only by having this larger point of view of a *data set*, will you later be able to link your micro analyses to relevant practices and/or discourses.

Systematically Working with Multimodal Data: Research Methods in Multimodal Discourse Analysis,
First Edition. Sigrid Norris.
© 2019 John Wiley & Sons, Inc. Published 2019 by John Wiley & Sons, Inc.
Companion website: www.wiley.com/go/Norris/multimodal-data

Example: Ellentube
Identifying Your Data Set

When working with a YouTube clip such as Ellentube, the data set is the entire screen layout on the day that you have first chosen to work with your clip. I first located the Ellentube clip on 2 July 2016, and thus took a screenshot on that day as illustrated in Figure 4.4.

Task 1: YouTube
Take a screenshot of the entire screen with your open YouTube clip and the surrounding areas on your screen.

Note 1: YouTube
You can easily take a screenshot on your Mac by pressing shift + command + 4 and then delineating the area you wish to take a picture of; or you can use the snipping tool on your PC easy to locate by searching on your computer.

Figure 4.4 illustrates the YouTube clips and the positioning on the online page. Next, we want to draw a site of engagement that includes ourselves, the researcher, as the viewer of the clip.

This larger perspective will become relevant at a later stage, when we want to link the micro analyses to intermediate and macro analyses. Certainly, you will see how YouTube clips and their positioning change, giving insight into online time-dimensions. Taking a screenshot of the entire screen when you first choose your YouTube clip, will allow you to link your micro to the intermediate and macro analyses (Phase V). For now, a quick screenshot of the page is all you need in order to illustrate your data set. But next, you want to think about your own involvement in data analysis and illustrate the site of engagement that includes the researcher/viewer and the data set.

Figure 4.4 The site of engagement of the *data set*: YouTube clip from Ellentube on 2 July 2016.

Step 2: Understanding the Site of Engagement That Includes the Researcher and the *Data Set*

The site of engagement, as discussed in the previous section as well as in Chapter 2, is the window opened up through practices (and discourses) (Norris 2014b; Norris and Jones 2005d; Scollon 1998, 2001a) that make the particular real time mediated actions possible. Real time mediated actions are frozen in video data and video recording devices thus making the analysis of previous real time mediated actions possible. While we do want to continue to problematize the notion of "real time," we do want to also realize that the mediated actions that are frozen in videos were performed in some "real time" and "did not change afterward."

Task 2: YouTube

Discuss how the notion of "did not change afterward" needs to be problematized since YouTube clips and other online videos or films are often edited.

Task 3: YouTube

Discuss how the actual mediated actions that are presented *were* performed by someone at some point in time.

Task 4: YouTube

Discuss why YouTube videos offer a great opportunity for multimodal scrutiny of actions and interactions that people perform.

The fact that YouTube clips and other downloadable/viewable videos are often edited adds another dimension for analysis. Often, such material is (heavily) edited to the point that illustrated mediated actions performed by a social actor are not necessarily performed at the same time or in the same order as shown in the clip. This is necessary to realize when working with online or pre-fabricated material such as film; however, the viewer still sees the mediated actions unfolding as presented and these unfolding mediated actions are well worth our study. Thus, in Step 2, we want to identify the site of engagement that the researcher is a part of.

Here, the site of engagement of Ellen and Kai (inter)acting *and* our watching it and thus *(inter)acting with the clip* is made possible through multiple practices and discourses (Figure 4.5).

Task 5: YouTube

Have a close look at your data set on the screen and think about why it is important to embed yourself in the data set as shown in Figure 4.5. Discuss.

Next, you want to identify your data piece.

Practice of watching
and re-watching videos

Practice of analyzing data

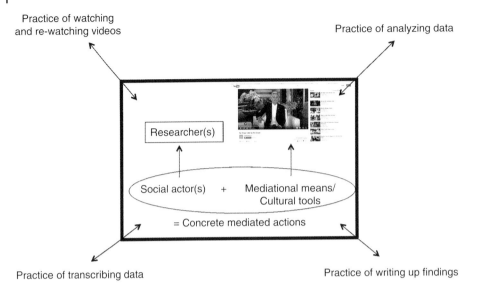

Researcher(s)

Social actor(s) + Mediational means/
Cultural tools

= Concrete mediated actions

Practice of transcribing data

Practice of writing up findings

Figure 4.5 The site of engagement of a YouTube video data set that includes the researcher as relevant social actor.

Step 3: Identifying a *Data Piece*

Of course, you found the YouTube video that you want to work with online, and thus it is not a difficult task to identify your data. However, it is important to understand the difference between the *data set* as described above and the actual *data piece*.

Example: Ellentube
A data piece for the Ellentube clip is the video called *Kai Sings "Cake by the Ocean"* (Figure 4.6).

Figure 4.6 A *data piece*: *Kai Sings "Cake by the Ocean"*.

Task 6: YouTube
Take a snapshot of a data piece that illustrates your data.

Next, we again want to demonstrate our involvement in data analysis and identify the site of engagement.

Step 4: Identifying the Site of Engagement That Embraces the Researcher/Viewer in Relation to the *Data Piece*

Reminding ourselves that all actions are mediated actions and further reminding ourselves that researchers/viewers also produce mediated actions as they are watching and analyzing a YouTube clip, we realize that it is relevant for our analysis to show just where and how the data is observed. The relationship between viewer, computer/laptop/screen, and clip is illustrated in Figure 4.7.

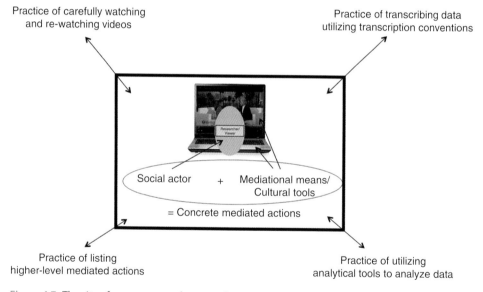

Figure 4.7 The site of engagement of a researcher/viewer watching/analyzing the clip *Kai Sings "Cake by the Ocean"*.

A very important person for a YouTube clip is the *viewer*. Without a viewer, nobody watches the clip, and the clip does not communicate to anyone. In fact, from your own perspective, a particular clip simply does not exist until you have found it, watched it, or have talked or read about it. Only when a person (inter)acting with the clip, such as the one of Ellen and Kai discussed here, comes into play, do the stage and the people on and off stage become relevant. For this reason, we need to incorporate the researcher/viewer as they are highly relevant for the watching, and/or analysis of the YouTube clip. Also, important here is to illustrate how the actual viewer watches the clip. In my case, illustrated in Figure 4.7, the viewer watched the clip full-screen. You may watch a YouTube clip differently, so that other clips show up on the side of the screen. Whichever way the viewer watches the clip, is the way to be represented in this step.

Task 7: YouTube

Illustrate the viewer(s), the screen, and the device that you are using to watch your chosen YouTube clip and add an image of the actual clip onto the image of the device. Or, better yet, have someone take a photo of you watching the chosen YouTube clip.

Note 2: YouTube

In order to illustrate the viewer and the data piece, you want to move to a part in the video of your chosen clip on the screen that allows you to demonstrate a part of the actual clip *and* the external researcher(s)/ viewer(s).

Now, that you have gained a good understanding about your chosen data set and your chosen data piece, it is time to re-formulate your research question.

Step 5: Phrasing a Research Question That Encircles Your Data

No doubt, you had set out on your research project with some clear research questions similar to the research questions presented at the beginning of Chapter 3.1. These research questions *guided your initial thoughts* about your YouTube data and they may, again, come in handy later. However, at this point, you want to phrase one general research question. *This new research question shall clearly, and only, encircle your data*. Such a data-focused research question will allow you to examine your data with an open mind. Thus, from here on, you want to work data driven. This means you have found your data (e.g. your YouTube clip) and you will not return to data collection.

Example: Ellentube
Phrasing a Research Question That Encircles the YouTube Clip
While I set out to answer the research questions when I first found the data (described in Chapter 3.1), I am eager to not force the answers to these questions. Rather, I want to let the data tell its own story and allow the data to guide me in directions that I may not have thought of before.

Thus, I put the original research questions aside and develop a data driven research question, which is more general, without however, losing my focus. A good general question is:

> *How do social actors (inter)act in a YouTube show?*

This is general, but still the question does embed some theoretical notions:

1) That you are interested in studying social actors (usually human, but sometimes also animals if you can make the argument that they are acting or interacting as social actors rather than mediational means as discussed in Chapter 2); and
2) That you are interested in what the social actors do (i.e. you are interested in their mediated actions).

Task 8: YouTube

Phrase a general research question for your selected YouTube clip.

Phase II: Summary

In Phase II of systematically working with multimodal data, you have gained a deep understanding of your YouTube data. In Phase II, consisting of five steps, you have:

1) Identified your *data set*;
2) Illustrated the site of engagement that includes you, the researcher, and your *data set*;
3) Identified a *data piece*;
4) Illustrated the site of engagement that includes you, the researcher and viewer *and* the *data piece*;
5) Rephrased your initial research questions so that you have developed one general research question that only *encircles your data*.

Task 9: YouTube

Follow the five steps of Phase II before moving on to Phase III.

Note 3: YouTube

Understanding the Dimension of Your Study

Grasping your data set(s) in the form of a data image for a small project allows you to understand the position of your data piece online.

Note 4: YouTube

Setting Up the Data to Work in a Data Driven Way

By asking a relatively general research question, you open up the possibility to work in a data driven way. Using this multimodal framework, we are generally interested in social actors' (inter)actions and this interest largely focuses our research questions. Therefore, we can simply ask *How do social actors (inter)act in a YouTube clip?* This way of asking leads us to the next analysis phase, in which we demarcate higher-level actions within our data piece(s).

4.2

Systematically Working with Medium-Sized Data Sets

Phase II Delineating the Data

In this section, I demonstrate the same phases and steps as outlined in Chapter 4.0. But this time, I am showing how Phase II is used in a medium-sized data set with an example from the experimental study of dyads working in teams via video conferencing technology, which I discussed in Chapter 3.2. Chapter 4.2 is thus a direct continuation of Chapter 3.2. This section will be particularly useful for small research teams and Masters or PhD seminars.

A Step-by-Step Guide to Analyze Experimental Data

Phase II: Delineating the Data

Data sets vary greatly in research so that you may be looking at a relatively small data set such as a YouTube video surrounded by other videos to examine for a class project; or you may be looking at a larger data set which may consist of data that you yourself or a team of researchers have collected such as the dyadic teamwork study presented in Chapter 3.2 and continued below. You may also be in a position where you can use some of the data of such an experimental study already collected and select your data set from what has been collected. *Your selection* of a part of the data would then be *your own data set.* The reason you need to delineate your data set (Steps 1 and 2) is that you cannot draw conclusive connections between the micro analyses if you have not worked with all of your data in your data set; besides being able to draw connections, understanding the *completeness of your data set* will later allow you to *position* the micro analyses within the larger picture, *your data set.* This positioning will be particularly important for you in order to draw verifiable conclusions. Of course, you also have to understand the actual data (Steps 3 and 4) that you have collected or selected and that you are focusing on. Then, you want to re-formulate your previously (Chapter 3) formulated research questions into one research question that encircles your data (Phase II Step 5) in order to allow you to work in a data driven way as you continue your data analysis as discussed in the remainder of this book.

Systematically Working with Multimodal Data: Research Methods in Multimodal Discourse Analysis, First Edition. Sigrid Norris.
© 2019 John Wiley & Sons, Inc. Published 2019 by John Wiley & Sons, Inc.
Companion website: www.wiley.com/go/Norris/multimodal-data

Step 1: Identifying Your *Data Set*

Here, you want to gain a clear picture of all of the data that you have collected (or selected if you are working with corpus data). Only by having this larger point of view, will you later be able to position your micro analyses within the data set that you are analyzing.

Example: Dyadic Teamwork via Video Conferencing Technology
Identifying the Data Set

In this larger project, there in fact are two *data sets* that have to be taken into account: (i) the full data set, and (ii) the data set of each dyad.

The Full Data Set of All Dyads

In the medium-sized project outlined in Chapter 3.2, we have a data set that consists of 12 dyads working in teams and completing two tasks each, 24 individual video recorded interviews, as well as some observational notes. For the example presented here, I shall view the medium-sized project as a corpus and select three dyads to work with. My selection criterion in this instance is the fact that these three dyads have worked close to 15 minutes on each task, while other dyads either worked much less (as little as three minutes on a task) or much longer (as long as 32 minutes on a task). Thus, in the example below, three dyads, including their working on both tasks, six individual interviews, and some notes build my data set.

Table 4.2 The *data set:* comprising three dyads working on two tasks each, plus individual interviews clearly showing the length of the recordings, as well as notes. Reproduced with permission of the participants.

Name of data piece	Length of recording	Participants 1–3 important mediational means/ cultural tools	Notes (relationship and interview foci)
Dyadic Teamwork 1 Task 1 (Amsterdam)	00:00.00–15:22:24 **About 15 min**	*Alisa* Google Maps, Zoomato.com, Restaurant Websites *Milena* Google Maps	Sisters-in-Law
Dyadic Teamwork 1 Task 2 (Recycling)	15:22:24 – 32:01:01 **About 17 min**	*Alisa* Changemakers.com, North Star Recycling. com, bigbelly.com, recycling boutique, circle economy. *Milena* Recycling.co.nz, Wikipedia	

Table 4.2 (Continued)

Name of data piece	Length of recording	Participants 1–3 important mediational means/ cultural tools	Notes (relationship and interview foci)
Dyadic Teamwork 1 Interview A	00:00:00–07:24:24 **About 7 min**	*Alisa*	1) Ease of communication, video or face-to-face: video does not allow one to be very personal; but both face-to-face and video conferencing allows one to read nonverbal communication. 2) Similar tasks in day-to-day life: Yes 3) Video conferencing in day-to day life: Planning to but not at the moment
Dyadic Teamwork 1 Interview B	00:00:00–05:13:00 **About 5 min**	*Milena*	1) Ease of communication, video or face-to-face: wasn't as much as being there; distanced; face-to-face is easier 2) Similar tasks in day-to-day life: Yes 3) Video conferencing in day-to day life: a little bit with family (maybe twice a month); but don't really use it for this
Dyadic Teamwork 2 Task 1 (London)	00:00:00–17:31:18 **About 17 min**	*Brownie* Technology fault: No screen recording *Ivana* TripAdvisor, Google maps	Friends
Dyadic Teamwork 2 Task 2 (Bullying)	17:31:18 – 30:50:40 **About 13 min**	*Brownie* Computer (for Skype) *Ivana* Laptop (for Skype)	
Dyadic Teamwork 2 Interview A	00:00:00–04:36:00 **About 4 min**	*Brownie*	1) Ease of communication, video or face-to-face: first task harder via video but about the same as face-to-face for the second task; makes me want to use video conferencing more 2) Similar tasks in day-to-day life: yes a little bit 3) Video conferencing in day-to day life: Used to use it quite a bit with friends and family; but the last three months have had computer problems

(Continued)

Table 4.2 (Continued)

Name of data piece	Length of recording	Participants 1–3 important mediational means/ cultural tools	Notes (relationship and interview foci)
Dyadic Teamwork 2 Interview B	00:00:00–15:56:30 **About 16 min**	*Ivana*	1) Ease of communication, video or face-to-face: finds Skype awkward; prefers face-to-face or the phone 2) Similar tasks in day-to-day life: not via Skype; face-to-face or via phone 3) Video conferencing in day-to day life: yes, but rarely; usually just audio
Dyadic Teamwork 3 Task 1 (Vancouver)	00:00:00 – 17:00:54:12 **About 18 min**	*Dunja* Google maps, Vancouver's best place narcity.com, restaurant website *Sara* Google maps narcity.com, restaurant website	Sisters
Dyadic Teamwork 3 Task 2 (Public transport)	17:54:12 – 28:09:00 **About 10 min**	*Dunja* Computer (for Skype) *Sara* Laptop (for Skype)	
Dyadic Teamwork 3 Interview A	00:00:00–05:10:00 **About 5 min**	*Dunja*	1) Ease of communication, video or face-to-face: easier in person but depends on what you are doing; more difficult for first task, but pretty much the same as face-to-face for second task 2) Similar tasks in day-to-day life: yes 3) Video conferencing in day-to day life: yes, very often, every second day or so with friends or family
Dyadic Teamwork 3 Interview B	00:00:00–04:00:00 **About 4 min**	*Sara*	1) Ease of communication, video or face-to-face: I feel like she is sitting opposite – not much difference to face-to-face 2) Video conferencing in day-to day life: yes, family and friends – we Skype together, talking to our sister or Mum. She's in Europe right now

A table, as presented above, allows you to systematically present your data set. When taking a close look at Table 4.2, you see that the exact times in the video data are listed here, at the very same time as a bolded rounded number of minutes is listed. The bolded number of minutes allows for a quick understanding of the approximate amount of data that you have gathered. The exact time codes in a video allow you to find a particular segment (such as a dyad working on one particular task) easily without having to re-watch your entire video collection. Besides the times and length of segments, the data set table clearly shows some important cultural tools, allowing you to easily select video data in which particular mediational means (such as Google maps) have been used by the participants. Further, a data set table includes valuable notes (such as the relationship between the participants) and the foci of the individuals with particular interview questions.

Task 1: Experimental Study

Produce a data set table that includes all of your collected (or selected) data similar to the one shown in Table 4.2.

A Sub-Data Set of One Dyad

Each one of the 12 dyads comprises a data set of their own as the dyads worked on their tasks together on different days and/or times. Each data set is thus somewhat unique, but all of these (individual dyad) data sets also overlap. An example of a *one-dyad data set* is shown in Figure 4.8.

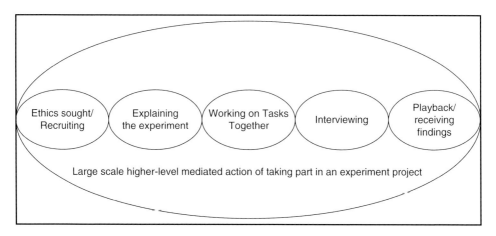

Figure 4.8 *Sub-data set*: comprising the large scale higher-level mediated action of one dyad taking part in the experimental study with many smaller scale higher-level actions.

Here, the large scale higher-level action is that the dyad is participating in an experimental study. This *participating in an experimental study* is the largest scale higher-level action that we as researchers have collected data on. Taking note of this level of analysis will allow us to put micro actions into a bigger perspective at a later time. Both *data sets* for this study thus differ and allow us to gain insight into our data from different perspectives.

Task 2: Experimental Study

Produce a graph that illustrates a sub-data set for a study similar to the one illustrated in Figure 4.8.

Step 2: Understanding the Site of Engagement That Includes the Researcher and the *Data Set*

Here, we want to utilize the notion of a *site of engagement* to make sense of our part as researcher(s) in relation to the data set and in relation to data analysis. The site of engagement, defined by Scollon (1998, 2001a) as the window opened up by intersecting practices to make concrete mediated actions possible, allows us to visualize researcher involvement (Figure 4.9).

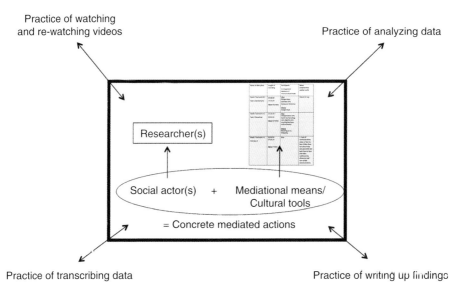

Figure 4.9 Site of engagement of the entire data set including the researcher(s).

When presenting the data set (Table 4.2) in relation to the researchers, we can visualize a site of engagement in which the practices of watching and re-watching videos, the practice of transcribing data using transcription conventions, the practice of analyzing data utilizing analytical tools, and the practice of writing up findings converge to make the concrete higher-level action of conducting research possible. In this graph (Figure 4.9), we see that the researcher(s) are here the social actor(s) engaged in conducting research and the collected data are the mediational means or cultural tools in this mediated action.

Task 3: Experimental Study

Why do you think it is important to visualize a site of engagement that clearly illustrates the relationship between the researcher and the data set? Discuss.

Task 4: Experimental Study

Discuss how actual mediated actions are frozen in the videos that you have collected or selected.

Task 5: Experimental Study

Think about yourself in relation to the data set. Then outline some of the mediated actions that you, as researcher, are performing.

Task 6: Experimental Study

Discuss the difference between mediated actions and practices.

Next, you want to identify a data piece.

Step 3: Identifying a *Data Piece*

The actual data for this study comprises the data from a dyad as they are working on a task via video conferencing technology. This data can be illustrated by a snapshot taken from one of the (inter)actions as shown in Figure 4.10.

Figure 4.10 Data: a screenshot of a dyad working on a task via video conferencing technology. Reproduced with permission of the participants.

> **Task 7: Experimental Study**
>
> Take a snapshot of one of your data pieces that illustrates your data.

Next, we once again want to demonstrate our researcher engagement in data analysis and identify the site of engagement.

Step 4: Identifying the Site of Engagement That Embraces the Researcher in Relation to the *Data Piece*

All actions are mediated actions. Just as anyone else, researchers also produce mediated actions when examining a video recorded (inter)action. A positioning of the researcher in relation to a data piece clearly shows where and how the data is analyzed. The relationship between researchers and video excerpt is illustrated as shown in Figure 4.11.

Figure 4.11 Site of engagement: researcher analyzing the recorded (inter)action of a team working on a task via video conferencing technology. Reproduced with permission of the participants.

Here, the mediated action, or better yet, the many mediated actions that a researcher performs when examining a data piece, come about through the practice of watching and re-watching the recorded video, the practice of listing higher-level mediated actions (Phase III), the practice of transcribing data utilizing transcription conventions (Phase IV), and the practice of analyzing data excerpts by utilizing analytical tools (Phase V).

> **Task 8: Experimental Study**
>
> Illustrate yourself as the researcher, the device that you are using to watch the video, and the video clip on screen.

At this point, you are quite clear about your data set, your data piece, and your relationship to both the data set and the data pieces. Now it is time to re-formulate your research question in order to make it possible for you to work in a data driven way.

Step 5: Phrasing a Research Question That Encirlces Your Data

Up until now, your previously formulated research questions *guided your data collection*. Those questions may be valuable again, later. However, at this point, you want to phrase one general research question. *This new research question shall clearly, and only, encircle your data.* Such a data-focused research question will allow you to examine your data with an open mind.

From here on, you want to work data driven. Because of a strong theory and abundant choices in analytical tools, a researcher has many choices on the one hand, but is also tightly interconnected in a framework on the other hand. This gives you the freedom to allow your data to tell its own story and drive your analysis without losing analytical rigor.

But before setting out on a data driven analysis, you will need to phrase *just one* research question that encircles all of your data.

Example 2: A Dyadic Team (Inter)action via Video Conferencing Technology
Phrasing a research question that encircles the dyadic teamwork via video conferencing data
While we set out to answer research questions when collecting the data, we do not want to force the answers to these questions, but rather, once having collected the data, we want to let the data tell its own story, allowing it to lead us into possibly quite different directions.

Working in a data driven way, the original research questions are thus put aside after data collection and we encircle our data by formulating a new research question that can lead us into unknown territory during data analysis. Thus, here we want our research question to be more general, without, however, losing its focus. Thus, we now ask:

> *How do social actors (inter)act when performing tasks together* via *video conferencing technology?*

A question such as this one is quite general, but clearly embeds the following theoretical notions:

1) We are interested in studying the social actors.
2) We are interested in how the social actors act and (inter)act, i.e. what they do, when engaged in teamwork via video conferencing technology.

Thus, the question is also quite concrete, encircling only our video data. As you recall, part of our data set are interviews. However, rather than going through the process of analyzing the video recorded interviews, let me just mention that the process is the same as the one outlined for other video recorded (inter)actions. Within the confines of this book, I shall only allude to the use of interviews and observational notes. But you can find more on how to analyze these multimodally in Norris (2011a).

Task 9: Experimental Study
Phrase a general research question that encircles your collected video data.

Note 1: Experimental Study
If you are looking at interviews as another primary data source, phrase a research question that encircles the recorded interview data.

Note 2: Experimental Study
Also, be aware that it always depends upon your data at which level you can ask a general research question.

Phase II: Summary

In Phase II of systematically working with multimodal data, you have gained a deep understanding of your data of an experimental study. In Phase II, consisting of five steps, you have:

1) Identified your *data set*;
2) Illustrated the site of engagement that includes you, the researcher, and your *data set*;
3) Identified a *data piece*;
4) Illustrated the site of engagement that includes you, the researcher, *and* the *data piece*;
5) Rephrased your initial research questions so that you have developed one (or, depending upon your data, several) general research question(s) that only encircle your data.

Task 10: Experimental Study
Complete the five steps before moving on to Phase III.

Note 3: Experimental Study
Understanding the Dimension of Your Study
Grasping your data set(s) in the form of a data table for the complete data set of a medium-sized project allows you to understand the exact dimensions of your study. Once you have worked out the larger picture that each data piece is a part of, you can begin to make sense of your data.

Note 4: Experimental Study

Setting Up the Data to Work in a Data Driven Way

By asking a relatively general research question, you open up the possibility to work in a data driven way. Using this multimodal framework, we are generally interested in social actors' (inter)actions and this interest largely focuses our research questions. Therefore, we can simply ask *How do social actors (inter)act when working on a task X?* This way of asking leads us to the next analysis-phase, in which we demarcate higher-level actions within our data piece(s).

4.3

Systematically Working with Large Data Sets

Phase II Delineating the Data

In this section, I demonstrate the same phases and steps as outlined in the previous sections. But this time, I show how Phase II is used when working with video ethnographic data, which (usually) comprises a large and diverse data set. Here, I illustrate the five steps in Phase II with the same video ethnographic study introduced in Chapter 3.3 of 17 New Zealand families video conferencing with family members at a distance (naturally occurring (inter)actions). This section will be particularly useful for upper-level classrooms such as PhD seminars and for established researchers working with large data sets.

For a video ethnography, it is important to understand that the phases and steps for such a large study are not necessarily all temporally ordered as presented. Particularly researchers engaging in video ethnographic studies may want to begin data analysis while data collection is still ongoing. In that case, the researchers will want to produce the data collection table (Phase I Step 8) as they are collecting data, and simultaneously begin working on other steps of Phase I, as well as beginning to work on some steps of Phase II outlined below. Doing so will be useful not only in order to speed up the process of analysis, but also in guiding data collection *and* limiting over-collection of video data.

A Step-by-Step Guide to Analyzing Video Ethnographic Data

Phase II: Delineating the Data

Even though I am discussing large data sets, for space reasons, I will limit my examples to only several families of the original project. My primary objective is to demonstrate how to work with a diverse data set. When collecting diverse data sets, it may be useful to delineate a full data set as well as sub-data sets as shown in Step 1 below. Next, we want to understand our own, the researcher's, position in relation to the data sets (Step 2). Only once we are clear about our own position, do we want to identify a data piece (Step 3). Following the illustration of a data piece, we again want to bring ourselves into the picture and demonstrate how the researcher is positioned in relation to the data

Systematically Working with Multimodal Data: Research Methods in Multimodal Discourse Analysis,
First Edition. Sigrid Norris.
© 2019 John Wiley & Sons, Inc. Published 2019 by John Wiley & Sons, Inc.
Companion website: www.wiley.com/go/Norris/multimodal-data

pieces (Step 4). Once our data is clearly delineated, we end Phase II by rephrasing our research question to open up our study to a data driven examination.

Step 1: Identifying Your *Data Set*

Here, you want to gain a clear picture of all of your data collected (the full data set) and also gain a clear understanding of individual sub-data sets (which may be quite different from one another depending upon your study). Only by having this larger point of view, will you later be able to link your micro analyses of individual data pieces to relevant practices and discourses in relation to your data sets.

Example: Family Video Conferencing (Inter)actions
Identifying the Data Set
In this larger project, there are in fact two *data sets* that have to be taken into account: (i) the full data set; and (ii) the sub-data set of each family.

The Full Data Set of All Families
In the study of families (inter)acting outlined in Chapter 3.3, we have a data set that consists of 17 video-recordings of families (inter)acting via video conferencing technology, 1 video-recorded interview with all family participants of one family conducted via video conferencing technology, one second session of a family video conferencing (inter)action that emerged immediately after the interview, 15 audio-recorded phone interviews with 1 member of each of 15 families, and 1 interview with 2 members of the family (in Auckland with one participant visiting from Australia) and field notes of various length per family. Each family was video recorded and the files were then saved in a folder. Thus, when listing our data in a data set table, we only need to show the length of the recordings and not the timing of each video.

The study of family members (inter)acting via video conferencing technology includes middle-class participants in Australia, Canada, New Zealand, the United Kingdom, and the United States. These participants are dispersed. They own technological devices that make video conferencing possible and they (inter)act with one another across distances and time zones. The full data set includes the data listed in Table 4.3. Here, I only present the data of three families that we will be working with in this section and the rest of the book.

Table 4.3 is an example of how video and audio-recorded (inter)actions of participants in a large project can be systematically represented. I illustrate the table by giving the details about the data of three families that took part in the project and that I continue to work with below. I chose these three examples particularly, because they are quite different from each other. In fact, the three families differed in many respects. As can be seen in the table, the family constellation differed as did the extent to which participants were familiar with video conferencing. As a result, we conducted phone interviews with Families 1 and 3. During the time the interview was conducted with participants from Family 1, Mic and his sister Jo, who also had participated in the Skype (inter)action was visiting from Australia. Thus, here, we interviewed two family members. While we had the chance to video record the interview with Family 3. Here, immediately after the interview, another video conferencing (inter)action among the family members naturally emerged.

Table 4.3 (Part of) *a full data set:* comprising participants (adults and children), their relationships, devices, and animals present in the video conferencing project as well as the length of the recordings. Reproduced with permission of the participants.

Name of data piece	Length of recording	Participants 1–3 important mediational means/ cultural tools	Notes (relationship, pets, people not participating)	1–3 Observational notes and/or special points in interviews (brief generally relevant notes)
Auckland Family 1 Video conference	about 20 min	3 adults 3 children 2 researchers research laptop iPad	uncle and aunt *Mic* and Abbie (NZ) mother (uncle's sister) *Jo* 3 children (3,6,8) dog (Australia)	All are used to video conferencing; at least once or twice a week with family; love it particularly with the kids; they run around and show things; video conferencing is better because it is face-to-face
Auckland Family 1 Phone interview	about seven min	*Mic* and *Jo*		
Auckland Family 2 Video conference 1	about 1 hr and 10 min	3 adults + 2 children 3 researchers research laptop desktop computer	mother 2 children (4, 9) caterpillar in NZ 1 (NZ) adult not participating grandmother (mother of mother) in Canada 1 (Canada) adult not participating	This family is new to video conferencing; a great deal of connection problems the first time and better the second time; are using it ever since; like being there in person; much better than phone with the kids; now, the little boy uses it on the phone to show his grandmother around and show her his things
Auckland Family 2 Video-Interview	about 15 min within emerging video conferencing interaction	3 adults 1 child 2 researchers research laptop stationary computer	mother child (4) in NZ grandmother in Canada	
Auckland Family 2 Video conference 2	About 30 min including interview	3 adults 1 child 2 researchers	participants and cultural tools same as during interview Naturally emerged after interview	
Auckland Family 3 Video conference		2 adults 5 children 1 researcher research laptop iPad	mother and triplets (NZ) (triplets are nine months) uncle and 2 sons (11 and 12) (Canada)	All are used to video conferencing; 2–3 times a month; better with the kids because of the visual
Auckland Family 3 Phone interview	3.5 min	*Clara*		

Thus, the important point here is to notice that we are *not* trying to collect a perfect data set in a video ethnography. When studying participants ethnographically, you want to collect whatever data is necessary to help you make sense of what is going on. You also want to have the option of changing your data collection depending upon the situation. Thus, rather than forcing the video recording of certain interactions or interviews, you will want to be flexible and work with your participants. Some may prefer to be video recorded, others may prefer to have interviews audio recorded, or again others may prefer if you take field notes. Similar to participants' preferences, you may find that researcher preference of data collection changes. You may find that it is too cumbersome to video record interviews and switch to audio recording (as we did in the project described here).

Especially in video ethnographies, you have to work with what is right for the situation and all people involved. In such studies, it is particularly important to realize that data will vary and that forcing a particular kind of data collection onto an ethnographic project in fact will go against the intent of the study.

The data set table is primarily for you, the researcher, to get a clear overview of what exactly it is that you have collected and what you have to work with. Secondly, the data set table allows you to clearly show the data when writing up your findings in a thesis. For examiners, such an overview of data is important and the clearer you can illustrate the data, the better. At the same time, you do not want to add more detail than necessary in a data set table, because a data set table with too much detail becomes difficult to read.

Task 1: Video Ethnographic Study

Produce a data set table that includes all of your collected data similar to the one shown in Table 4.3.

A Sub-Data Set of One Family

Each one of the 17 families comprises a data set of their own as the families do not know each other and were recorded at different times and in different places. Each data set is thus somewhat unique, but all of these (individual family) data sets also overlap. An example of a *one-family data set* is shown in Figure 4.12.

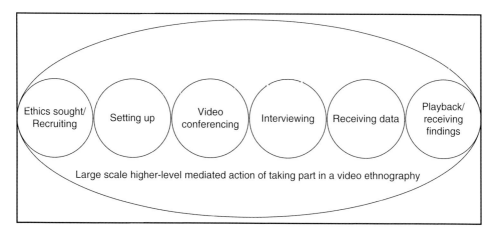

Figure 4.12 *Sub-data set*: comprising the large scale higher-level mediated action of one family taking part in the video ethnography with many smaller scale higher-level mediated actions.

Here, the large scale higher-level action is that the family is participating in a research project. This *participating in a research project* is the largest scale higher-level action that we as researchers have collected data on. Taking note of this level of analysis will allow us to put micro actions into a bigger perspective at a later time. Both *data sets* for this study thus differ and allow us to gain insight into our data from different perspectives.

Task 2: Video Ethnographic Study

Produce a graph that illustrates a sub-data set for your study similar to the one illustrated in Figure 4.12.

Step 2: Understanding the Site of Engagement That Includes the Researcher and the *Data Set*

Here, we want to utilize the notion of a *site of engagement* to make sense of our part in data analysis. The site of engagement, defined by Scollon (1998, 2001a) as the window opened up by intersecting practices to make concrete mediated actions possible, allows us to visualize researcher involvement (Figure 4.13).

When presenting the data set (Table 4.3) in relation to the researchers, we can visualize a site of engagement in which the practices of watching and re-watching videos, the practice of transcribing data using transcription conventions, the practice of analyzing data utilizing analytical tools and the practice of writing up findings converge to make the concrete higher-level action of conducting research possible. In this graph

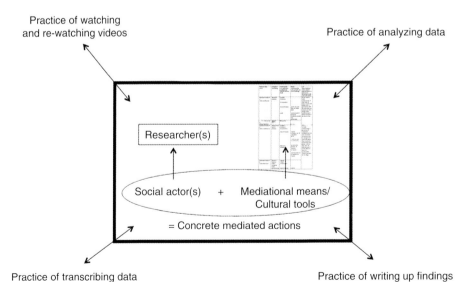

Figure 4.13 Site of engagement of the entire data set including the researcher(s).

(Figure 4.13), we see that the researcher(s) are here the social actor(s) engaged in conducting research and the collected data are the mediational means or cultural tools in this mediated action.

Certainly, just as we can argue that the family video conferencing project consists of a large – all families encompassing data set – as well as individual family data sets, so we can visualize two sites of engagement that researchers are involved in. First, the site of engagement illustrated in Figure 4.13 and second, the site of engagement of studying individual families as shown in Figure 4.14.

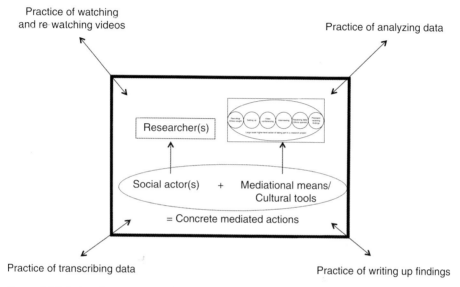

Figure 4.14 A site of engagement that embraces the researchers and a one-family data set.

Visualizing a site of engagement that incorporates the researcher(s) is important in order to be clear about our own (the researcher's) position in relation to the data set. Bringing ourselves, the researchers, into the picture of data analysis both broadens our understanding of a particular event and it also demonstrates the limitations of what can be surmised from our data.

Task 3: Video Ethnographic Study

Discuss how overtly positioning ourselves as researchers in relation to the data set both broadens and limits what we can say about the data.

Task 4: Video Ethnographic Study

Discuss how mediated actions are frozen in the videos that you have collected.

Task 5: Video Ethnographic Study

Think about yourself in relation to the data set. Then outline some of the mediated actions that you, as researcher, are performing.

Task 6: Video Ethnographic Study

Discuss the difference between mediated actions, practices, and discourses.

As our next step, we want to identify a data piece and illustrate it.

Step 3: Identifying a *Data Piece*

The actual data for this study comprises the data from a one-family data set, since we are interested in family video conferences. This data can be illustrated by a snapshot taken from one of the family video conferencing (inter)actions as shown in Figure 4.15.

Figure 4.15 Data: a screenshot of a recorded video conferencing (inter)action. Reproduced with permission of the participants.

Here, we see one data piece, which is the third higher-level action in the large scale higher-level action of participating in a research project illustrated in Figure 4.12.

Task 7: Video Ethnographic Study

Take a snapshot to illustrate a data piece.

Step 4: Identifying the Site of Engagement That Embraces You, the Viewer/Researcher and the *Data Piece*

Reminding ourselves that all actions are mediated actions and further reminding ourselves that researchers also produce a mediated action as they are watching and re-watching a video-recorded (inter)action, we realize that it is relevant for our analysis to show just where and how the data is analyzed. The relationship between researchers and video excerpt is illustrated as shown in Figure 4.16.

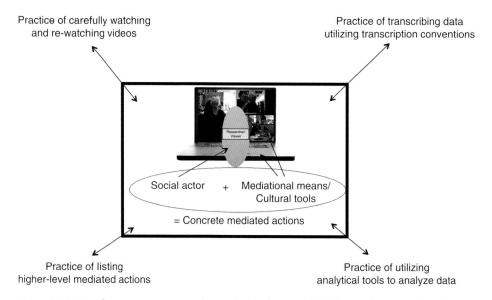

Figure 4.16 Site of engagement: researcher analyzing the recorded video conferencing (inter)action. Reproduced with permission of the participants.

Here, the mediated action, or better yet, the many mediated actions that a researcher performs to analyze data, is made possible through the practice of carefully watching and re-watching the recorded videos, the practice of listing higher-level mediated actions (Phase III), the practice of transcribing data utilizing transcription conventions (Phase IV), and the practice of analyzing data excerpts by utilizing analytical tools (Phase V).

Task 8: Video Ethnographic Study

Illustrate yourself, the researcher, the device that you are using in order to watch the video data, and a video clip on screen.

Next, in order to work in a data driven way, in which you let your data tell its story, you want to think about *one new research question*.

Step 5: Phrasing a Research Question That Encircles Your Data

No doubt, you had set out on your research project with some clear research questions. These research questions *guided your data collection* and they may, again come in handy later. However, at this point, you want to phrase one general research question. *This new research question shall clearly and only, encircle your data.* Such a data-focused research question will allow you to examine your data with an open mind.

From here on, you want to work data driven. The good thing about having a strong theory and abundant choices in analytical tools is that you really cannot get lost. You have collected your data. You have formulated a research question that encircles your data, which gives you a more or less general direction and with that, you are now open to allow your research focus be driven by your data.

But how do you phrase just one research question that encircles all of your data?

Example 2: Family Video Conferencing (inter)actions
Phrasing a Research Question That Encircles the Family Video Conferencing Data
While we set out to answer three research questions when collecting the data, we did not want to force answers to these questions, but rather, once having collected the data, we wanted to let the data tell its own story, allowing it to lead us into possibly quite different directions.

Working in a data driven way, the original research questions were thus put aside after data collection and we encircled our data by formulating a new research question that could lead us into unknown territory during data analysis. Now, our primary research question became in some way more general than the research questions during data collection, without, however, losing its focus and was now simply:

> *How do social actors (inter)act* via *Skype?*

Task 9: Video Ethnographic Study

Phrase a general research question that embraces your collected data.

Note 1: Video Ethnographic Study

If you are beginning your analysis before you have finished data collection, phrase a research question that encircles the sub-data set that you are looking at.

Note 2: Video Ethnographic Study

Also, be aware that it always depends upon your data at which level you can ask a general research question: for our family (inter)action study via Skype, we could ask one general question. However, if your data set is very diverse, it may be more useful to work at a different level (grouping some data pieces together, for example) and asking different research questions for each group of data.

Phase II: Summary

In Phase II of systematically working with multimodal data, you have gained a deep understanding of your data of a video ethnographic study. In Phase II, consisting of five steps, you have:

1) Identified your *full data set* as well as your *sub-data set(s)*;
2) Illustrated the site of engagement that includes you, the researcher, and your *data set* and *sub-data set(s)*;
3) Identified a data piece;
4) Illustrated the site of engagement that includes you, the researcher, and a *data piece*;
5) Rephrased your initial research questions so that you have developed one (or, depending upon your data, several) general research question(s) that only encircle your data.

Note 3: Video Ethnographic Study

Understanding the Dimension of Your Study

Grasping your data set in the form of a data table for the complete data set of a large study *and* the large scale actions as sub-data sets (in our case the individual families) allows you to understand the exact dimensions of your study. Once you have worked out the larger picture that each data piece is a part of, you can begin to make sense of your data.

Note 4: Video Ethnographic Study

Setting Up the Data to Work in a Data Driven Way

By asking a relatively general research question (or several general research questions), you open up the possibility to work in a data driven way. Using this multimodal framework, we are generally interested in social actors' (inter)actions and this interest largely focuses our research questions. Therefore, we can, for example, simply ask *How do social actors (inter)act* via *Skype?* This way of asking leads us to the next analysis-phase, in which we demarcate higher-level actions within our data piece(s).

Chapter 5

Systematically Working with Multimodal Data: Phase III

5.0

Phase III: Selecting Data Pieces for Micro Analysis

In the last chapter, in Phase II, we learned to delineate the data. We completed Phase II by phrasing one or several new research questions. Thus, while in Phase I, we developed research questions that *guided our data collection*, we phrased new research questions in Phase II to *guide us in our analysis*. The reason we want to phrase a research question that encircles our data is to allow us to work in a data driven way. We want to let the data tell its own story.

   In Phase III, we begin to make deeper sense of our entire data set. Here, we conduct a crucial analysis *of all data pieces that we have collected*. The analysis of all data pieces (Phase III) is crucial in order to be able to systematically *select* data pieces for micro analysis. Only when all data has gone through Analysis-Phase III, can we determine what kind and which data pieces are best suited for micro analysis. We may want to select data pieces of a particular kind because they occur often, or we may want to select data pieces because they appear seldom. Once having gone through Phase III, we can show others what we selected and the frequency of occurrence of our selection in our data set, and then explain our reasoning why we find a particular kind of data of interest to examine in more detail. Thus, rather than simply selecting data pieces that we *think* may be of interest, or that we *think* occur often or less frequently, we work in a systematic way to allow other researchers to have insight into the kind of data that we are working with, to allow for replicability of our study, and to ensure reliability of our findings. Thus, similar to qualitative corpus analysis (Hasko 2012), we deal with our data like a corpus from which we select particular data pieces for micro analysis. However, unlike much of qualitative corpus analysis, we actually produce our own data set (however small or large), work through *the entire data set*, and then make informed decisions about what to select for micro analysis. *Thus, we let the entire data set drive further analysis.*

Note 1

The objective of Phase III is to guide us in the selection of data pieces for micro analysis.

Systematically Working with Multimodal Data: Research Methods in Multimodal Discourse Analysis, First Edition. Sigrid Norris.
© 2019 John Wiley & Sons, Inc. Published 2019 by John Wiley & Sons, Inc.
Companion website: www.wiley.com/go/Norris/multimodal-data

So, Where Do We Begin?

In order to work through the entire data set, we begin by demarcating higher-level mediated actions. Higher-level mediated actions come about through – and simultaneously build – the coming together of chains of lower-level mediated actions. As an example, you can think of yourself, sitting in front of your computer or in a chair with a book, reading these pages, and trying to understand what Phase III is about. Your reading is a higher-level mediated action. You are sitting (a chain of lower-level mediated actions with your shifts in posture), reading either on a screen or in a book (a chain of lower-level mediated actions of reading word after word, line after line), gazing up once in a while, thinking about what you have just read (a chain of gaze shifts and a chain of thoughts), and so on. Your higher-level mediated action of reading is thus built from many chains of lower-level mediated actions and, simultaneously, your higher-level level mediated action produces the many chains of lower-level mediated actions.

While, when reading the above, what a higher-level mediated action is seems clear enough, it becomes a little less clear when you are actually starting to work with it. Suddenly, a clear demarcation of higher-level mediated actions seems difficult. The reason for this is that higher-level mediated actions can be demarcated differently, depending upon your research questions(s) and depending upon your focus. Here, a most important point to realize is the fact that higher-level mediated actions have to be demarcated by the researcher *based on their research project.*

For example, your reading of this book is a higher-level mediated action. How you demarcate this higher-level mediated action, however, can be quite different for different people. One researcher may want to delineate this higher-level mediated action in a way so that your sitting down and beginning to read becomes the beginning of the higher-level mediated action and getting up after you have stopped reading becomes the ending of the higher-level mediated action. Another researcher may wish to demarcate this higher-level mediated action in a different way so that opening the book or file becomes the beginning and the closing of the book or file becomes the ending of the higher-level mediated action. While we can all agree that there are different ways to look at beginning and ending points of higher-level mediated actions, we now want to see how we can perform a demarcation. The following steps demonstrate how to best delineate higher-level mediated actions in practical terms.

Phase III: Selecting Data Pieces for Micro Analysis

Selecting data pieces for analysis should not be random. It should also not be based on the research questions that you had devised for data collection in Phase I. Those research questions were discarded in Phase II and new research questions were developed to encircle the data. Next, the selection of data pieces for micro analysis needs to proceed through analysis of all data pieces in the entire data set. This kind of analysis will make it possible for you to actually examine all of your collected data, it will allow you to investigate which individual data pieces will be most important or useful to undergo micro analysis, and it will allow you to position your micro analyzed data pieces within your data set. Thus, this way of working will encompass your project in a way that it becomes possible for you to make stronger claims about your analyzed data.

Phase III will ensure that your study is verifiable, that it is replicable, and that the findings are reliable. Further, Phase III ensures that your micro analysis (in Phase V) is possible to understand in relation to the entire data set(s). In order to help us do this in a systematic way, we utilize the mediated action as our unit of analysis.

Step 1: The MEDIATED ACTION: Rephrasing Your General Research Question

Since we work in the philosophically and theoretically founded way outlined in Chapter 2, we take the social action as our guiding principle and the mediated action as our primary unit of analysis. As we learned in Chapter 2, the mediated action is defined as social actor(s) acting with or through mediational means/cultural tools (Scollon 1998, 2001a; Wertsch 1998).

All actions are mediated in multiple ways, all actions are performed by social actors, and there always exists a tension between social actors and cultural tools. Further, cultural tools are mediational means that mediate an action and mediational means are cultural tools that mediate the actions. Mediational means and cultural tools are the very same thing, with each term only emphasizing a different aspect: the term "mediational means" emphasizes the notion of mediation, while the term "cultural tool" emphasizes the notion of culture which always underlies everything social. Since a mediated action is a social action that is mediated in multiple ways, both terms, mediational means and cultural tools can be used interchangeably.

In Step 1 of Phase III, we now want to utilize the research question that encircles our data and rephrase this question into a statement about our data. Thus, if your data driven research question is *How do social actors (inter)act on a TV show?* all we need to do is to build it into the statement:

Social actors (inter)acting on a TV show

This formulation provides the three components of a mediated action:

1) Social actors
2) The action = (inter)acting
3) A relevant mediational means/cultural tool (TV show)

Task 1

Rephrase your research question produced in Phase II Step 5 into a statement of a MEDIATED ACTION

Note 2

Social actors + the mediational means/cultural tools = mediated action
Social actors + TV show = the mediated action that we are interested in, i.e. (inter)acting

---

With this in mind, we are ready for Step 2, in which we will begin to demarcate higher-level mediated actions.

Step 2: Demarcating Higher-Level Mediated Actions

Let us begin learning this step with a task.

Task 2

Think of what you (the social actor) are doing (the mediated action) at the moment *and* in which way this action is mediated (the mediational means/cultural tools that you are using to do what you are doing). Formulate your actions as mediated actions and list them. Then share and discuss.

Working on the above task will open up many questions: What is a higher-level mediated action as opposed to a lower-level mediated action? What is the beginning of a higher-level mediated action? What is the end point of a higher-level mediated action? Interestingly, all of this seems quite clear when you read about it, but when the time comes to actually delineate one mediated action from another, everything seems to become muddled.

Thus, let us begin by working through this together: A lower-level mediated action does not ever exist by itself. Therefore, *whatever you do will always be a higher-level mediated action.* Parts of this higher-level mediated action (the lower-level mediated actions) *can* be separated theoretically and for the purpose of analysis. But for a person (inter)acting, a singling out of particular lower-level mediated actions is relatively rare and the production of just one lower-level mediated action is impossible. With this in mind, we can leave the lower-level mediated action behind for the time being and move on to the higher-level mediated action.

Everything you do is a higher-level mediated action. For example, when you greet somebody, you perform a higher-level mediated action. This higher-level mediated action comes about through your using language, head movement, posture, facial expression, gesture, and proxemics. Here you see that even a short higher-level mediated action such as a greeting comes about in complexly multimodal ways.

So now we want to think about you getting up this morning. List what you did: you got up, brushed your teeth, etc. Each one of these higher-level mediated actions can be listed separately, and for a study in which you are examining a five-minute YouTube video you would want to list higher-level mediated actions on this level.

Now think about what you did last month. You got up early every morning except for the weekends. You went to university or work from morning to late afternoon. You went skiing each Saturday and visited family on Sundays. Here you see that we no longer worry about each time you brushed your teeth. We work on a different scale when we work with data over a whole month. Here, we work with larger higher-level mediated actions, or we bundle a number of higher-level mediated actions together.

Working in a data driven way means that the researcher wants to make sense of their data. We want to find out what is going on in the data that we have gathered. For this, we begin by demarcating higher-level mediated actions in a list or a table. Important here is to list higher-level mediated actions in the data *and* to list the times in the video clip. Table 5.1 illustrates such a table with an imaginary example of friends meeting at a coffee shop.

Table 5.1 Higher-level mediated action table of an imaginary data set.

Time stamp in video at the beginning of a higher-level mediated action	Brief description of a higher-level mediated action
00:00:00	Friends greeting (entering the café and meeting each other)
00:03:10	Friends ordering coffee
00:05:23	Friends ordering a cake
Many more time stamps listed on this side of the table	Many more higher-level mediated actions listed on this side of the table
01:05:10	Friends greeting (leaving the café and each other)

Task 3
Produce a table of all higher-level mediated actions in your entire data set.

Task 4
Show your data and your higher-level mediated action table to other researchers and see if they can understand how you have delineated the higher-level mediated actions.

Certainly, you will list various kinds of smaller and larger higher-level mediated actions, but the point is to really get to know the mediated actions that social actors perform in your data. When working in this way, you will at first go back and forth between various data pieces, trying to find your "right" size of higher-level mediated action to work with. It does take a little practice to delineate higher-level mediated actions in a useful way and the following sections in this Chapters 5.1–5.3, will help you learn to demarcate higher-level mediated actions in practice. Once we have demarcated higher-level mediated actions, we are in a position to develop an overview of the higher-level mediated actions found in our data.

Note 3
Here, you see the importance of time stamping your video as outlined in Phase I Step 10. Time stamps are our way of noting down particular higher-level mediated actions in our data *and* our way to locate these again later without having to watch and re-watch each entire video.

Step 3: Developing an Overview of Higher-Level Mediated Actions in Your Data Set

In order to develop an overview of the higher-level mediated actions in your data set, you will want to produce a table in which you bundle some higher-level mediated actions. An example of how to do this is shown in Table 5.2.

Table 5.2 Bundled higher-level mediated action table of an imaginary data set.

Time stamp (as shown in the previous table listing your higher-level mediated actions)	A bundle of higher-level mediated actions
00:00:00, 01:05:10	Social actors greeting
00:03:10, 00:05:23	Social actors ordering

Task 5

Bundle higher-level mediated actions in your data set.

Once you have produced this kind of table (Table 5.2), you will have produced an overview of all of your data in the data set that you are studying. From this overview of all higher-level mediated actions occurring in your data set, you can then make an informed selection and begin to focus upon certain higher-level mediated actions to study further.

Note 4

The bundling of higher-level mediated actions and their positions in your video data, allows you to:
1) Move on to micro analysis without having to re-watch your entire data.
2) Clearly position your micro analyzed data pieces into the larger data set.

Note 5

Working in this way permits us to:
1) Make informed decisions to focus on this or that higher-level mediated action for further analysis based on our own data set.
2) Recognize how pertinent or how rare the moments are that we are focusing on.
3) Know exactly where to find the relevant data pieces that we want to examine more closely.

Note 6

Working in this way prohibits us from:
1) Examining a minute detail that almost never occurs in our data set without clearly revealing its rarity.
2) Over-emphasizing something that is rare, or de-emphasizing something that occurs frequently in our data set.
3) Finding only what we are looking for.

Step 4: Narrowing the Site of Engagement

In Chapter 2, we learned that a site of engagement is the window opened up through practices and discourses that makes particular concrete social actions possible (Norris 2014b; Scollon 1998, 2001a). Then, in Chapter 4, we utilized the notion of a site of engagement to position ourselves, the researchers, in relation to our data sets (Phase II Step 2) and data pieces (Phase II Step 4). Thus, there we learned that the site of engagement that includes ourselves and the data set (or data piece) comes about through the intersection of practices and discourses that make our concrete higher-level mediated actions of analyzing the data possible.

At this point, we have demarcated the higher-level mediated actions in our entire data set. We have created a table that clearly shows the overview of all higher-level mediated actions performed in our data, and we are now ready to select particular higher-level mediated actions for closer examination. In order to move forward in a theoretically founded way, we again want to use the site of engagement as our starting point.

Site of Engagement as Window for Analysis

Here, I would like you to actually think of a window that can be opened and closed. Further, imagine that the window is covered so that you cannot see through it when the window is closed. However, this is not much of a problem, because you are the one who can open and close this window. Your view of the outside world is thus either widely visible to you when you are opening the window all the way, or your view is rather limited when you are opening the window only a small slit. Next, you want to think of your data as that outside world that you are looking at when opening this window.

While in Phase II Step 2, you produced a graph that showed your entire data set plus yourself and you produced a graph of yourself and a data piece in Phase II Step 4, you now want to think of this window here in *Phase III Step 4 to only show your data*. Thus, when you open this window here as wide as you can, you will be able to see your entire data set.

Next, you want to think of closing this window to a particular higher-level mediated action that you want to investigate in detail. Maybe you have picked this data piece because higher-level mediated actions like this one occur in your data frequently. Or maybe you have selected this data piece because higher-level mediated actions like this one are very rare in your data set. Or maybe you have selected this data piece because this kind of higher-level mediated action is something that you are particularly interested in. You will have your own reasons why you chose this particular higher-level mediated action in your data to examine more closely and all of your reasons can be justified.

In order to select this data piece in a theoretically founded way, we utilize the notion of a site of engagement. By doing this, we can never forget that this concrete higher-level mediated action comes about through intersecting practices and discourses, which may direct or change the concrete higher-level mediated action that you are studying and which in turn may be directed or changed through this concrete higher-level mediated action.

Note 7

Working in this way allows us to:
1) Select data pieces for micro analysis in a theoretically founded and systematic way.
2) Focus on *any* higher-level mediated action in our data that we wish without losing sight of the way it is positioned in relation to other higher-level mediated actions in our data set.
3) Never lose sight of the coming together of concrete mediated actions, practices, and discourses.

Phase III: Summary

In Phase III of systematically working with multimodal data, we gain a deep understanding of our entire data set. Phase III consists of four steps:

1) The MEDIATED ACTION: rephrasing your general research question
2) Demarcating higher-level mediated actions
3) Developing an overview of higher-level mediated actions in your data set
4) Narrowing the site of engagement

Now that you have learned the individual analysis steps of Phases III, you will find an illustration of this Step-by-Step analysis in the next sections. First, in Section 5.1, I demonstrate Phase III of the Step-by-Step process with the YouTube video from Sections 3.1 and 4.1. Then, in Section 5.2, I illustrate how the four steps of Phase III are utilized in the experimental study from Section 3.2 and 4.2, for which we collected data of 12 dyads (inter) acting via Skype to each perform two tasks together. In Section 5.3, I then show how the Step-by-Step process of Phase III works in an even larger study. Here, the examples come from the study that was conducted by a group of researchers in New Zealand to examine family (inter)action via video conferencing technology, shown in Sections 3.3 and 4.3.

The Step-by-Step analysis of the YouTube clip demonstrates how the analytical framework can be used for smaller data pieces; the Step-by-Step analysis of the dyadic teamwork illustrates how to use the framework for medium-sized projects; and the Step-by-Step analysis of the project of family video conferencing (inter)actions shows how researchers can use the methodology to systematically make sense of larger data sets. Video excerpts from this larger study for classroom use can be found at www.wiley. com/go/Norris/multimodal-data. For each data piece in this section, slightly longer video clips are available online and the student/novice researcher can begin to work through the steps by continuing the analyses of the examples given.

Phase III: Selecting Data Pieces for Micro Analysis – Things to Remember

---

Things to Remember 1

Before delving into a micro analysis of individual data pieces, we want to make sure that we continue to work in a theoretically founded manner. For this, you learned to rephrase your research questions encircling your data into a theoretically founded statement.
- Rephrase your research questions produced in Phase II Step 5 as a statement of a MEDIATED ACTION.

Things to Remember 2

We want to let the data tell the story. In order to truly allow the data to speak to us, we need to demarcate all higher-level mediated actions in our data set. If it is not possible for you to work through the entire data set delineating all higher-level mediated actions, you are either working with a data set that is too large for what you are trying to accomplish or you are listing the higher-level mediated actions at too small a scale.

In fact, it makes little sense to work only with particular higher-level mediated actions in a very large data set, because we have no way of knowing the relationship of these particular higher-level mediated actions to the entire data set. Without being able to relate specific higher-level mediated actions to the entire data set that we are examining, we do not have much to say about the relevance of our analysis. Thus here, you have learned:

- How to produce a table of all higher-level mediated actions in your entire data set.
- That your guiding principle when listing higher-level mediated actions is that you can show your data to other researchers and they can understand how you have delineated the higher-level mediated actions. In other words, when you explain to others how you delineated the higher-level mediated actions in your data and show them your video(s), they will easily be able to see sense in what you did.

Things to Remember 3

In order to truly understand the entirety of higher-level mediated actions in your data set, you will next want to bundle similar higher-level mediated actions.

Things to Remember 4

Once you have worked through your entire data set, it is time to choose particular data pieces for micro analysis. Of course, we want to continue working in a theoretically founded way and to do so, we utilize the notion of a site of engagement as a window opened up through practices and discourses that make concrete social actions possible (Norris 2014b; Scollon 1998, 2001a). By working with the site of engagement as our theoretical concept to narrow our view to analyze specific higher-level mediated actions, we incorporate social actors (including their cognition, history, memory, emotion), mediational means/cultural tools (their origins, the ways they are used, their make-up), the practices (actions with a history), and the discourses (actions with a history that have an institutional and/or ideological dimension). Thus, even when examining minute actions found in our data pieces, their links to practices and discourses can never get lost.

Task 6

Draw an image of a site of engagement, in which you see within the window the concrete higher-level mediated action and where the window is crisscrossed by practices and discourses.

5.1

Systematically Working with Small Data Sets/Data Pieces

Phase III Selecting Data Pieces for Micro Analysis

In this section, I exemplify the four steps of Phase III outlined in the beginning of this chapter with the same YouTube video that I introduced in Chapter 3.1. and continued to work with in Chapter 4.1. This part, a continuation of Chapter 3.1 and 4.1 may be particularly useful for classroom use. Here, the tasks guide the student to engage in how to analyze an entire data set.

A Step-by-Step Guide to Analyze a YouTube Video

Phase III: Selecting Data Pieces for Micro Analysis

First, we want to rephrase our research question that encircles our data, which we produced in Phase II Step 5. Here, we rephrase the question into a theoretically founded statement, a mediated action (Step 1). Next, we learn to demarcate higher-level mediated actions (Step 2). We want to demarcate higher-level mediated actions in our entire data set in order to later make connections between the actions we analyze in minute detail (Chapter 7) and the data set that we have collected (Chapter 3). Once we have listed all higher-level mediated actions in our data set, we want to bundle higher-level mediated actions into groups (Step 3). By doing this, we arrive at an overview of higher-level mediated actions performed by social actors in our data set. Working in this way makes sure that we do not later have to go back and re-watch entire videos, but rather, we can focus on the particular segments in Phases IV and V without losing sight of their position in relation to our entire data set. At the end of Phase III, we want to emphasize the theoretical view that all concrete actions are produced by social actors drawing on (and possibly changing) intersecting practices and discourses. For this, we want to utilize the site of engagement as our concept that helps us to select concrete higher-level mediated actions to analyze in more detail (Step 4). We begin by rephrasing our data driven research question into a MEDIATED ACTION.

Systematically Working with Multimodal Data: Research Methods in Multimodal Discourse Analysis, First Edition. Sigrid Norris.
© 2019 John Wiley & Sons, Inc. Published 2019 by John Wiley & Sons, Inc.
Companion website: www.wiley.com/go/Norris/multimodal-data

Step 1: The MEDIATED ACTION: Rephrasing Your Data Driven Research
Question

Task 1: YouTube
Before opening your video, take out a piece of paper *and* open a new document on your computer and write on top in large letters: MEDIATED ACTION

The mediated action is your guiding principle that helps you to always be clear about what it is that you are looking for. I suggest a piece of paper *and* a document in Task 1, because you can always have a piece of paper physically present as you work with your data. Putting it next to your computer allows you to glance at it each time when your mind is straying and you get overwhelmed in trying to make sense of your video data.

Still focused on your piece of paper with the words MEDIATED ACTION at the top, you want to realize that your video data consists of many concrete and *always mediated* actions that participants performed, and it is the concreteness of these actions that will keep you grounded and clear in your pursuit of analyzing the data.

Even before watching your video, you want to name the mediated action that your study is about. Here, you *rephrase your general research question that you developed in Phase II Step 5* into an action. You place this action below the words MEDIATED ACTION into your documents.

Example: *Kai Sings "Cake by the Ocean"*
The MEDIATED ACTION
For our YouTube study, the documents read:

MEDIATED ACTION
Social Actors (Inter)Acting in a YouTube Show

This formulation provides the three components of a mediated action:

1) Social actors
2) The action = (inter)acting
3) A relevant mediational means/cultural tool (YouTube show)

With this formulation, we highlight the relevance of the YouTube show in this (inter) action. Quite obviously, this is not an everyday naturally occurring (inter)action. The YouTube clip is staged; it has been produced and has no doubt been heavily edited. Some of the shots may even come from different shows/times and we have no way of knowing this from watching and analyzing the clip. This is something we could only determine if we had access to the production of the show itself. However, because we know that this is so, we can also see that this makes the analysis of a YouTube clip an assemblage of various facets that are produced to show "ostensible real time" (inter) action, quite interesting.

Task 2: YouTube
Formulate one mediated action that comprises your general research question developed in Phase II Step 5.

Next, you want to demarcate higher-level mediated actions. In the beginning, the notion of demarcating higher-level mediated actions can seem difficult. However, if you work systematically, you will quickly learn how to delineate them. Always keep in mind that higher-level mediated actions are produced through various chains of lower-level mediated actions – or that lower-level mediated actions are produced in chains by social actors as they are producing higher-level mediated actions. People can never just *produce* one lower-level mediated action alone, but we can *analyze* a specific lower-level mediated action. However, here we will not go into lower-level mediated actions. This is something that is addressed in Chapters 6 and 7. Here, we want to focus on understanding the higher-level mediated actions in your data. The following step will help you to demarcate higher-level mediated actions, all of which are MEDIATED ACTIONS.

Step 2: Demarcating Higher-Level Mediated Actions

Now, you are ready to open your YouTube clip and begin to list the higher-level mediated actions that you see. At this point, you want to note the beginnings of higher-level mediated actions, but do not want to worry about the ending points or the duration of a higher-level mediated action. That is something that comes later. Here, you want to just jot down what you see and/or hear.

As you are watching the first few minutes, you will wonder how to "cut up" the actions as separate from one another. This can be tricky, but does not have to be. Just begin by writing the first action down that you see. Name it by what is going on. Then, don't worry about the fact that you will find many different kinds of higher-level mediated actions, some of which will last a few seconds and some of which will last a long duration of time. The basic question here is: What are the people in your video clip doing?

For a YouTube clip or movie, you will also want to list the camera angles. Sometimes the camera angle corresponds to who is talking, but that is also quite often not the case. When using a table that shows the times when the camera angle shifts and what is happening in the video during that time for each individual, we gain insight into the relationship between the camera angle and what is shown. If we do not repeat the same time for all three (the camera angle, Ellen, and Kai), but rather only include a time stamp when and where the change occurs, we can glance at our table later and see just how often the camera angle was used to shift the viewers' attention to a particular social actor or to specific mediated actions.

Example: *Kai Sings "Cake by the Ocean"*
Listing Higher-Level Mediated Actions
Please watch the EllenTube clip *Kai Sings "Cake by the Ocean"*

www.youtube.com/watch?v=h9fZY0KFNQM

When listing higher-level mediated actions, you are analyzing what your video clip is about. Here, you want to be relatively general. This is not the place and not the time to transcribe your video. The first few seconds of listing the higher-level mediated actions and noting down the camera angles (since this is an edited clip) in the EllenTube video *Kai sings "Cake by the Ocean"* are as shown in Table 5.3.

Table 5.3 Higher-level mediated action table YouTube example.

Time	Camera angle	Ellen and Kai
00 : 00	Full shot, chair relatively straight towards camera	Ellen introduces the next guest, Kai Audience claps
00 : 06	Change of angle: Ellen and Kai sitting across from one another	Ellen queries Kai as the audience claps Audience claps
00 : 08	Change of angle: Kai full head/shoulder; part of Ellen's left side of face in view	Kai begins to explain the loss of his teeth
00 : 10		Ellen has moved out of shot and begins to ask Kai about his teeth
00 : 12	Change of angle: frontal view of Ellen and back of Kai	Ellen continues to query Kai about his teeth making a joke about his inability to pronounce "th"
00 : 13		Kai agrees and explains how he lost his teeth Audience laughs
00 : 21		Audience laughs

Task 3: YouTube

Practice listing higher-level mediated actions for the next 30 seconds in the YouTube example.

Task 4: YouTube

Next, list higher-level mediated actions for your chosen clip and place them in a table like the one illustrated as Table 5.3.

As mentioned above, listing higher-level mediated actions (and camera angles for edited videos) is an analysis step. It is *not* a transcription step. Thus, you do not want to arrive at a table like the one illustrated as Table 5.4.

In this crossed out table, the language has been transcribed verbatim and particular lower-level mediated actions such as pointing have been added. Such a table may seem like a good idea as you are noting down actions in great detail. However, such detail at this early

Table 5.4 *Incorrect* higher-level mediated action table YouTube example.

Time	Camera angle	Time	Ellen	Time	Kay
00:00	Full shot, chair relatively straight towards camera		Ellen: our next guest is one of the cutest singers to ever be on my stage from Spring Texas please welcome Kai Langer		
00:06	Change of angle: Ellen and Kai sitting across from one another		Ellen: what's going on? pointing at her own teeth as audience claps		Kay sitting across from Ellen
00:08	Change of angle: Kai full head/shoulder; part of Ellen's left side of face in view				Kai: Ahm, lost two teeth, ahm one of them I lost
		00:10	Ellen has moved out of shot and begins to ask "two how many?"		
00:12	Change of angle: frontal view of Ellen and back of Kai		"two teeth?" showing her own teeth		
				00:13	Kai points to his mouth and says yeah. I lost one of them ahm...

point will not only not be helpful in the analyses to come; such detail here, will in fact, ensure that you get lost in your data.

A good point to remember is that we are trying to *understand* our data. We will transcribe *SOME* data later, but first we need to discern which parts to transcribe. When working with a YouTube clip, it may seem plausible to transcribe the entire clip. But even when working with little data (as in our example with 6 minutes 17 seconds), a full transcription of the video will be more confusing than helpful. Next, we want to bundle higher-level mediated actions.

Step 3: Developing an Overview of Higher-Level Mediated Actions in Your Data Set

The aim is to understand the data, to make sense of what we see and hear and to note down our understanding of the clip. When we list the higher-level mediated actions (rather than transcribing every word or lower-level mediated action), we can begin to see some interesting aspects in our data. After listing the higher-level mediated actions (Table 5.3), we can highlight what comes up and can continue to make sense of our data (Table 5.5). Now we want to highlight those higher-level mediated actions with the same color that are similar enough to fit into the same kind. Each of the highlighted verbs in Table 5.5 below portrays an action. Some actions recur (such as the action of explaining) and other actions can be understood as being of the same kind (such as query and ask).

Thus, once you have completed your higher-level mediated action table, you are ready to produce a new data table, a color coded bundles of higher-level mediated action table. Looking at your higher-level mediated action table in this way allows you to find topics, which is a very similar way to logging your data as one does in discourse analysis (Tannen 1984) or critical discourse analysis (Wodak 2001).

As you color-code your higher-level mediated actions, you now begin to distil the higher-level mediated actions into groups, and by doing this you solidify some of the things that you noticed in your data while creating your higher-level mediated action table. What you have noticed will show up in your data tables as the very actions that you have summarized. Further, similar actions will often be combined as a set of actions (i.e. queries, asks); and actions that you found to be of great interest will be separated out (i.e. humor), already illustrating some possible foci.

Table 5.5 Color coded bundles of higher-level mediated action table YouTube example.

Time	Camera angle	Ellen and Kai
00:00	Full shot, chair relatively straight towards camera	Ellen introduces the next guest, Kai Audience claps
00:06	Change of angle: Ellen and Kai sitting across from one another	Ellen queries Kai as the audience claps Audience claps
00:08	Change of angle: Kai full head/shoulder; part of Ellen's left side of face in view	Kai begins to explain the loss of his teeth
00:10		Ellen has moved out of shot and begins to ask Kai about his teeth
00:12	Change of angle: frontal view of Ellen and back of Kai	Ellen continues to query Kai about his teeth making a joke about his inability to pronounce "th"
00:13		Kai agrees and explains how he lost his teeth Audience laughs
00:21		Audience laughs

Task 5: YouTube

Color-code higher-level mediated actions of a similar kind in your own data.

Note 1: YouTube

Always record the time from the beginning of a higher-level mediated action.

Next, you create a new table that shows how you bundled the higher-level mediated actions. Table 5.6 gives an example.

Example: *Kai Sings "Cake by the Ocean"*

Making sense of the higher-level mediated actions in the U-Tube clip Kai Sings "Cake by the Ocean"

Table 5.6 Bundled higher-level mediated action table YouTube example.

Time	A bundle of higher-level mediated actions
00:00	Ellen introducing a guest
00:06, 00:10, 00:12	Ellen questioning
00:12	Ellen making a joke
00:08, 0013	Kai explaining
00:13	Kai agreeing
00:00, 00:06, 00:13, 00:21	Audience clapping/laughing

Task 6: YouTube

Bundle your color coded higher-level mediated actions of a similar kind and produce a table as shown as Table 5.6.

Here, the higher-level mediated actions are shown by the social actor (inter)acting. We need to remind ourselves that each of the higher-level mediated actions comes together multimodally, is produced in and with the environment, objects within and with other social actors present or imagined. We want to go beyond analyzing the verbal mode and examine the introduction, question, explanation, humor, agreement, or the clapping/laughter of the audience in their multimodal complexity.

When distilling the higher-level mediated actions as explained above, you may already find something specific that you are interested in. For example, you may wonder how various talk-show hosts introduce guests, leading you to examine a good number of different YouTube clips. Thus, had you begun by examining the YouTube clip of Ellen and Kai by transcribing the entire clip, you would have wasted much precious time that you can use instead to find different, but similar, videos to examine introductions by hosts.

Since we work in a data driven way, we want to let the data speak to us. This means, we want to first understand as much as possible about the data that we have collected in order to then begin micro analyses. When we are ready to conduct a micro analysis, we want to recall that we are working in a theoretically founded way. The concept of the site of engagement helps us to never lose sight of the complexity of social action.

Step 4: Selecting Data Pieces for Micro Analysis: Narrowing the Site of Engagement

As we are now ready for micro analysis of particular higher-level mediated actions from our data set, we want to utilize the site of engagement, the window opened up through practices and discourses that make concrete higher-level mediated actions possible.

A sketch of a higher-level mediated action as a window becomes useful here. You will recall, we used the concept of a site of engagement previously. In Phase II Steps 2 and 4 we illustrated the position of the researcher in relation to the data set and data pieces. Here, we want to utilize the concept by narrowing the window so that all we can see is a particular data piece, which we wish to examine in great detail.

Here, we want to focus our first analysis on how Ellen introduces a guest. Therefore, we narrow the window (our site of engagement) to a point that we can only see the first six seconds of the You Tube clip. It is during these first six seconds that Ellen introduces her guest, Kai (Figure 5.1).

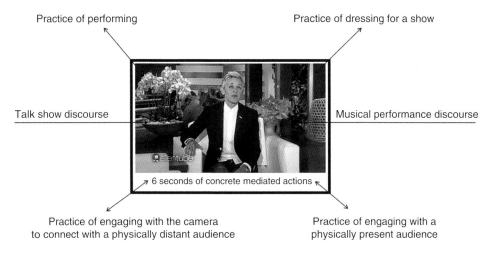

Figure 5.1 A narrow site of engagement for micro analysis example YouTube.

Phase III: Summary

In Phase III of systematically working with multimodal data, you have gained a deep understanding of the higher-level mediated actions in your selected YouTube data. In Phase III, consisting of four steps, you have:

1) Rephrased your research question that encircles your data into a MEDIATED ACTION
2) Demarcated the higher-level mediated actions in your entire data set
3) Developed a table that bundles all higher-level mediated actions in your data set and shows an *overview* of your entire data
4) Narrowed the site of engagement, selecting a data piece for micro analysis

Task 7: YouTube
Follow the four steps of Phase III before moving on to Phase IV.

5.2

Systematically Working with Medium-Sized Data Sets

Phase III Selecting Data Pieces for Micro Analysis

In this section, I demonstrate the same phases and steps as outlined in Chapter 5.0. But this time, I am showing how Phase III is used in a medium-sized data set with an example from the experimental study of dyads working in teams via video conferencing technology. Section 5.2 is a direct continuation of the examples in Chapters 3.2 and 4.2. This section will be particularly useful for small research teams and Masters or PhD seminars.

A Step-by-Step Guide to Analyze Experimental Data

Phase III: Selecting Data Pieces for Micro Analysis

We begin Phase III by rephrasing our research questions that encircle our data, which we produced in Phase II Step 5. In Step 1, we rephrase the question into a mediated action. By doing this, we make sure that we continue to work in a theoretically founded way. Once we have rewritten our data-encircling research question, the statement (the mediated action) guides us when demarcating higher-level mediated actions. In Step 2, we always want to keep in mind the notion that a mediated action is defined as social actor(s) acting with or through mediational means or cultural tools. When remembering this, a demarcation of higher-level mediated actions becomes possible. What is important is to delineate all higher-level mediated actions in our data set before setting out to analyze specific actions in minute detail. Only by working through all of our data, can we later make informed claims about the value of our micro analyses. Next, once we have listed all higher-level mediated actions in our data set, we move on to Step 3, in which we want to bundle higher-level mediated actions into groups. When we group higher-level mediated actions found in our data set, we develop an overview of our entire data. This way of working ensures that we do not have to go back later and re-watch entire videos, but rather, we can focus on particular segments without losing site of their position in relation to our entire data set. At the end of Phase III, in Step 4 we want to overtly remember our theoretical position by utilizing the site of engagement as our concept for narrowing our view to select particular data pieces for detailed micro analysis. The concept of a site of engagement always reminds us that all concrete actions

Systematically Working with Multimodal Data: Research Methods in Multimodal Discourse Analysis, First Edition. Sigrid Norris.
© 2019 John Wiley & Sons, Inc. Published 2019 by John Wiley & Sons, Inc.
Companion website: www.wiley.com/go/Norris/multimodal-data

are produced by social actors drawing on (and possibly changing) intersecting practices and discourses. We begin our investigation by rephrasing our data driven research question into a MEDIATED ACTION.

Step 1: The MEDIATED ACTION: Rephrasing Your Data Driven Research Question

Let us begin this step with a task:

Task 1: Experimental Study

Before opening a video, take out a piece of paper *and* open a new document on your computer and write at the top in large letters:

MEDIATED ACTION

As you recall from Chapter 2, the mediated action is the theoretically founded unit of analysis that incorporates the tension between social actor(s) acting and the mediational means or cultural tools that are being used. The mediated action, in Multimodal (Inter)action Analysis delineated into lower-level, higher-level, and frozen mediated actions, is the overarching unit of analysis.

Making it overt that you are analyzing mediated actions will help you to always be clear about what it is that you are looking for. I suggest a piece of paper *and* a document, because you can always have a piece of paper physically present as you work with your data. Putting it next to your computer allows you to glance at it each time when your mind strays and you begin to list what people say, rather than what people do. *Making sense of video data means to make sense of what people do*, which includes, but is never limited to, what people say.

Considering the MEDIATED ACTION on screen and your piece of paper, you want to realize that your data consists of many concrete and *always mediated* actions. This focus upon concrete actions will keep you grounded and clear in your pursuit of analyzing the data. But now, even before beginning to watch your first video, you want to utilize your data driven research questions developed in Phase II Step 5 and formulate a MEDIATED ACTION.

Example: Dyadic Teamwork Via Video Conferencing Technology

The data driven research question that we developed for this experimental study was: *How do social actors (inter)act when performing tasks together* via *video conferencing technology?*

The MEDIATED ACTION

For our experimental study, the document reads:

MEDIATED ACTION
Social actors working on tasks together via Skype with computer/laptop

This formulation also provides the three components of a mediated action:

1) Social actors
2) The action = working
3) Some relevant mediational means/cultural tools (tasks, Skype, computer or laptop)

With this formulation, we highlight the mediational means, the tasks, as well as the technological cultural tools that the social actors used, namely Skype and computer or laptop.

Because we are here working with an experiment, the naturalness of the mediated actions is limited. On the one hand, social actors act as they are able to in or with their own repertoire of actions. Thus, they are performing each mediated action naturally and in their own ways. On the other hand, the setting, the tasks themselves, and the computer and laptop provided by the researchers, make the mediated actions not natural on a larger scale. Since our interest here, however, is primarily the way that our participants perform the mediated actions of working together on two tasks, our analysis lies predominantly in the area of *naturally occurring*. However, when we later link our micro analyses to the larger picture (Phase V Steps 3 and 4), we can determine the level of *non-naturally occurring* in regard to larger scale mediated actions.

Task 2: Experimental Study

Formulate one mediated action that comprises your general research question developed in Phase II Step 5.

Now that you have formulated the mediated action that you are interested in, you are ready to list higher-level mediated actions. The notion of demarcating higher-level mediated actions may seem difficult at first. However, when you work systematically, you will quickly learn how to delineate higher-level mediated actions. As outlined in Chapter 2, higher-level mediated actions are produced through the coming together of various chains of lower-level mediated actions. Simultaneously, lower-level mediated actions are produced by social actors as they are producing higher-level mediated actions. The lower- and the higher-level thus constitute each other. What is important to realize here is that people never can *produce* just one lower-level mediated action alone. While one lower-level mediated action can be transcribed and analyzed (see Chapters 6 and 7), we do not work on this level just yet. Here, we want to focus on recognizing and demarcating *higher-level mediated actions* in your data. The following steps will help you in this endeavor.

Step 2: Demarcating Higher-Level Mediated Actions

Now, you are ready to open your first video file and begin to list higher-level mediated actions. Important here is to realize that you do not need to worry about the endings or the duration of higher-level mediated actions. Rather, our interest here is the beginning of a higher-level mediated action.

When you begin to watch a video, you are likely to be puzzled about how to "cut up" higher-level mediated actions and you may wonder how to separate one from another.

While this may seem tricky, it is really not that difficult. Simply begin by noting down the first action that you see. Jot down the beginning of the higher-level mediated action, and name the social actor and the action. Then, move on to the next one. Try not to worry about the fact that you will find many different kinds of higher-level mediated actions in your data, some of which will last a few seconds and some of which will last a long duration of time. The basic question here is: What are the people in your video clip doing?

In order to illustrate our purely data driven approach, I give an example from the experimental study that we began working with in Chapters 3.1 and 4.1. In this example, I illustrate demarcating higher-level mediated actions in the first couple of minutes of two individuals working on Task 1 together. The two are ostensibly staying in Amsterdam at a specific hotel and have been given the task of finding a restaurant for dinner. The clip can be watched online and can be utilized as a teaching or learning tool in class or for self-study. By using this clip, you will learn the listing of higher-level mediated actions before you embark on your own data analysis.

Example: Dyadic Teamwork Via Video Conferencing Technology
Listing Higher-Level Mediated Actions
Delineating higher-level mediated actions for *teamwork* from the dyadic teamwork via Skype study, the following is listed for approximately the first two and half minutes (Table 5.7).

Task 3: Experimental Study
Watch the teamwork video. Read the higher-level mediated action table (Table 5.7) while watching and see if you can find the sense in describing what is going on in the clip in this way. Then, discuss in class.

Table 5.7 Higher-level mediated action table teamwork example. Reproduced with permission of the participants.

00:06:29	Greeting, Play-acting, Getting into the task
00:26:48	Milena logs into Google and begins to search for options
00:29:10	Alisa (inter)acts with Milena to figure out options
00:41:20	Milena responds as she is looking up the hotel
00:46:26	Alisa clicks on Google maps and begins to scroll
00:56:32	Alisa inquiries about what Milena is searching/wants to eat
01:00:21	Milena explains and Alisa begins to search the hotel
01:18:16	Alisa begins typing
01:23:30	Milena speaking through what she is doing
01:29:28	Alisa looking at and commenting on the hotel, then Milena looks at the hotel
01:48:05	Milena speaking through what she is doing
01:56:46	Alisa begins to talk through what she is doing/thinking
02:29:27	Milena is looking at Google Maps and Alisa is going there

When listing higher-level mediated actions, we want to ensure that we do not work at a very small level (see Table 5.8). The point of developing higher-level mediated action tables is to make sense of our data in a way that we can later have an overview of what is going on. Especially when working with medium (and large) sized data sets, we want to work on a level that allows us to see a bigger picture rather than focusing on the minute micro actions that individuals perform. The micro, too, is important, but that is something we will examine in Phase IV, when we multimodally transcribe micro actions.

Table 5.8 *Incorrect* higher-level mediated action table teamwork example. Reproduced with permission of the participants.

00:06:29	Milena looks at screen and says "Hi, Alisa" and puts a hand on the keyboard.
00:07:33	Alisa looks at Milena through the screen and says "Hey, hi, ciao", then briefly looks at her piece of paper.
00:9:45	Both laugh. Milena has her arms on the desk and looks at the piece of paper lying next to her laptop.
00:11:00	Alisa continues to look at the screen and says "Nice to be in Amsterdam, huh?"
00:11:28	Milena moves back, laughs and looks at the screen.
00:12:49	Milena says "yeah, it's nice to be here" as she again has her arms on her desk and looks at the piece of paper again.
00:14:48	Both laugh.

Working on the level demonstrated in Table 5.8 at this time of analyzing our data will cause more confusion than clarity. Further, here we will fall into the trap of realizing that whatever we put into such a table is flawed. No matter how much we try, there is always more going on than we can easily sum up in such a table. The only way to do it seems to go down to a smaller and smaller level up to the point when we begin to list lower-level mediated actions in elaborate tables. If we go down this path, we will find that a certain movement – say a movement of the head to and from the screen – may come up again and again. We can then say that this head movement occurs 1000 times in 15 minutes. But so what? What point would we be able to make with such a "finding"? The pure fact that someone doing something on a computer looks at the screen is hardly worth mentioning. Further, if we have detailed tables that list everything that anybody does, we still have no idea what is actually going on in an (inter)action. Instead, we have lost sight of what we want to find out, namely: How do people work in teams via Skype? We want to look at multiple dyads, and not at a five-minute interval of one video, describing *only* what happens there. We want to understand the bigger picture and then draw on that understanding before we move to transcription and micro analysis. Therefore, working too detailed at this stage is a downfall (see Table 5.8).

Task 4: Experimental Study

Watch Video 5.1 and continue the higher-level mediated action table in Table 5.7 (being very careful not to fall into the trap of too much information as shown in Table 5.8). Then share your tables and discuss.

Task 5: Experimental Study
Begin to list higher-level mediated actions for your own project.

Note 1: Experimental Study
Always record the time from the beginning of a higher-level mediated action

Listing higher-level mediated actions will give you great insight into your data. It is an easy and relatively quick way to systematically understand what your data is all about. Thus, when working with your own collected data, *you want to list all higher-level mediated actions in your data set.* You list the higher-level mediated actions with their beginning points in the clip. The point here is to make it possible for you later to easily find the higher-level mediated actions that you wish to examine in more detail. But, again, be careful not to go overboard. It is not necessary to list these beginning points too correctly up to the millisecond. If you can easily locate the millisecond of a beginning, by all means do that. However, often there is so much going on that this is more difficult. When your data are very complex, it may be more useful for you to work on approximately a second-level when listing the beginnings of higher-level mediated actions. Remember you are listing these higher-level mediated actions in order to make sense of your entire data set.

When demarcating higher-level mediated actions, it is not important that two researchers list the same higher-level mediated actions. What is important is that others can understand how you listed the higher-level mediated actions when they watch your video and follow along with your list. Therefore, you always want to give your higher-level mediated action tables to other researchers and let them watch the video to check and see if they can understand your way of seeing the data. If others understand what you have done, you are on track. While higher-level mediated actiontables of the same video can differ from one researcher to the next, the selected excerpts transcribed using the transcription conventions that we will learn in Phase IV, will be the same for different researchers. But first, we need to bundle our higher-level mediated actions in order to establish an overview of all higher-level mediated actions in our data.

Step 3: Developing an Overview of Higher-Level Mediated Actions in Your Data Set

The goal here is to make sense of all of our data. For this, let us revisit Table 5.7 and color-code bundles of higher-level mediated actions that may be of particular interest (Table 5.9).

When you look at Table 5.9, you will see that I have marked particular higher-level mediated actions, and sometimes, you find that I have chosen to mark one higher-level mediated action with two colors. The two-toned higher-level mediated actions will be represented in two different higher-level mediated action bundles in the next table, where we arrive at an overview of higher-level mediated actions in our entire data (Table 5.10).

Table 5.9 Color coded bundles of higher-level mediated action table teamwork example. Reproduced with permission of the participants.

00:06:29	Greeting, play-acting, getting into the task
00:26:48	Milena opens Google and begins to search for options
00:29:10	Alisa (inter)acts with Milena to figure out options
00:41:20	Milena responds as she is looking up the hotel
00:46:26	Alisa clicks on Google maps and begins to scroll
00:56:32	Alisa inquiries about what Milena is searching/wants to eat
01:00:21	Milena explains and Alisa begins to search the hotel
01:18:16	Alisa begins typing
01:23:30	Milena speaking through what she is doing
01:29:28	Alisa looking at and commenting on hotel, then Milena looks at hotel
01:48:05	Milena speaking through what she is doing
01:56:46	Alisa begins to talk through what she is doing/thinking
02:29:27	Milena is looking at Google Maps and Alisa is going there

Table 5.10 Bundled higher-level mediated action table teamwork example. Reproduced with permission of the participants.

00:06:29 01:29:28	Play-acting
00:26:48 00:41:20 00:46:26 01:00:21 01:18:16 01:23:30 01:48:05 01:56:46 02:29:27	Searching
00:29:10	Speaking with the other participant without searching anything
00:56:32	Inquiring what the other participant is searching/ wants to eat
01:00:21	Explaining to the other what the participant is doing
01:23:30 01:48:05 01:56:46	Participant speaking through what she is doing

When you have bundled the higher-level mediated actions in your entire data, you will see that some themes and topics emerge. Examining and color-coding your higher-level mediated action tables produced in Phase III Step 2, allows you to find topics (similarly to the way we log data in discourse analysis (Tannen 1984) or critical discourse analysis (Wodak 2001)).

What you also may notice as you are color-coding the higher-level mediated actions is that you listed many of the higher-level mediated actions in accordance with what people say. This is *not necessarily* a problem, *but it is something that you will want to be wary of.* Listing actions in words forces us to produce tables as text. This word-oriented approach to our understanding of what is going on in the data however, can be changed once you begin to create your bundled higher-level mediated action table. As you create your bundled higher-level mediated action table, you distil the higher-level mediated actions into groups; and by doing this, you also solidify some of the actions that you noticed in your data while producing your earlier tables. Now you will see just how well you have understood your data, how much you already have noticed, and how particular aspects drive your curiosity. What you have noticed, no doubt will show up in your data tables as the higher-level mediated actions that you have summarized. You will find that similar higher-level mediated actions are now easily combined as a bundle of actions, while you will want to separate out some other higher-level mediated actions that you have found in your data – already illustrating your focus.

Making Sense of the Higher-Level Actions in Video 1 of the Teamwork Data
In this data driven way, we let the data speak to us. But of course, we are social actors with particular interests and thus while working with our data in this way, we see what catches our interest. Now it is time to begin to focus further and select data pieces for micro analysis.

Step 4: Selecting Data Pieces for Micro Analysis: Narrowing the Site of Engagement

Now, you are ready to select particular higher-level mediated actions from your data set for micro analysis. In order to continue working in a theoretically founded manner, we want to utilize the site of engagement, the window opened up through practices and discourses that makes concrete higher-level mediated actions possible. Drawing a window in which a higher-level mediated action is illustrated becomes useful here. You will recall that we used the concept of a site of engagement previously. In Phase II Steps 2 and 4 we illustrated the position of the researcher in relation to the data set and in relation to data pieces. Here, we want to utilize the concept by narrowing the window, focusing upon a particular data piece, which we wish to examine in great detail.

Here, we want to focus our first analysis on how Alisa is speaking with Milena, while Alisa is not searching. Thus, we now narrow the window (our site of engagement) to a point that we can only see the beginning of this higher-level action (00 : 29 : 10) in our window (Figure 5.2).

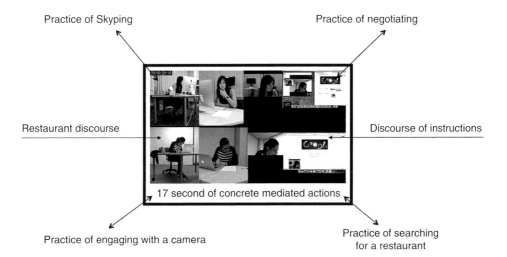

Figure 5.2   A narrow site of engagement for micro analysis teamwork example. Reproduced with permission of the participants.

Phase III: Summary

In Phase III of systematically working with multimodal data, you have gained a deep understanding of the higher-level mediated actions in your experimental data. In Phase III, consisting of four steps, you have:

1) Rephrased your research question that encircles your data into a MEDIATED ACTION
2) Demarcated the higher-level mediated actions in your entire data set
3) Developed a table that bundles all higher-level mediated actions in your data set and shows an *overview* of your entire data
4) Narrowed the site of engagement and selected a data piece for micro analysis

Task 6: Experimental Study
Follow the four steps of Phase III before moving on to Phase IV.

5.3

Systematically Working with Large Data Sets

Phase III Selecting Data Pieces for Micro Analysis

In this section, I demonstrate the same phases and steps as outlined in the previous sections. But here, I show how Phase III is used when working with video ethnographic data, which comprises a large and diverse data set. I illustrate the four steps in Phase III with the same video ethnographic study introduced in Chapters 3.3 and 4.3 of 17 New Zealand families video conferencing with family members at a distance. This section will be particularly useful for upper-level groups such as PhD seminars and for established researchers working with large data sets.

A Step-by-Step Guide to Analyze Video Ethnographic Data

Phase III: Selecting Data Pieces for Micro Analysis

In the beginning, the notion of demarcating higher-level mediated actions can seem difficult. However, if you work systematically, you will quickly learn how to delineate them. Always keep in mind that higher-level mediated actions are produced through various chains of lower-level mediated actions – or that lower-level mediated actions are produced in chains by social actors as they are producing higher-level mediated actions. People never can *produce* just one lower-level mediated action alone, but we can *analyze* a specific lower-level mediated action. However, analyzing a specific lower-level mediated action takes practice and will be something I shall illustrate in Phase IV. Here, you want to focus on understanding the *higher-level mediated actions* in your data. The following steps will help you to demarcate higher-level mediated actions, all of which are mediated actions.

We begin our investigation of higher level mediated actions by rephrasing our general research question in Step 1.

Systematically Working with Multimodal Data: Research Methods in Multimodal Discourse Analysis, First Edition. Sigrid Norris.
© 2019 John Wiley & Sons, Inc. Published 2019 by John Wiley & Sons, Inc.
Companion website: www.wiley.com/go/Norris/multimodal-data

Step 1: The MEDIATED ACTION: Rephrasing Your Data Driven Research Question

We begin Step 1 with a task:

Task 1: Video Ethnographic Study
Before opening a video, take out a piece of paper *and* open a new document on your computer and write at the top in large letters: <div align="center">MEDIATED ACTION</div>

The mediated action is your guiding principle that will help you to always be clear about what it is that you are looking for. I suggest a piece of paper *and* a document, because you can always have a piece of paper physically present as you work with your data. Putting it next to your computer allows you to glance at it each time when your mind is straying and you become overwhelmed by trying to make sense of your video data.

Still focused on your piece of paper with the words MEDIATED ACTION at the top, you want to realize that your video data consists of many concrete and *always mediated* actions that participants performed, and it is the concreteness of these actions that will keep you grounded and clear in your pursuit of analyzing the data.

Even before watching your video, you want to name the mediated action that your study is about. Here, you *rephrase the general research question that you developed in Phase II Step 5 into an action*. You place this action below the words MEDIATED ACTION into your documents.

Example: A Family Video Conference
The MEDIATED ACTION
For our video conferencing study, the document reads:

MEDIATED ACTION
Social actors (inter)acting via video conferencing technology
with desktop /laptop/iPad

This formulation also provides the three components of a mediated action:

1) Social actors
2) The action = (inter)acting
3) Some relevant mediational means/cultural tools (video conferencing technology, desktop, laptop, or iPad)

With this formulation, we highlight the technological mediational means/cultural tools of Skype/Facetime and desktop/laptop/iPad. The (inter)actions are not completely natural as they have been recorded and observed by researchers. However, the actions that the social actors produce (i.e. how they speak, move, gesture, and so on) are naturally produced, thus naturally occurring, which makes this data quite different from the YouTube data. Here, we also have no editing, but snippets of actual (recorded) "real time" (inter)action.

Task 2: Video Ethnographic Study

Formulate one mediated action that comprises your general research question developed in Phase II Step 5.

Now that you have formulated the mediated action that you are generally interested in, you can begin to list higher-level mediated actions.

Step 2: Demarcating Higher-Level Mediated Actions

Now, you are ready to open your first video file and begin to list the higher-level mediated actions that you see. At this point, you do not need to worry too much about the exact length of the higher-level mediated actions. That is something that may become relevant later. Here, you want to just jot down what you see and/or hear.

As you are watching the first few minutes, you will wonder how to separate the actions from one another. This can be tricky, but does not have to be. Just begin by writing down the first action that you see. Name it by what is going on. Then, do not worry about the fact that you will find many different kinds of higher-level mediated actions, some of which will last a few seconds and some of which will last a long duration of time. The basic question here is: What are the people in your video clip doing?

In order to illustrate our purely data driven approach, I now give an example from the video conferencing project. In the following example, I illustrate demarcating higher-level mediated actions in the first few minutes of a Skype call in our family video conferencing project. The clip can be watched online and can be utilized as a teaching or learning tool in class or for self-study. By using this clip, you will thus learn the listing of higher-level mediated actions before you embark on your own data analysis.

Example: A Family Video Conference
Listing Higher-Level Mediated Actions for Video 5.2 of the Family Video Conferencing Project
Delineating higher-level mediated actions for *family interaction* from the video conferencing study, the following is listed for approximately the first three minutes in this interaction (Table 5.11).

Task 3: Video Ethnographic Study

Watch video 5.2 of the video ethnographic study. Read the higher-level mediated action table (Table 5.11) while watching and see if you can find the sense in describing what is going on in the clip in this way. Then, discuss in class.

Table 5.11 Higher-level mediated action table video ethnography example. Reproduced with permission of the participants.

Time	Higher-level mediated action
00:00:06:00	Mic calling, (inter)acting with researchers
00:00:16:08	Abbie (inter)acting with Mic
00:00:20:25	Adults greeting
00:00:23:11	Checking if they can be seen
00:00:28:29	Mother prompts Sophie to greet uncle
00:00:34:15	Mother prompts Sophie to look at the screen
00:00:38:06	Uncle can see Sophie
00:00:41:18	Mother points out Sophie is dressed up
00:00:53:21	Sophie wants to visit her uncle
00:01:47:01	Technology cut-off
00:01:48:01	(Inter)action between uncle Abbie (in NZ)
00:01:53:19	Mic tries to re-connect
00:02:00:28	Mic greets and notices Ayla, Mother prompts Ayla to greet
00:02:12:10	Mic notices Ayla's hair
00:02:16:12	Sophie announces they have ice cream
00:02:40:06	Mic notices Ayla's blue tongue
00:02:48:00	Mic takes a sip of beer
00:02:52:23	Mic checking if he is heard
00:03:02:11	Mic asks about the dress of the child
00:03:10:14	Mother announces that they are disconnecting

When producing your higher-level mediated action table, be careful not to fall into the trap of working at a very micro level as demonstrated in Table 5.12.

Table 5.12 *Incorrect* higher-level mediated action table video ethnography example. Reproduced with permission of the participants.

Time	Higher-level mediated action
00:00:06:00	Mic calling
00:00:07:28	Mic appears on screen
00:00:08:01	Mic: (…) go on?
00:00:09:08	Mic appears on external camera, sitting slightly slouched forward
00:00:09:14	Researcher 1: I'm gonna start recording
00:00:10:22	Researcher 2: Yep
00:00:12:21	Mic moves back in his chair and turns to researchers
00:00:12:27	Mic: Am I sitting up straight?

When you work at the very micro level shown in Table 5.12, you will get lost in your data, rather than finding the clarity that you are seeking. The micro level is important, but it is not important at this point in our analysis process.

Task 4: Video Ethnographic Study

Begin to list higher-level mediated actions for your own project. Always record the time from the beginning of a higher-level mediated action.

Listing higher-level mediated actions will give you great insight into your data. It is an easy and relatively quick way to systematically understand what your data is all about. Thus, when working with your own collected data, you want to list *all* higher-level mediated actions in your entire data set, ensuring that you note the times in the clip as accurately as possible. Of course, noting time is not quite as straightforward as it may seem. The best way to note times is to note the starting moment of the higher-level mediated action that you are listing, without, however, becoming too bogged down in the detail here as well. You want to be consistent so that you can later easily find the beginning of certain actions.

Note 1: Video Ethnographic Study

Researchers may demarcate higher-level mediated actions differently. However, that does not make one way of listing them correct and another way incorrect. In fact, we can always list higher-level mediated actions in different ways, looking at different levels of action. Thus, the actual way of how you demarcate higher-level mediated actions is not so important.

Note 2: Video Ethnographic Study

What is important, however, is that others can understand how you have demarcated the higher-level mediated actions. In other words, you have to be able to show your list to others as they are watching the video and they have to be able to see what you have listed.

Note 3: Video Ethnographic Study

The best way to check for correctness is to do a data show with others following your demarcated higher-level mediated actions.

Note 4: Video Ethnographic Study

While your list of higher-level mediated actions can differ from those of other researchers studying the same clip, your detailed data analysis that is conducted during transcription and your transcripts will not differ from others transcribing the same clip (Phase IV).

Step 3: Developing an Overview of Higher-Level Mediated Actions in Your Data Set

Once you have completed your higher-level mediated action table, you are ready to produce a table that shows particular topics that emerge in your data and the times when these emerge. Looking at your higher-level mediated action table(s) produced in Step 2 and color-coding similar higher-level mediated actions allows you to find topics (similarly to the way we log data in discourse analysis (Tannen 1984) or in critical discourse analysis (Wodak 1995)) (Table 5.13).

Table 5.13 Color coded bundles of higher-level mediated action table video ethnography example. Reproduced with permission of the participants.

Time	Higher-level mediated action
00:00:06:00	Mic calling and (inter)acting with researchers
00:00:16:08	Abbie (inter)acting with Mic
00:00:20:25	Adults greeting
00:00:23:11	Checking if they can be seen
0000:28:29	Mother prompts Sophie to greet uncle
00:00:34:15	Mother prompts Sophie to look at the screen
00:00:38:06	Uncle can see Sophie
00:00:41:18	Mother points out that Sophie is dressed up
00:00:53:21	Sophie wants to visit her uncle
00:01:47:01	Technology cut-off
00:01:48:01	(Inter)action between Mic and Abbie (in NZ)
00:01:53:19	Mic tries to re-connect
2:00:28	Mic greets and notices Ayla, Mother prompts Ayla to greet
00:2:12:10	Mic notices Ayla's hair
00:02:16:12	Sophie announces they have ice cream
00:02:40:06	Mic notices Ayla's blue tongue
00:02:48:00	Mic takes a sip of beer
00:02:52:23	Mic checking if he can be heard
00:03:02:11	Mic asks about the dress of a child
00:03:10:14	Mother announces that they are disconnecting

What you may notice now, is that many of the actions that you have listed are listed in accordance with what people actually say. This is particularly evident in the Skype data discussed here. While listing higher-level mediated actions by what people say is not necessarily a problem, it is something that you will want to be wary of. Listing actions in words forces us to work in a word-oriented approach. This language-focused approach to our understanding of what is going on in the data, however, can be changed once you begin to make a more general higher-level mediated action table, always listing your video time stamps, showing where these topics occur in your video (Table 5.14).

As you produce your action tables, you distil the higher-level mediated actions into groups; and by doing this you solidify some of the things that you noticed in your data while making your lists. What you have noticed will show up in your data tables as the very actions that you have summarized. Some similar actions taken will easily be combined as a set of actions, while you will want to separate out some other actions found in your data – already illustrating your focus (Table 5.14).

Example: A Family Video Conference
Developing an overview of higher-level mediated actions in video 1 of the video conferencing data

Table 5.14 Bundled higher-level mediated action table video ethnography example. Reproduced with permission of the participants.

Substance of the higher-level mediated action	Time in video
Technology related	06:00, 23:11, 34:15, 38:06, 1:47:01, 153:19, 2:52:23, 3:10:14
Greeting	20:25, 28:29, 2:00:28
Façade	41:18, 2:12:10, 2:40:06, 3:02:11
Topics introduced by child	53:21, 2:16:12
(Inter)actions in NZ home	06:00, 16:08, 1:48:01
Drinking	2:48:00

Task 5: Video Ethnographic Study

Produce a bundled higher-level mediated action table for your video ethnographic study.

You see here, I have named the gist of the higher-level mediated actions in quite different ways. Listing them as such makes sense to me and what I am interested in. I am interested in technology related higher-level mediated actions. I am fascinated by how family members use greetings when Skyping. I am highly interested in how family members address each other's façade and I am interested in child-initiated actions and topics as well as those (inter)actions that occur outside of the Skype (inter)actions by family members in the same location. Thus, you can already see *how I* view this data.

Task 6: Video Ethnographic Study

Think about how higher-level mediated actions in Table 5.11 could be listed differently and what kind of an effect that would have on the bundling of higher-level mediated actions as shown in Table 5.14. Discuss.

When listing higher-level mediated actions (Table 5.11) and making sense of them (Table 5.13) in order to bundle similar higher-level mediated actions (Table 5.14), you are analyzing your data by working in a purely data driven way. Of course, you have collected the data because you were interested in specific aspects of human (inter)action. Then, when you begin Phase III, you will find other aspects in your data that may be equally interesting, or you may find aspects that for now you are not really interested in (such as Mic taking a sip of beer). However, you still want to list such higher-level mediated actions as you may find many instances of family members eating or drinking during video conferencing (inter)actions. If that is the case, we may want to have a closer look at such higher-level mediated actions and will be glad to have named and bundled them at this point. Thus, you want to be careful to not only list those higher-level mediated actions that you are interested in, but rather list all of the higher-level mediated actions that are in your data.

Since we work in a data driven way, we want to let the data speak to us. This means, we want to first understand as much as possible about the data that we have collected in order to then begin micro analyses. When we are ready to conduct a micro analysis, we want to recall that we are working in a theoretically founded way. The concept of the site of engagement helps us to never lose sight of the complexity of social action.

Step 4: Selecting Data Pieces for Micro Analysis – Narrowing the Site of Engagement

We are now ready for micro analysis of particular higher-level mediated actions from our data set. We want to utilize the site of engagement, the window opened up through practices and discourses that make concrete higher-level mediated actions possible. A sketch of a higher-level mediated action as a window becomes useful here. Previously, we used the concept of a site of engagement in Phase II Steps 2 and 4 to illustrate the position of the researcher in relation to the data set and in relation to data pieces. Here, we want to utilize the concept by narrowing the window so that all we can see is a particular excerpt from a data piece, which we wish to examine in great detail.

Here, we want to focus our first analysis on the higher-level mediated action of Mic connecting. Therefore, we narrow the window (our site of engagement) to a point that we can only see 17 seconds (between 00 : 06 : 00 and 00 : 23 : 00) of the family's video conferencing (inter)action. It is during these 17 seconds that Mic establishes a Skype connection (Figure 5.3).

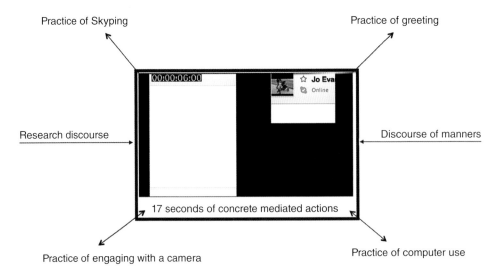

Figure 5.3 A narrow site of engagement for micro analysis example family video conferencing. Reproduced with permission of the participants.

Phase III: Summary

In Phase III of systematically working with multimodal data, you have gained a deep understanding of the higher-level mediated actions in your video ethnographic study. In Phase III, consisting of four steps, you have:

1) Rephrased your research question that encircles your data as a MEDIATED ACTION
2) Demarcated the higher-level mediated actions in your entire data set
3) Developed a table that shows an overview of all higher-level mediated actions performed in your data set
4) Narrowed the site of engagement, selecting a data piece for micro analysis

Task 7: Video Ethnographic Study
Follow the four steps of Phase III and then move on to Phase IV.

Chapter 6

Systematically Working with Multimodal Data Phase IV

6

Phase IV: Transcribing Data Using Multimodal Transcription Conventions

Now, that you know your data set, and you have a very good understanding of your data, you are ready to conduct micro analysis of particular data pieces. However, before utilizing specific analytical tools to analyze specific excerpts from your data, you want to familiarize yourself with multimodal transcription conventions, which allow us to reliably transcribe video data.

This chapter is dedicated to the conventions that we use in order to understand particular excerpts in our data in great detail. The conventions described here are the same for any kind of video data, *hence conventions*. The reason we adhere to transcription conventions (using our units of analysis, the lower-level, higher-level, and frozen mediated actions as our point of departure) is that these conventions make our research replicable. This means if two (or many more) researchers transcribe the very same excerpt of an (inter)action, using these transcription conventions, the *final transcripts* will be identical. Thus, just as discourse analysts transcribe all verbal utterances, verbal noises, and laughs, we in addition transcribe all nonverbal movements as well as the objects and environment relevant to the (inter)action. Moreover, we are even more interested in language use than many discourse analysts, because we also pay attention to the intonation that people use when verbalizing utterances, or noises. For this, we follow Ladefoged's (1975) notion of intonational curves.

As you will see, producing a multimodal transcript is a lengthy process in Multimodal (Inter)action Analysis. Further, transcription and analysis go hand in hand: first, this means that you only want to transcribe those parts that you wish to analyze; and second, by transcribing you will analyze and embed your analysis in the transcript itself. Thus, multimodal transcription *is* analysis. But so are Phases I, II, and III, which are explained in the previous chapters. As we saw in the last chapter, Phase III leads us to the aspects that we are interested in, and which we want to transcribe and analyze in detail. However, before we can set out to do so, we need to understand the *conventions* used to transcribe in a way so that other researchers can replicate your transcripts and analyses. In order to exemplify transcription conventions in Multimodal (Inter)action Analysis, I hone in on examples from each of the discussed studies and show how to embed the analysis in the transcripts.

Upfront, we want to make it overt that *all* mediated actions, lower-level, higher-level, and frozen, communicate. As discussed in Chapter 2, we communicate even when we do nothing. For example, if I sit in a chair and look out of the window, my sitting still and

Systematically Working with Multimodal Data: Research Methods in Multimodal Discourse Analysis,
First Edition. Sigrid Norris.
© 2019 John Wiley & Sons, Inc. Published 2019 by John Wiley & Sons, Inc.
Companion website: www.wiley.com/go/Norris/multimodal-data

looking at some far-away or middle-distance point communicates to others, i.e. my sitting has meaning. I had mentioned earlier that lower-level and higher-level mediated actions have a beginning and an ending point. Lower-level mediated actions are bracketed by pauses. But make no mistake and think that the term *pause* here refers to non-movement. In order to illustrate what I mean, I would like us to think further about the example of my sitting in a chair and looking out of a window, doing absolutely nothing. My sitting still, a lower-level mediated action, is bracketed by pauses of not-sitting. Just as my looking out of the window, another lower-level mediated action, is bracketed by pauses of my not-looking out of the window. Lower-level mediated actions chain together seamlessly in everyday life. Our finding beginning and ending points is useful only in so far as it allows us to transcribe what is going on in an (inter)action as closely as possible. Keeping this in mind, we now turn to our multimodal transcription conventions.

So, Where Do We Begin?

We are now in a position to learn about lower-level mediated actions in greater detail. As explained earlier, one lower-level mediated action never comes about alone. However, as analysts, we can delineate a lower-level mediated action by its beginning and ending point. This is the one thing that helps us greatly. No matter what a person does, we can transcribe the action from one beginning to the next. As we will learn in this chapter, we may be speaking about the mode of gesture, but mean something quite different with the term *gesture* than many other researchers do. While this brings with it possible confusion, it is of utmost importance for us to realize that terminology *can* be used vastly differently in research. This does not mean that one way of using the term gesture is right and another way of using the term gesture is incorrect. All it means is that researchers from different backgrounds theorize what a gesture is quite differently. For us, gesture is a mode, and as you will see in Step 1, modes are theoretical concepts and the term mode embeds a great amount of theory in Multimodal (Inter)action Analysis.

Note 1
Transcription conventions are of great importance. When researchers follow the same transcription conventions, they make sure that their findings can be replicated, making their findings more reliable.

Note 2
Lower-level mediated actions are bracketed by pauses. Movements, for example, can be bracketed by stillness and stillness can be bracketed by movements.

Note 3
All mediated actions communicate, i.e. have meaning.

Phase IV: Transcribing Data Using Multimodal Transcription Conventions

In this chapter, we learn how to produce multimodal transcripts that allow us to analyze the (inter)actions in detail, allow us to embed aspects of analysis, and further allow us to demonstrate our analysis to others. Thus, multimodal transcription has three functions:

1) Multimodal transcripts allow us to analyze data in great detail.
2) Multimodal transcripts allow us to embed aspects of analysis.
3) Multimodal transcripts allow us to illustrate our findings as exactly as possible.

In the following steps, we learn how to transcribe one mode at a time. Here, I use examples from the three studies in order to demonstrate transcription conventions. Then, in the last step, I discuss how to produce final transcripts, in which all individual modal transcripts are collated.

Step 1: Identifying a Mode

Mode is defined as a system of mediated action (Norris 2013a). What this means is that each and every mediated action that a social actor performs continuously builds and/or reinforces a system of mediated action that we call *mode*. By thinking of a mode as a system of mediated action, we embed the social actor *and* the mediational means/cultural tools in the definition of mode. Thus, the social actor is as much a part of the mode as are the mediational means/cultural tools used to perform the action.

> By theorizing modes as systems of mediated action, the mere definition of the term mode includes the irreducible tension between social actor and mediational means. This tension is easily missed when defining modes as semiotic systems or as systems of representation; but it is also missed when we define modes as mediational means or cultural tools...
>
> *(Norris 2013a, p. 274)*

Let us take language as an example of a mode (or system of mediated action). My son spoke his first word at seven and half months. He was upstairs in a safe playroom and I was making lunch in the kitchen downstairs. He had been babbling for some time and I was listening to the sounds. Suddenly, he loudly said *Mama*. I stopped what I was doing and ran upstairs, picked him up, held him in the air and kept repeating *Mama*, *Mama*, with small pauses in between. He was delighted and after a while, I put him back into the playroom and went downstairs to continue making lunch. After only a few minutes, I heard him again, clearly enunciating *Mama*. Up I went again, happily picking him up, laughing and repeating *Mama* as before. You can imagine what happened next. He loved the reaction and tried out *Mama* as often as he could that day, always with my happy reaction to follow. Here, we see that the system of mediated action is acquired not as an individual, but as a social being in social interaction with another. In fact, we cannot be sure that the first time he called out, *Mama* actually was a word, but after a few more tries, it most certainly was. Word + reaction helps the baby acquire the system of mediated action (or mode) of spoken language. The same is true for learning the mode of touch, smell, gesture, object handling, layout, and so on. Some modes (or systems of mediated action) can only be learned in connection with other social actors. Other modes can be learned by acting and interacting with the environment (such as walking on stone, wood, or sand). But all modes are acquired through mediated action.

Take a pointing gesture, for example. As we learned previously, a complete pointing gesture is a lower-level mediated action. This lower-level mediated action is made up of a social actor acting with or through multiple mediational means/cultural tools (such as the hand/arm/fingers, the environmental space, the air, the knowledge of the meaning of the gesture, etc.). Each time this social actor points at something, this social actor builds up their system of mediated action (or mode) of pointing gesture. Mode, therefore, is always made up of many lower-level mediated actions of social actor + multiple mediational means/cultural tools. We could also think of modes as practices (actions with a history) that have to do with a certain kind of lower-level mediated action as for example the practice of handing (Scollon 2001a). But I would like to suggest to think of modes as a shortcut of building common understanding between researchers. If I speak of head movement as a mode, pretty much everyone who reads these pages will have a good idea about what I mean by this terminology. The mode of head movement simply alludes to the way a person may hold or move their head. Or, as alluded to above, gesture is not defined by what others have termed *gesture* (Kendon 2004; McNeill 1992). Rather, in Multimodal (Inter)action Analysis, we analyze all actions that utilize hands, arms, or fingers as the mode of gesture (or often I refer to the mode of hand-arm-finger movement to make the distinction clear). Thus, we do not limit our analysis to some pre-defined notion of what the mode of gesture is, but examine how hands, arms, or fingers are held or moved at all times. However, we also do not disregard the definitions of gesture by other researchers, but rather utilize these definitions whenever they are useful. For example, a beat gesture, usually an up-down or back-forth movement is a nice way of describing what is going on. But, just as you can never not act (as I said before, even when you are asleep, you perform an action), so you can never not use the mode of hand/arm/finger movement (or the mode of gesture). Even when you are holding your hands, arms, fingers still, you are utilizing the mode of gesture as defined here. Thus, what I term the mode of gesture is a larger mode than the mode of gesture that most gesture researchers would refer to. It includes all movements and non-movements of the hands, arms, and fingers. But this brings me to the next point: one mode can never be used alone. Think of self or other touching, for example. There, we find the mode of gesture (as defined here) and the mode of touch playing a part. Or think about the mode of object handling. Just a second ago, I picked up my tea cup. In order to perform this mediated action, I extended my arm, touched the cup, picked it up, etc. But thinking of these as three modes does little to help us understand the action of picking up a cup. Instead, it is more useful if we just realize that the mode of object handling inevitably entails the use of the hand/arm (or for some people the leg/foot) + an object + the touch.

What we see here, is that the definition of what a mode may or may not be, in fact, is quite up to us, the researchers. We define how we want to think about a particular mode before we begin to transcribe. As we will see, it makes no difference at all to a final transcript if one researcher transcribes the picking up of the cup under the rubric of object handling, another under gesture, and a third under touch. Once the transcripts are collated, the final transcripts will still look exactly alike. Thus, we do not want to get hung up on the concept of mode when transcribing. There is little point in discussing whether one lower-level meditated action belongs to one mode or another. It is much more important to correctly transcribe the lower-level mediated action.

Why Is Mode an Important Concept If We Are Really Only Looking at Lower-Level Mediated Actions?

The term mode in Multimodal (Inter)action Analysis has two functions. First, it embeds a great deal of theory, which we want to carry with us throughout our analyses and discussion of findings; second, speaking of a mode allows us to create a quick (and to some extent common) understanding between researchers. For example, when speaking with researchers coming from a different theoretical perspective, we can say "I am analyzing the gesture in this excerpt" (common understanding somewhat reached) "but my definition of gesture is that it is a system of mediated actions and that everything that somebody does with the arms, hands, and fingers falls under my definition of this mode" (difference of understanding clarified). As we will see below, it in fact becomes extremely important to clearly define our own understanding of mode. Only when we clearly define what we mean by a mode, can we make sure that others are able to replicate our modal transcripts.

Mode: Embedded Theoretical Notions

When thinking of modes as systems of mediated actions, we embed in the pure definition of modes the:

1) Cognitive-psychological (thoughts and feelings)
2) The socio-cultural (self always with others)
3) Physical body, environment, objects (incl. biological senses and Umwelt)

Modes are theoretical notions that allow us to talk about particularities in action and interaction. Modes, defined as systems of mediated action, can possess very different structures, materiality, and make-up. Because of their definition as systems of mediated action, they are nevertheless compatible and in action and interaction together build one system of communication. Thus, all teasing apart of modes is entirely theoretical in nature. In real life, people do not usually think of communicating in separate modes. Thus, how does our theoretical understanding, the actual concept of mode as a system of mediated action relate to our notions of perception and embodiment?

Perception

While individual modes are not usually perceived as such, and while the term *mode* here is used as a conceptual way of delineating and dissecting complex actions and interactions for analysis, we can certainly learn to perceive the world multimodally. This perception is learned and this book will guide the reader in learning to perceive various modes for the purpose of analyzing multimodal discourse. But not only researchers can delineate modes. A common mode that every person perceives is the mode of language. Some other modes that are readily perceived by all are facial expression and gesture. What, however is usually not perceived by many people is the fact that neither of the modes is necessarily more important than any other. As shown in Norris (2014a, b), because we are taught to prioritize the meaning of language particularly in formal schooling, people often do not perceive the other modes as strongly as they communicate.

Embodiment

Modes are concepts for analysis and only become embodied when someone is learning the concept to delineate complex actions and interactions for analysis. Thus, as you are reading about modes, using the concept of modes to examine an (inter)action in its multimodal complexity, defining each mode that you are transcribing clearly, the notion of mode becomes embodied for you. But, at the same time, when a person perceives a mode as such (for example the mode of language), then it is evident that modal production (such as speaking or writing) are embodied.

Note 4
Mode = A system of mediated action

Note 5
Mode = A theoretical concept

Modes and Transcription Conventions

Transcription conventions outlined here, were developed in order to make our work systematic to the point that it is possible for others to replicate our work. Such replicability is possible because of the analytical units that we employ in a Multimodal (Inter) action Analysis.

However, modes – different from actions – are not clearly and easily delineated. In fact, my delineation of an "individual mode" (in so far as we can actually speak of one mode at all), may be quite different from the way you would delineate a mode. Besides our different ways of seeing the world, modes depend upon the (inter)action that we are analyzing.

So, how can it be possible that two people can actually transcribe the same excerpt in the very same way? The answer is easy: we do not actually care about the delineation of modes, but what we do care about is the transcription of the lower-level mediated actions that are performed. We use the theoretical concept of mode as discussed above, because it helps us to cut up a much too complex (inter)action. Our goal is to transcribe the entire excerpt in a final transcript as detailed as possible. In other words, we want to show in a final transcript what has occurred in the excerpt of video-recorded (inter) action. Thus, for example, I can place a particular movement in the "individual" transcript that I call my head-movement transcript, and you can transcribe the same movement in the "individual" transcript that you call your posture transcript. At the end, this movement will be transcribed in my final transcript just like it is transcribed in your final transcript. The importance lies in the fact that we both have transcribed the movement correctly and that this is illustrated in the final transcript.

The notion of modes, thus is useful only in so far as it helps us to talk about something in a theoretically founded way. As long as we define (first of all for ourselves) what we mean by a certain mode, we can stay consistent in our transcription and that consistency is what helps us to grasp and analyze highly complex and intricately interconnected human (inter)actions.

Step 2: Transcribing Layout

I define layout as a mode that tells us about the distance that is taken up between objects and the environment and the people (inter)acting. In order to demonstrate how we can transcribe the mode of layout, I return to the YouTube clip of Ellen and Kai. Here, we find that there are different kinds of layout that can be transcribed.

Task 1

Watch the clip *Kai Sings "Cake by the Ocean"* at: www.youtube.com/watch?v=h9fZY0KFNQM.

Transcribing the Layout of the Stages

Here, I define layout as the broad views of where people and objects are positioned in the environment depicted. In this clip, we have a number of different broad views of layout:

1) Ellen's full shot (similar to the Kai over the shoulder shot for layout)
2) A side-by-side shot
3) Kai's full shot
4) A further distance shot, showing the side view of Ellen and Kai *and* the full screen behind
5) A lower part of the stage, where a screen opens
6) The difference in height of the stages as Ellen and Kai walk down two steps
7) A side view of the lower stage; and
8) A different part of the room below the stages where the audience is positioned.

Each time, we see a different aspect of the stages and room-layout as illustrated in Figure 6.1. Thus, here, we are interested in transcribing the broader layout depicted.

Figure 6.1 Transcript of the broader layout of the stages in the YouTube clip *Kai Sings "Cake by the Ocean."*

Task 2
Have a close look at the Ellen and Kai video clip and discuss why I chose the particular images above to demonstrate the layout of the stages.

Task 3
Choose a YouTube clip to work with and take snapshots to represent the broader layout in your chosen clip.

Once we have transcribed the broad layout, taking all participating individuals into consideration, we realize that this YouTube clip actually represents a multi-party (inter) action. There are the main participants, Ellen, Kai, the audience in the clip, and the viewer watching the video on screen. But then, there are also the camera crew, the editors, and the production team. Some of these people have left traces in the form of frozen mediated actions. The production team no doubt arranged the stage in this certain way, put up the various video clips that are shown during the show behind Ellen and Kai, have gotten the team ready to present the contract to Kai, and so on. The camera crew has taken the video and the editors have carefully chosen the shots, which we can now analyze as the layout of the video clip.

Transcribing the General Layout of the Video Clip
Now, I define layout as the way the video clip is constructed, i.e. we are now interested in the layout of the video clip itself. Taking a close look at how the video clip is constructed, allows us to gain insight into the produced nature of the clip. For this, you want to take a snapshot of each new camera angle. I have taken snapshots of the camera angles in the first 40 seconds. Because I am here interested in the camera angles, I am here not paying attention to slight camera movements, fade-ins or fade-outs. Here, I only show the clip without the laptop screen, because as viewers, we hone in on watching the unfolding actions in the video and most often dismiss the surrounding area – whether laptop, computer, mobile phone, or TV. When watching the technology, which is streaming the video, the technology often becomes ubiquitous for the viewer. In a transcript, we can show this ubiquitous nature by zooming into the clip itself as shown in Figure 6.2.
 Transcribing the changing camera angles allows us to gain insight into the pace of the video clip that we are watching. In this clip, in only the first 40 seconds we find 12 different angles, making the clip quite fast-paced. But then, we also find the clip slows down between second 14 and 25. Interesting questions that arise here could be:

1) How do longer shots emphasize certain aspects in the (inter)action? or:
2) What kind of an impact does the fast-pace in the clip, i.e. a quick succession of camera angle changes, have in this (inter)action?

Task 4
Continue transcribing the camera angles for *Kai Sings "Cake by the Ocean"* for the next 30–40 seconds and discuss your thoughts regarding the questions of pace posited above.

Figure 6.2 Layout of the first 40 seconds in the video clip – camera angles.

Transcribing the Higher-Level Mediated Action of Introducing a Guest
Here, I define layout as a mode that tells us about the distance between objects and the environment to the people (inter)acting.

Task 5: YouTube

Watch the beginning of the Ellentube clip at www.youtube.com/watch?v=h9fZY0KFNQM as you are following the transcript in Figure 6.3.

In about the first six seconds of the Ellentube video, we find that the layout changes due to the camera angle shown. First, we see Ellen sitting facing the camera as she introduces the next guest (Image 1). During this time, the camera moves ever so slightly and comes to a halt at 00 : 01 : 29 (Image 2). For the rest of the introduction, the camera angle first stays in this position until 00 : 06 : 00, at which point a fade-in occurs (Image 3), showing a completely different angle and therefore, a different layout. Here, at 00 : 06 : 01, the fade-in becomes visible (Image 4) with a new view of the stage, a different layout.

What Is Problematical About the Mode of Layout?
When reading the above, watching the clip, and transcribing as discussed here, the mode of layout may seem easy enough to transcribe. However, once you are examining

00:06:00   00:06:01

3   4

Figure 6.3 Layout transcript for the first 6 seconds, YouTube example.

your own video data, this clarity may quickly turn into confusion. As I said above, I define layout as a mode that tells us about the relationship of people to objects and the environment. But people do not stay in one place. People move. A lift of the arm changes the relationship between a person and a cup; a movement closer to a laptop changes the relationship of a person to the environment and objects within. Thus, here we notice that the mode of layout is not something that is easily and clearly defined. Here, it becomes obvious that modes are only theoretical concepts. Thus, if you say that you want to represent the layout of the environment and objects within in relation to the people (inter)acting in general (as shown above), but you leave the way people move their arms to your gesture transcript and the way they move their torso closer to a screen to your posture transcript, then you can stay clear about what to transcribe when to transcribe it and how to transcribe it. In fact, when transcribing "individual" modes, it becomes very clear that "individual modes" do not exist at all. But our theoretical *concept of mode* exists and that becomes very useful when transcribing because it allows us to think through the concreteness of actions in helpful ways. Further, we see that how we transcribe layout differs depending upon our focus of study. Are we interested in the layout of the various stages (Figure 6.1)? Are we interested in the layout depicted by different camera angles (Figure 6.2), or are we interested in the detailed layout in a specific higher-level action (Figure 6.3)? In order to be clear about what and how we transcribe, we need to be clear about our definition of layout in each instance. It is not that we transcribe layout differently depending upon who is transcribing. Rather, we transcribe layout differently depending upon how we are *defining* the mode of layout that we wish to transcribe. Once we all agree on the same definition, we all transcribe the layout in the very same way. When defining the mode of layout as the layout of the stages, we all transcribe layout as shown in Figure 6.1. When defining layout as the layout demonstrated by different camera angles, we all transcribe the mode of layout as shown in

Figure 6.2. Yet, when transcribing the mode of layout shown in the particular higher-level mediated action of Ellen introducing a new guest, we all transcribe the mode of layout as demonstrated in Figure 6.3.

What we learn here is that there is *no inherently correct* way to transcribe the mode of layout. The mode of layout, in fact, is not real in the same sense as a cup of tea is. The mode of layout – just like every other mode – has to be clearly defined by the researcher(s) in order to achieve replicability. Every time you are telling others what it is you are transcribing, such as the mode of layout in a specific higher-level mediated action, then others can read your transcript correctly and they can replicate your work. As illustrated in the discussion about the mode of layout, many different layout transcripts can be produced, can be equally correct, but will each require a clear definition of the concept mode of layout and have relevance for different ways of working with your data.

Note 6

It is most important to define what you mean by the mode of layout (or any other mode). Your transcription is solely based on your understanding of what the mode of layout (or any other mode) is for you. This understanding always needs to be clarified by each and every researcher in order to make your individual mode transcripts replicable and thus reliable.

Step 3: Transcribing Proxemics

I define proxemics as a mode that tells us about the distance that people take up to one another and to objects in the environment while (inter)acting. In order to demonstrate how we can transcribe the mode of proxemics, I now turn to a video clip from the video ethnographic study discussed in this book in Chapters 3.3, 4.3, and 5.3. However, while the excerpt transcribed is part of that study, the excerpt (Video 6.1) is here used as a stand-alone example that you can work with in class or in self-study.

Task 6

Watch Video 6.1 Transcribing proxemics at www.wiley.com/go/Norris/multimodal-data.

In the following transcript (Figure 6.4), only the proxemics that the mother of the triplets takes up to the children, the environment (the walls), and the objects within (table, chairs) have been transcribed. As transcripts are becoming longer, we want to number the individual images used as illustrated in Figure 6.4. Here, the black space at the bottom right of each screenshot makes it easy to place a readable number. If there is no convenient space in your data, however, we usually place the number of each screenshot in the bottom or top right-hand corner and use color to make it visible. Numbering screenshots allows for an easier writing about the images and a quicker reading of your text and transcript. Of course, you always have the actual times in the clips available in the top left-hand corner of each screenshot. But it can become cumbersome when you want to explain what is going on in the transcript when you always

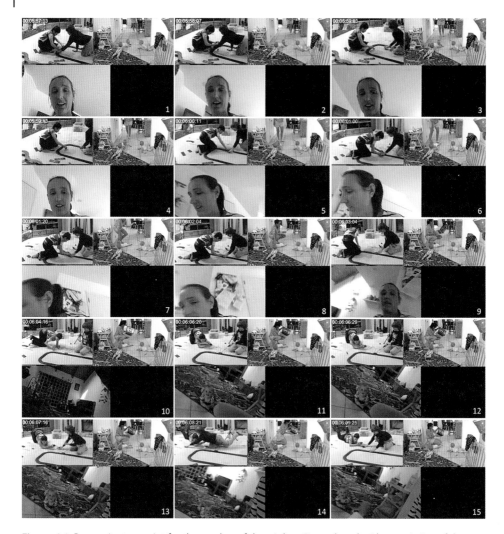

Figure 6.4 Proxemics transcript for the mother of the triplets. Reproduced with permission of the participants

have to refer to the exact times in the clip. Relevant here is to note that time as such is useful for our transcription purposes because we can use time to order and organize transcripts. However, time is not an organizing principle in *(inter)action*.

In the proxemics transcript (Figure 6.4), you see that each screengrab (numbered from 1 to 15) consists of three images, two at the top and one at the bottom plus a black space at the bottom. The top-left image shows two boys playing with a toy race track. This image is the Skype video image that appears on the laptop that the woman (the mother of the triplets) in the top-right image is holding. The top-right image is an external camera view, filmed in the house of the woman with the triplets. The bottom image is the Skype video view that is displayed on the screen as self-image as well as in the house of the two boys playing with the toy race track.

When reading the transcript, please have a look at the top-right image and watch the proxemics that the woman is taking up to the three babies, the environment, and objects within. Due to the camera positioning, focusing on the babies playing on the floor, we first only see the woman's legs (Images 1–6). Then, she begins to crouch down (Image 7) and right after that, we see her entire body (Images 8–15). The transcript in Figure 6.4 illustrates the woman's proxemic positions and changes. In Image 1, she is standing in the dining area next to a chair and table. In Image 2, we see her taking a step towards the babies, changing her proxemics position, moving away from the table and chair and closer to the children. As she walks, she begins to step closer to the wall to her right in Image 3, moving further away from the chair and table and closer to the children. Then, she walks along the wall (Image 4) without changing her distance to the wall, but further changing her proxemics to the chair and table and the children. In Image 5, the woman has moved closer to the children, further away from the chair and table, and is moving closer to the wall. The woman is now beginning to crouch down (Images 6–9), positioning her torso close to the wall. In Image 7, the woman has reached the closest distance that the woman is taking up to the children. Next, the woman moves her head and shoulders forward, changing the head and shoulder proxemic position away from the wall, while the rest of her body stays in the same position as before (Images 10–12). Following this, the woman begins to reposition herself in relation to the wall by first moving her head and shoulders back a little (Image 13) and then moving her entire torso forward as she is going onto her knees, thereby changing the proxemics to the wall behind her, the space in front of her, and the relation to the wall slightly to her right front (Image 14). Right after this (Image 15), the woman brings her back towards the wall behind her with similar proxemics to the babies and all surrounding environment and objects within as in Image 9.

Task 7

Re-watch Video 6.1 Transcribing Proxemics at www.wiley.com/go/Norris/multimodal-data and produce a proxemics transcript for one of the older boys (in the top left of the image).

Step 4: Transcribing Posture

I define posture as a mode that tells us about the way individuals hold their bodies. Here, we are particularly interested in the torso, i.e. slouching or holding it upright, and the lower extremities, i.e. standing, sitting, crossing legs, and such. If there is leg or foot movement in a particular (inter)action, these can be teased apart further, and a transcript of leg-foot movements becomes valuable. If, on the other hand, few leg-foot movements are produced, we can transcribe the ones that are produced as a part of the posture transcript. In order to demonstrate how we can transcribe the mode of posture, I now turn to a video clip from the experimental study discussed in this book in Chapters 3.2, 4.2, and 5.2. However, while the excerpt transcribed is part of that study, the excerpt (Video 6.2) is here used as a stand-alone example that you can work with in class or in self-study.

Transcribing Upper-body Posture

Task 8
Watch the Video 6.2 Transcribing Posture at www.wiley.com/go/Norris/multimodal-data and watch the man's upper-body postural changes.

We begin by transcribing upper-body posture. Figure 6.5 illustrates a posture transcript for the man in the dyad.

Figure 6.5 Upper-body posture transcript for the man in the dyad. Reproduced with permission of the participants.

In Figure 6.5, we again used the black space as a good position for numbering the screenshots. The first screenshot is our base that we are working from. This is the beginning of the video excerpt that we are transcribing, so we begin here. Image 2 illustrates that the man has moved his upper-body downward. Then in Images 3 and 4 we see that he is moving his shoulders up. Image 5 shows that he has straightened his upper body even further and Image 6 demonstrates how he is moving a little forward again. When watching the video, you will see that his upper-body movement, especially as illustrated in Image 6, is clearly connected to his typing. You will want to note observations about such modal connections in a separate document for you to further examine later, when producing the final transcript.

Arrow, Circle, and Such in a Transcript

Each time, we use an arrow to show what it is we are interested in. Here, it is important to realize that you are first of all transcribing the data for yourself in order to make sense of it. Weeks later, you do not want to look at your transcript wondering what you had transcribed. Thus, you want to embed your analysis right in the transcript. When you use arrows and circles (or whatever else is helpful to illustrate what it is you need) to note clearly what is going on in the (inter)action, then you can come back to your transcripts weeks later and continue where you left off. Another thing to remember is to not worry whether something is actually relevant to the (inter)action at hand. In fact, there is no way for you to know if anything is relevant until you have transcribed the entire data piece and have made sense of what you have found by utilizing analytical tools discussed in the next chapter. Thus, do not jump to conclusions. This is not an interpretation exercise. This is transcription.

Transcribing Leg and Foot Movements

Task 9
Watch Video 6.2 Transcribe Posture again and take a close look at the man's leg and foot movements at www.wiley.com/go/Norris/multimodal-data.

We can transcribe even subtle leg and foot movements in our posture transcripts. In Figure 6.6, we see the man's movements that he produces with his right leg transcribed.

In screenshot number 1 we see the base position of the man's legs and feet. Image 2 in Figure 6.6 illustrates his movement of the right knee outward. Because this is a subtle movement, which can easily be overlooked, we indicate the point of interest in the transcript with an arrow as above in the upper-body posture transcript. Next, the man begins to move his foot (Image 3) and repositions his heel (Image 4). Then, he moves his right knee inward (Image 5) and outward (Image 6).

Also, as you will have noticed, some software allows you to work in a highly detailed manner, while other software will be less detailed. This difference is not necessarily a problem. You can only do what you can do with the software that you have and with the data that you are examining. Similarly, it is not really important that everyone transcribing the same data piece arrives at exactly the same frame (the last number in the time stamp) in the video that they are transcribing. Sometimes, it is easy to determine where a movement begins, and sometimes it is not. What is important is that everyone transcribing the same data piece is transcribing the same *movements*. The legs are still (your first image), the leg moves outward (your second image illustrating the most outward placement). The foot begins to move to a different position (first image just before the movement begins and second image when the movement has been completed). Technology can drive a person crazy when taken too seriously, but it helps to remember that our focus is never what technology can do or how detailed and exact technology

Figure 6.6 Leg and foot movement transcript for the man in the dyad. Reproduced with permission of the participants.

can be used. Our interest is always and only in what a person does. Thus, the transcript will be viewed as the same transcript if the transcript illustrates the movements that a person has made.

When transcribing posture, it is also quite helpful when you move the cursor slowly through the video excerpt. This shows you how much a person moves and can help you in counting the back and forth movements for example. Having a piece of paper and a pen handy is always helpful.

Task 10

Watch Video 6.2 Transcribing Posture at www.wiley.com/go/Norris/multimodal-data and produce a posture transcript for the woman in the dyad.

Step 5: Transcribing Gesture

I define gesture as a mode that tells us about the way individuals hold and move their arms, hands, and fingers. Any kind of hand, arm, or finger positioning is transcribed in the gesture transcript. Thus, here it is particularly important to note that the mode of gesture in our way of working is not limited to what Kendon (2004), McNeill (1992), or others term as "gesture." Rather, for us, the mode of gesture is all about the arms, the hands, and the fingers no matter what they do. Thus, self-touching falls under this mode as well as keeping the arms, hands, fingers still, and so do any random or not so random movements of the hands, arms, and fingers. Certainly, what others term "gesture" also falls into our mode of gesture. In order to demonstrate how we can transcribe the mode of gesture, I now turn to a video clip from the video ethnographic study discussed in this book in Chapters 3.3, 4.3, and 5.3. However, while the excerpt transcribed is part of that study, the excerpt (Video 6.3) is used here as a stand-alone example that you can work with in class or in self-study.

Task 11
Watch Video 6.3 Transcribe Gesture at www.wiley.com/go/Norris/multimodal-data.

In the following gesture transcript, only the arm, hand, and finger movements of the bearded man sitting to the right in the image between 26 : 07 and 26 : 10 are transcribed. As you see, only approximately 3 seconds are transcribed, ending up in a transcript with 10 images. The reason I chose this very moment to transcribe is the detail that you arrive at when transcribing everything somebody is doing with their arms, hands, and fingers. In this instance, the man scratches the outside side right nostril several times. When we carefully transcribe these movements, we arrive at the transcript illustrated in Figure 6.8.

When working in such a detailed manner, you can easily get lost and take an infinite number of unnecessary screenshots. Always remember that we want to reflect the movements as clearly as possible in a transcript. In order to keep clarity, we want to transcribe high and low points of movement. But to do this is almost impossible if you follow the (seemingly correct) idea of moving through your video excerpt frame-by-frame. Doing this will rather confuse you, instead of leading you to some clarity. What works much better is to watch and re-watch the video excerpt first at normal speed, then at a slightly slowed down speed (if you have the option) and then again at normal speed. Then, you want to have a piece of paper and a pen handy and write down the times and what occurs on the piece of paper. No doubt, you will redo this several times before you will be happy with the results, checking and checking again to see if you have arrived at the right times. Once you have arrived at this point (Figure 6.7), you can then use your piece of paper and take the exact screenshots needed.

With a piece of paper as shown in Figure 6.7, it will take you less time to produce the transcript and it will be a cleaner, and more likely a correct transcript.

Looking at the man at the right in the image, we see in the first row of the transcript in Figure 6.8 (Image 1), how his right hand is positioned under his chin as he is watching the screen. Then, his hand moves to the right of his face and his pointer emerges from his fist (Image 2). Next, he moves his pointer to the outside of his right nostril and Image 3 shows the highest point. From there on, he strokes his nostril downward four times.

Figure 6.7 Noting times and actions.

26: 07: 11   — under chin

26: 07: 20   — moving up (mid-point)

26: 07: 29   — up

26: 08: 10   — down

26: 08: 16   — up

26: 08: 24   — down

26: 09: 01   — up

26: 09 : 06   — down

26: 09: 12   — up

26: 09: 16   — down

26: 09: 22   — lowering (mid-point)

26: 10: 08   — under chin

Figure 6.8 Gesture transcript of the man on the right in the images. Reproduced with permission of the participants.

Image 4 illustrates the lowest point from his first stroking the right side of his nostril downward. Image 5 demonstrates the second time he moves his pointer up to the highest point before he strokes his nostril downward. Image 6 illustrates the lowest point of the second time he strokes down. Image 7 illustrates the third time he moves his finger up and Image 8 the third time he moves the finger downward. Images 9 and 10 demonstrate the up and down points in the fourth stroking of his right nostril. He then moves his pointer into the fist (Image 11) and moves his fist back under his chin. Thus, what has been transcribed here is the first position of the man's right hand (under his chin, Image 1) and the change in position in Image 2 (a mid-point between the previous rest position and the stroking of the outside of the nostril). Then, high and low points of each stroke in Images 3–10 followed by a mid-position indicating the closing of the fist (Image 11) and the new rest position (Image 12).

Task 12

Watch Video 6.3 Transcribe Gesture at www.wiley.com/go/Norris/multimodal-data and produce a gesture transcript for the woman sitting on the couch.

Step 6: Gaze

I define gaze as a mode that tells us about the way individuals look at something or someone. Depending upon the data, it is not always easy to transcribe the mode of gaze, since we do not really know what people actually look at and since we cannot be certain that, even when we can determine what a person is looking at, the person actually sees (i.e. takes in the visual information) what they are ostensibly looking at. However, even though we often can say relatively little of what the person takes in, we can often determine what others in the (inter)action can determine, namely the gaze direction of another. Because we are transcribing what a person looks at, and since we are not interpreting the meaning of this gaze, we do not have to concern ourselves with the difficulty of really knowing what a person takes in and what a person does not see. Here, we are interested in the gaze itself, the gaze direction, and the gaze changes. We are thus not concerned with the actual *seeing* accomplished by a person. In order to demonstrate how we can transcribe the mode of gaze, I now turn to Video 5.1, which is here renamed Video 6.4, from the experimental study, which has been discussed in this book in the second sections of Chapters 3, 4, and 5. However, while the excerpt transcribed is part of that study, Video 6.4 is used here as a stand-alone example that you can work with in class or in self-study.

In Figure 6.9, we find a gaze transcript of the woman with the pony tail.

Task 13

Watch Video 6.4 at www.wiley.com/go/Norris/multimodal-data (which is the same as Video 5.1) and follow the transcript in Figure 6.9.

Figure 6.9 Gaze transcript for the woman with the pony tail. Reproduced with permission of the participants.

In Image 1 of Figure 6.9, we see the woman with the pony tail looking at the piece of paper lying next to her computer. Her gaze direction is indicated by the white arrow. Next, she shifts her gaze to the keyboard (Image 2) and then to the computer screen (Image 3). Image 4 illustrates her shift in gaze back to the piece of paper and Image 5–8 illustrates her gaze shifts between keyboard and piece of paper. The next images show how the woman looks at the screen (Image 9), looks back at the piece of paper (Image 10), looks at the screen (Image 11) and moves her gaze up on the screen (Image 12).

Task 14

Watch Video 6.4 Transcribing Gaze at www.wiley.com/go/Norris/multimodal-data and produce a gaze transcript for the other woman in the dyad.

Step 7: Transcribing Head Movement

I define head movement as a mode that tells us about the way individuals hold and move their heads. While this mode can be linked to the mode of gaze, i.e. a person wishes to look in a certain direction and in order to do so moves their head, head movements can and do also occur without a shift in gaze direction. Similarly, head movements may be linked to the mode of posture, i.e. a person turns their body to the side and simultaneously turns the head, but the head may also not move with the torso. Quite frequently, this mode is useful to transcribe separately. However, you could also transcribe head movement with either the mode of gaze or the mode of posture. Thus, similarly to the mode of leg and foot movements, you need to decide the importance of this kind of separating out details based on your data. In order to demonstrate how we can transcribe the mode of head movements, I now turn to a video clip from the experimental study discussed in this book in Chapters 3.2, 4.2, and 5.2. However, while the excerpt transcribed is part of that study, the excerpt (Video 6.5) is used here as a stand-alone example that you can work with in class or in self-study.

Task 15

Re-watch Video 6.4. This time we want to transcribe head movements at www.wiley.com/go/Norris/multimodal-data.

When transcribing gaze, you will have noticed that gaze is often closely related to head movements. However, you will also have realized that this is not always the case. People look at the same place and move their heads and people keep their heads still and look at different places. Because we can tease these two modes apart and because both modes are highly important in (inter)action, we want to produce a head-movement transcript separate from the gaze transcript. Certainly, there will often be much overlap, but modal overlaps in themselves can be very interesting.

When transcribing head movement, it may be valuable to move the video clip forward slowly and watch how the head moves before starting to take stills. Then, it will be valuable again to use a piece of paper to note down times and movements before actually taking the screenshots.

When comparing the head-movement transcript (Figures 6.10 and 6.11) with the gaze transcript (Figure 6.9), we realize the need for separate transcripts for this excerpt. While we needed 12 images (Figure 6.9) to transcribe the gaze, we needed 18 images (Figures 6.10 and 6.11) to transcribe the head movement for the woman with the ponytail.

Figure 6.10 Head-movement transcript (Images 1–8) for the woman with the pony tail. Reproduced with permission of the participants.

Figure 6.11 Head-movement transcript (Images 9–18) for the woman with the pony tail. Reproduced with permission of the participants.

Task 16

Re-watch Video 6.4 Transcribe Gaze at www.wiley.com/go/Norris/multimodal-data and produce a head-movement transcript for the other woman in the dyad.

Step 8: Transcribing Facial Expression

I define facial expression as a mode that tells us about the way individuals maintain and move their expressions of the face. Rather than interpreting the meaning of facial expressions as in the work of Ekman (2006) for example, we simply want to demonstrate what a person does in the excerpt that we are transcribing. Sometimes, people in (inter) action use elaborate facial expressions, while at other times, faces remain relatively even throughout an (inter)action. Thus, the extent of a facial expression transcript, just as the extent of any other modal transcript explicated here, will vary greatly. Facial expression may coincide with the mode of head movement or gaze. However, when you are transcribing an excerpt in which facial expression is extensive, it is useful to transcribe this mode separately. As we will see in Step 11, the overlaps of the modal transcripts are edited out at that point. In order to demonstrate how we can transcribe the mode of facial expression, I now turn to a video clip from the video ethnographic study discussed in this book in the third sections of Chapters 3, 4, and 5. However, while the excerpt transcribed is part of that study, the excerpt (Video 6.5) is here used as a stand-alone example that you can work with in class or in self-study.

Task 17

Watch Video 6.5 Transcribing Facial Expression at www.wiley.com/go/Norris/multimodal-data (Figure 6.12).

The woman in Video 6.5 produces quite an elaborate facial expression. Thus, this is a good video clip to learn how to transcribe this mode. When transcribing facial expression, you want to try not to use too many in-between expression stills. However, you also want to be careful to demonstrate eyebrow raises and such.

Task 18

Watch Video 6.5 Transcribing Facial Expression once again at www.wiley.com/go/Norris/multimodal-data.

Task 19

Continue transcribing facial expression from the point left off in Figure 6.12.

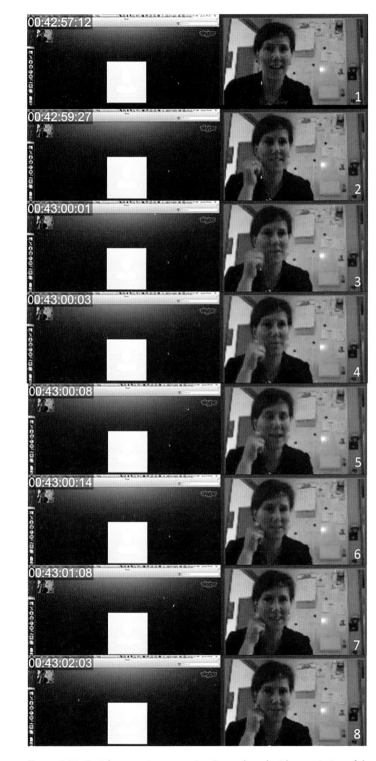

Figure 6.12 Facial expression transcript. Reproduced with permission of the participants.

Step 9: Transcribing Object Handling

I define object handling as a mode that tells us about the way individuals use objects. Of course, when someone handles an object, they also touch the object. Thus, the mode of touch is intricately intertwined with the mode of object handling. The mode of touch, as the mode of leg and foot movements or positions, can be separated out if that is useful for the data that you are transcribing. Here, I collapse the modes of object handling and the mode of touch, speaking of the mode of object handling since we cannot handle objects without touching them. In order to demonstrate how we can transcribe the mode of object handling, I once again turn to a video clip from the experimental study discussed in this book Chapters 3.2, 4.2, and 5.2. However, while the

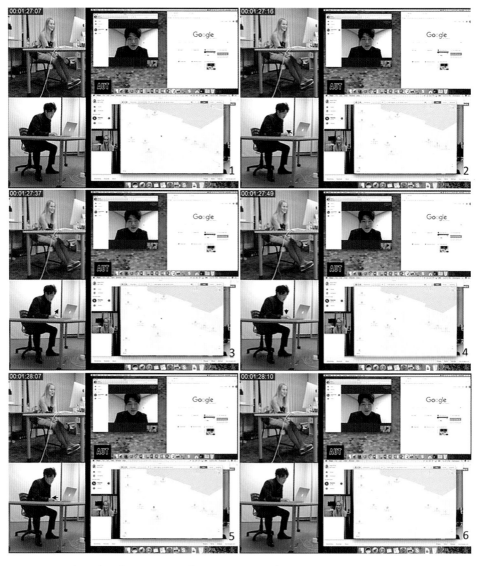

Figure 6.13 Object handling transcript for the man in the dyad. Reproduced with permission of the participants.

excerpt transcribed is part of that study, the excerpt (Video 6.6) is here used as a stand-alone example that you can work with in class or in self-study.

Task 20

Watch Video 6.6 Transcribing Object Handling at www.wiley.com/go/Norris/multimodal-data.

When transcribing the mouse movements that the man produces, it is a good idea to also (but not only) have a look at the movements registered on the screen. Because his hand/finger movements are very subtle, the screen can help determine when and where he moves the object. You will have noticed that I also transcribed the lifting and lowering of his hand in Images 3 and 4. Here, we can either transcribe these movements as part of the object handling transcript or we can transcribe these as part of a gesture transcript. In many cases, we will transcribe these in both transcripts, because, depending upon what we will be examining later, we may need them in both transcripts. Besides, in the final transcript, one set of these same movements will be edited out. So, transcribing a movement in more than one individual transcript is not a problem.

Task 21

Watch Video 6.6 Transcribing Object Handling once again at www.wiley.com/go/Norris/multimodal-data.

Task 22

Continue Transcribing Object Handling from the point left off in Figure 6.13.

Step 10: Transcribing Language

The mode of language is the mode that is most researched. We can separate out the mode of spoken language and the mode of written language. Certainly, depending upon your data, you will also differentiate between various languages spoken or written. For us, when transcribing (inter)action, we take particular care to transcribe the actual language used.

Transcribing Spoken Language

We begin by transcribing spoken language using transcription conventions like the ones used by Tannen (1984), where a comma is used to indicate a slight rising intonation (indicating more to come). A period is used to illustrate lowering of intonation. A dash is used to show a sudden stop in the middle of a word (a glottal stop), and question marks to indicate rising intonation. For a complete list of transcription conventions used by Tannen, please refer to her book. First writing down the utterances is a relatively quick way to transcribe language. We use numbers in parentheses to indicate lines (utterances).

Task 23

Re-watch the Video 6.3 at www.wiley.com/go/Norris/multimodal-data and read the transcript below.

In Tannen (1984), you already see the notion of indicating intonation. Here, in Multimodal (Inter)action Analysis, we go even further and show intonation in our final transcripts as wave forms. The wave forms illustrate the pattern of pitch changes, timing, and loudness that speakers use. For a very nice discussion of intonation and good illustrations of intonation waves, I would like to refer the reader to Ladefoged (1975).

In this video clip, man A is sitting on the right in the image, man B on the left, and the woman in the middle. Man C is the one on the other side on Skype (not visible).

1) Woman: hhh
2) Man A: thh
3) Man C: Cody,
4)   supposed to be dancing,
5)   Cody?
6) Woman: Cody you could,
7)   show uncle Cameron your music machine?

Multimodal Transcription of Spoken Language

Now we can do several things in order to come close to the intonation pattern. One, we can become very apt at hearing the rhythm of speech; two, we can embed the spoken language in a separate language analysis program such as PRATT (http://www.fon.hum.uva.nl/praat), but while PRATT does many things, you will still need to do your own analysis, since, as Nolan (2014) points out "the patterning of pitch in speech is so closely bound to patterns of timing and loudness, and sometimes voice quality, that we cannot consider pitch in isolation from these other dimensions." Thus, even when we come very close in showing an intonation wave, we still are missing quite a bit of information about how the person's language actually sounds, i.e. the voice quality. This, however is becoming less and less of a problem for Multimodal (Inter)action Analysis since we sometimes as in this book can (and hopefully soon even more often will be able to) attach the actual video or voice recording to our analyses.

When we transcribe spoken language multimodally in order to illustrate intonation, we have several tools that we can use to represent the speaker's intonation. First, we can use the waves to show the rhythmic pattern of speech. Then, we use font size to demonstrate loudness in relation to other speakers or loudness changes for one speaker. Plus, we can utilize space to illustrate timing, overlaps or contractions in speech. Figure 6.14 shows the first four lines from our verbal transcript above overlaid onto the gesture transcript from Video 6.3. Here, the woman's sounds are shown in yellow. Man A's sounds are represented in white and the utterances of man C (not seen in the image) are shown in red.

Task 24

Re-watch Video 6.3 at www.wiley.com/go/Norris/multimodal-data again and read the transcript below.

Task 25

Re-watch Video 6.3 at www.wiley.com/go/Norris/multimodal-data again and continue transcribing the spoken language from the point left off.

Note 7

If you are working in PowerPoint to produce your multimodal transcripts, the intonation curves can be produced in WordArt.

Figure 6.14 Spoken language transcript overlaid over the top of the gesture transcript. Reproduced with permission of the participants.

Transcribing Written Language and Images Used

Here, I define the mode of written language and image as that which is on a screen. You will see below why I define the mode as such here. When transcribing written language used in an (inter)action, the best way is to take snapshots or photos of the written words, or to add the written document to your transcripts. In a written document, you can highlight or underline the words read or used and you can take snapshots of these, adding the time stamp of your video at the top left-hand corner. An example of a written language transcript of the man from our object handling example (Video 6.6) is shown in Figure 6.15. Here, you see the map that the man is using and the writing that emerges as he is clicking on a restaurant site. In the first image, we find the beginning of the clip just as in the object handling transcript (Figure 6.13 above). Then, we see that the map has moved slightly. Here, we want to realize that we have already transcribed the man's mouse movements in the object handling transcript and can here simply focus on what is changing on the screen. In Image 3, we see a balloon opening up and in Images 4–6, the balloon extends. In Image 7, we have transcribed the beginning of the closing of the balloon and Image 8 shows the previous map without the balloon.

Task 26

Watch Video 6.6 at www.wiley.com/go/Norris/multimodal-data again and read the transcript below.

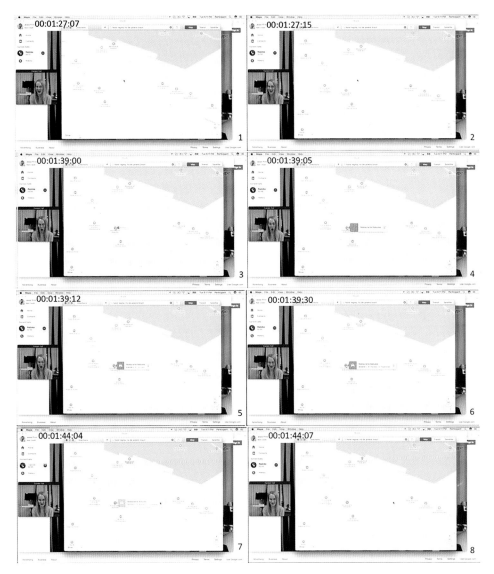

Figure 6.15 Written language/image transcript. Reproduced with permission of the participants.

Task 27

Re-watch Video 6.6 and continue transcribing the written language/image transcript for Video 6.6 from the point left off in Figure 6.15.

Step 11: Producing a Final Transcript

In our last step of Phase IV, we want to learn how to collate transcripts in order to produce final transcripts that show the essence of the (inter)action that we have transcribed. Now, even more than before, the time stamps in the images become important. However, you also want to realize that the last number in the time stamp, which is the number of frames, is not really *that* important. Frames depend upon the quality that the video is recorded in, the quality of the video as it is downloaded, and the quality that the video is saved as. For example, you may have noticed that the frames in the transcripts shown are not the same as shown in some of the programs that you may be using. The reason is that the video was collated and time stamped in its original high-quality version, but then was saved in a lower quality to make it easier to upload and download. Time stamps are useful for two reasons: first, they are useful to arrange images correctly in a transcript; and second, they are useful to see how quickly or slowly an (inter)action proceeds. When collating transcripts, you want to edit out the images that have the same time stamp and you also want to merge some images that are very close in time (especially if the frames are the only difference). An example of merging two transcripts, the beginning of the gaze and the head-movement transcripts from Figures 6.9 and 6.10 is shown in Figure 6.16.

Figure 6.16 Producing a final transcript: gaze and head-movement transcript collated. Reproduced with permission of the participants.

Task 28

Watch Video 6.4 at www.wiley.com/go/Norris/multimodal-data again and read the transcript (Figure 6.16).

Task 29

At this point you want to work with your individual transcripts and begin collating. In Figure 6.16, we see the first few images for the gaze and head-movement transcripts from Figures 6.9 and 6.10 collated. Next, work with the images in Figures 6.9–6.11 and make a list of the time stamps that you will use to fully collate these two transcripts. Then compare your work with others in your group and discuss.

Phase IV: Summary

In Phase IV of systematically working with multimodal data, we learn to systematically transcribe our data. In Phase IV you have learned to:

1) Identify a mode
2) Transcribe layout
3) Transcribe proxemics
4) Transcribe posture
5) Transcribe gesture
6) Transcribe gaze
7) Transcribe head movements
8) Transcribe facial expression
9) Transcribe object handling
10) Transcribe language
11) Produce a final transcript

Now that you have learned the individual steps of Phase IV, you are ready to transcribe your own data piece(s) that you have selected in Phase III Step 4.

Phase IV: Transcribing Data Using Multimodal Transcription Conventions – Things to Remember

---

Things to Remember 1

Before delving into transcription, we want to make sure we understand how we define the notion of mode in Multimodal (Inter)action Analysis.

Things to Remember 2

We want to transcribe one mode at a time (each time clearly defined by us) in order to gain new insight into how (inter)action proceeds multimodally. By transcribing in great detail, we often already come across interesting new findings, or we come across aspects that are puzzling to us, thus perking our interest in looking more deeply into these aspects. For this reason, I suggest always having something ready to write down your thoughts and ideas as you transcribe.

Things to Remember 3

When putting together final transcripts, we work with our multiple individual transcripts that we have already produced. Because of the great complexity, it is always a good idea to first combine two individual transcripts such as the gaze and the head-movement transcript illustrated in Figure 6.16. Then, we add another transcript and so on. While it may seem daunting in the beginning to collate the many transcripts, with a little practice, this actually turns into a really interesting exercise. At this point, you may also wish to add more arrows or numbers to indicate movements rather than showing the almost same movement in various images. Our gesture transcript would be a good example. There, we could just count the number of up-down movements of the finger, illustrate one up and one down movement each in the final transcript, and add a number next to each up and down movement. When you have repetitions like the one in the gesture transcript (Figure 6.8), you may also wish to add a *from-to-timestamp* at the top of the two images to indicate the length of time to produce multiple iterations of the (almost) same movement.

Chapter 7

Systematically Working with Multimodal Data Phase V

7

Phase V: Using Analytical Tools

In Phase V we learn to utilize analytical tools to conduct detailed micro analyses and to put our analyses into perspective in regards to the intermediate- and macro level of (inter) action. Theoretically founded analytical tools allow us to work in a reliable and replicable manner. In this chapter, you will learn to choose from seven analytical tools for micro analysis that allow you to discover different aspects in (inter)actions that social actors perform. Then, you will learn to integrate your micro analyses into a larger perspective by choosing from three analytical tools or tool sets depending upon your data. For example, you may examine the scales of actions that are apparent to position your micro analyses in a larger picture; you may examine the practices and discourses that come into play when concrete mediated actions are produced at a site of engagement; or you can investigate time cycles and rhythms that are at play when concrete mediated actions are produced.

Each of the analytical tools for micro analysis explicated in this chapter can be used alone or in union with other analytical tools explicated here.

The use of well-defined and tested analytical tools ensures that we are working in a systematic, replicable, and reliable way. While much of social science and some discourse analysis relies heavily on interpretation, we minimize interpretation in our way of working. The term *interpret* is defined in the Meriam-Webster dictionary as:

Interpret
Transitive verb
1) to explain or tell the meaning of: present in understandable terms
• interpret dreams
• needed help interpreting the results
2) to conceive in the light of individual belief, judgment, or circumstance: construe
• interpret a contract
3) to represent by means of art: bring to realization by performance or direction
• interprets a role
https://www.merriam-webster.com/dictionary/interpret
(accessed 5 November 2017)

Systematically Working with Multimodal Data: Research Methods in Multimodal Discourse Analysis,
First Edition. Sigrid Norris.
© 2019 John Wiley & Sons, Inc. Published 2019 by John Wiley & Sons, Inc.
Companion website: www.wiley.com/go/Norris/multimodal-data

Thus, the term *interpret* leaves room for different people to tell the meaning of something in vastly different ways. Interpreting can easily become a point of argument. I will come back to this point below, particularly when discussing the analytical tool called the modal density foreground-background continuum. In fact, we want to stay away from interpreting and instead want to think about our work as Multimodal (Inter)action Analysts as the work of analyzing what is actually happening without trying to read something into an (inter)action. We do this by using theoretically founded and well-tested analytical tools on the one hand, and by being meticulous about defining what it is that we are doing on the other. Through thorough defining and through the use of analytical tools, we arrive at replicable findings of high scientific value. Now, let us turn to selecting analytical tools that we can employ in our analysis in Phase V (Step 1), conducting micro analyses by using analytical tools (Step 2), selecting tools to put micro analyses into a larger perspective (Step 3) and putting micro analyses into a larger perspective (Step 4).

Note 1

The objective of Phase V is to guide us in selecting analytical tools to analyze our data in detail in a theoretically founded manner.

Step 1: Selecting Analytical Tools for Micro Analysis

In Step 1 of Phase V, we want to select analytical tools that help us to systematically conduct micro analyses of specific data pieces. For some analyses, we may want to select just one analytical tool, while for other analyses, we will want to select a few analytical tools that together allow us to gain new insight into our data. In order for you to choose, we now want to learn the seven analytical tools for micro analysis discussed in this book:

1) The lower-level mediated action
2) The higher-level mediated action
3) The frozen mediated action
4) Modal density
5) Modal configurations
6) The modal density foreground-background continuum of attention/awareness
7) Semantic/pragmatic means

Analytical Tool for Micro Analysis 1: The Lower-Level Mediated Action

---

The Lower-Level Mediated Action

This analytical tool is used in the following way:

1) The lower-level mediated action allows us to examine the *multiple mediation* within any one lower-level mediated action. With this tool, we can examine the embodied physical, the environmental physical, the cognitive, the psychological and emotional, as well as the historical and cultural aspects that mediate particular lower-level actions.

2) The lower-level mediated action is our smallest unit of analysis. You will have already used it as you were producing your transcripts, but it also plays an important part in many other analytical tools explained below.

The lower-level mediated action is defined as a social actor acting with or through mediational means or cultural tools. When utilizing the lower-level mediated action as our analytical tool, we can always only examine one social actor performing a particular lower-level mediated action at a time. As explained before, a lower-level mediated action is the smallest pragmatic meaning unit of a mode. This means that the lower-level mediated action is the smallest unit that in its entirety (however small) communicates some meaning. While a mode is a concept that comes about through the production of lower-level mediated actions, a lower-level mediated action is always concrete. This concreteness allows us to systematically, replicably, and reliably analyze the lower-level mediated action, no matter how small the lower-level mediated action is. For example, when a social actor produces a loud outbreath, this outbreath is a lower-level mediated action. In fact, all out-breaths or in-breaths or coughs or laughs can be termed lower-level mediated actions. Thus, when you now disregard anything else that is going on and just focus on the loud outbreath that a person performs, you can begin to untangle all of the mediational means and cultural tools that it takes to produce this loud outbreath. The mediational means here, are air (environmental physical), lungs (embodied physical), open lips, or nostril(s) (embodied physical), cultural knowledge of what it means to produce a loud outbreath at a certain moment in (inter)action (cultural and cognitive), emotion (psychological) to name a few. Each lower-level mediated action, however small, can thus be teased apart into the social actor performing the mediated action and the always multiple mediational means/cultural tools that are used in order to perform the action.

Task 1
Continue the list of mediational means/cultural tools used when producing the lower-level mediated action of a loud outbreath.

Task 2
Think about an artist producing the lower-level mediated action of one brushstroke on a canvas. Which mediational means and cultural tools are required for the artist to perform this lower-level mediated action?

At this point, relatively little work has been conducted to examine the multiple mediation in lower-level mediated actions. Thus, it is a worthwhile exercise to do so and to see where such an examination leads.

Task 3
Read the article: Norris, S. (2013a). What is a mode? Smell, olfactory perception, and the notion of mode in multimodal mediated theory. *Multimodal Communication* 2 (2): 155–169.

Task 4
Think about the relationship between a lower-level mediated action and a mode. Discuss.

Of course, we realize that, while we can analyze one lower-level mediated action at a time, lower-level mediated actions are never produced alone in (inter)action. This brings us to the next analytical tool, the higher-level mediated action.

But first, we want to think a little about perception and embodiment. Because this is discussed in Chapter 2 in detail, I only reiterate a few points here.

Perception: The Lower-Level Mediated Action

A lower-level mediated action can be perceived by the person producing it and a lower-level mediated action can be perceived by others. The reason for saying "can be" is the fact that quite often in (inter)action individual lower-level mediated actions are not individually perceived either by the performer, nor by others. Usually, lower-level mediated actions are chained in (inter)actions and are intricately interlinked with other chains of lower-level mediated actions. However, they are still units that have a clear beginning and ending point and are thus distinguishable by an analyst. The ability to perceive a lower-level mediated action gives it practical applicability because everyone can learn to distinguish these units.

Embodiment: The Lower-Level Mediated Action

Every lower-level mediated action that a person performs, experiences, and perceives is necessarily embodied and always mediated in multiple ways. Without a person performing, experiencing, or perceiving, a lower-level mediated action is not possible. The multiplicity of mediational means/cultural tools in every lower-level mediated action builds the glue that connects the body (including cognition and psychology) to the environment, the social, and the cultural. Thus, it is the notion of mediation which allows us to recognize and systematically analyze the embodiment in every lower-level mediated action that a social actor performs.

Analytical Tool for Micro Analysis 2: The Higher-Level Mediated Action

The Higher-Level Mediated Action
This analytical tool is used in the following way: 1) The higher-level mediated action allows us to examine the various chains of lower-level mediated actions that make up (or are produced by) this higher-level mediated action. With this tool, we can examine how the "same" higher-level mediated action (for example a meeting, a lesson, a conversation) can be produced through different chains of lower-level mediated actions. 2) The higher-level mediated action is an analytical unit that plays a role in many other analytical tools explicated below.

The higher-level mediated action is defined as the multiple chains of lower-level mediated action that come together to produce the higher-level mediated action at the same time as they are produced by the higher-level mediated action. Higher-level mediated actions define and are defined by the chains of lower-level mediated actions that come together as the higher-level mediated action is produced. Thus, we can find that certain chains of lower-level mediated actions are produced to construct the higher-level mediated action and simultaneously that certain chains of lower-level mediated actions are constructed by the performance of the higher-level mediated action. For example, think of a meeting. There are five participants in the meeting and the topic that is being discussed is a difficult and unpleasant one. The chains of lower-level mediated actions that come together clearly are the chains of spoken language, the chains of postural shifts, the chains of gaze shifts, the chains of writing notes and so on. But if you now introduced some other chains of lower-level mediated action to the meeting that would also intersect with all of the others, you could change the tone of the difficult meeting. For example, we could introduce cups of tea to the meeting and see how the addition of the new chains of lower-level mediated actions, the extending of the arms, holding the cups, moving the cups to the mouth, drinking sips of tea, etc. would have on the overall meeting. In fact, we could devise an experiment, seeing how the chains of lower-level mediated actions introduced would have an effect on the outcome of a difficult meeting. On the other hand, we may find that there is no change or that there is a negative change. These various findings will emerge, because different meetings require different chains of lower-level mediated actions in order to be successful. What this means is that it is not the tea that will make the difference, but the *chains of lower-level mediated actions* that people perform that make the difference in a meeting.

Task 5

Think about the example of a meeting as a higher-level mediated action and continue to list possible chains of lower-level mediated actions. Then compare and discuss what kind of an effect particular chains of mediated action may have.

Task 6

Think about an artist producing the higher-level mediated action of painting a canvas and list possible chains of lower-level mediated actions that can arise and how these would form the higher-level mediated action of painting a picture.

There is much work to be done to examine the chains of lower-level mediated actions and their effects on higher-level mediated actions and of course, this also means that there is much work that needs to be done to examine how particular higher-level mediated actions produce particular chains of lower-level mediated actions as these two levels of action always constitute one another. However, while they always come together, we can still look at these from two analytical perspectives.

Task 7
Read the chapter: Norris, S. (2012a). Teaching touch/response-feel: a first step to an analysis of touch from an (inter)active perspective. In: Multimodality in Practice: Investigating Theory-in-Practice-Through-Methodology (ed. S. Norris), London: Routledge.

Task 8
Think about the coming together of chains of lower-level mediated actions in a higher-level mediated action and discuss.

Now, I would like us to think a little about perception and embodiment in higher-level mediated actions. Because this is discussed in more detail in Chapter 2, I only reiterate a few points here.

Perception: Higher-Level Mediated Action

A higher-level mediated action is perceived by the person producing it and a higher-level mediated action can be perceived by others. The person performing the higher-level mediated action certainly perceives what it is they are doing. Similarly, when others are present and paying attention to the higher-level mediated action that is being performed by a person, they too perceive the higher-level mediated action.

Embodiment: Higher-Level Mediated Action

Since every lower-level mediated action that a person performs, experiences, and perceives is mediated in multiple ways, gluing the body (including cognition and psychology) to the environment, the social and the cultural, each higher-level mediated action, which is the coming together of chains of lower-level mediated action, is therefore necessarily embodied and always mediated in numerous ways.

Higher-Level Mediated Actions and Identity

Scollon (1997) made the point that all mediated actions are identity telling. When thinking of the higher-level mediated action (always simultaneously producing and coming about through chains of lower-level mediated actions), we can begin to analyze how particular mediated actions tell about the identity of the performer.

Task 9
Read the article: Norris, S. (2007). The micropolitics of personal national and ethnicity identity. *Discourse and Society* 18 (5): 653–674.

Task 10
Think about the coming together of chains of lower-level mediated actions in a higher-level mediated action and discuss how they produce identity.

The Frozen Mediated Action
This analytical tool is used in the following way:

1) The frozen mediated action allows us to examine (lower- or higher-level) mediated actions that were produced prior to the real time moment. For example, the lower-level mediated action of an artist's brush stroke is frozen in the very painting long after the artist has finished painting the picture and you can see and analyze particular brush strokes. Or, as another example, the mere presence of the painting placed on a wall in the artist's studio tells of prior higher-level mediated actions which are now frozen in the painting hanging in its place: the higher-level mediated action of positioning the painting on the particular wall in the particular way, the higher-level mediated action of painting the image, and so on.
2) The frozen mediated action is an analytical tool that plays a role in other analytical tools explained below.

The frozen mediated action is defined as the previously performed (lower-level or higher-level) mediated action. Frozen mediated actions are readily read off of objects and the environment by social actors as mediated actions. In other words, lower-level or higher-level mediated actions, performed at an earlier time, may become frozen in objects or the environment. For example, when roads are constructed, the mediated actions are frozen in the environment and you may hear a driver say *"Oh look. They cut up the mountain to build this street".* Here, the driver has read and reacted to mediated actions previously produced by other social actors. Or you may ask a person "Where did you buy that cup?" As soon as you have said this, you will see that you actually read the mediated action of buying the cup off of the object itself. Just as in the examples of the road and the cup, social actors quite readily assign mediated actions to objects and the environment. This assigning or reading of mediated actions that must have been performed earlier is what we mean when we speak of frozen mediated actions.

Task 11
Think about the example of a road or a cup entailing frozen mediated actions. Then, look around and find other frozen mediated actions in your vicinity. Discuss.

Task 12
Find one lower-level mediated action frozen in an object. Then, think about multiple frozen higher-level mediated actions that are found in the same object. Discuss.

Next, I would like us to think about the notion of perception and embodiment in regards to the analytical tool frozen action. Since this is discussed in Chapter 2 in more detail, I only reiterate a few points here.

Perception: Frozen Mediated Action

When encountering an object, we not only perceive the object itself, but quite readily assign mediated actions to the object as frozen within. Thus, we perceive the actions that must have been performed by a social actor as well as we perceive the object itself.

Embodiment: Frozen Mediated Action

A frozen mediated action can either be a lower-level mediated action or a higher-level mediated action. Since every lower-level mediated action that a person performs, experiences, and perceives is necessarily embodied and always mediated in multiple ways and since each higher-level mediated action that an individual performs, experiences, and perceives is necessarily embodied and always mediated in numerous ways, each frozen mediated action that we find embedded in objects and the environment is therefore necessarily embodied and always mediated in multiple ways.

Frozen Actions and Identity

Objects and the environment not only speak of the mediated actions that social actors have taken at an earlier time, these frozen mediated actions are also identity telling. Because frozen mediated actions are solidified in objects and the environment, the identity-telling aspect may be easier to examine and also may be of particular interest because these identity-telling mediated actions endure.

Task 13
Read the article: Norris, S. and Makboon, B. (2015). Objects, frozen actions, and identity: a Multimodal (Inter)action Analysis. *Multimodal Communication* 4 (1): 43–60.

Task 14
Take a look at a frozen mediated action in your environment and discuss how this frozen mediated action is identity telling.

Analytical Tool for Micro Analysis 4: Modal Density

Modal Density
This analytical tool is used in the following way: 1) Modal density allows us to examine the lower-level mediated action make-up of a higher-level mediated action performed by a social actor. 2) Modal density *is* lower-level mediated action density within a higher-level mediated action performed by one social actor. 3) Modal density may be quite different for each social actor involved in the (ostensibly) same higher-level mediated action.

Modal density is defined as the intensity and/or complexity of lower-level mediated actions that a participant produces as they are (at the very same time) producing a higher-level mediated action. Before discussing the theoretical and analytical make-up and use of the tool modal density and its direct link to the displayed attention levels (Analytical Tool 5) of a social actor in (inter)action, I shall give an example. In this example, you are one of the participants and I would like you to imagine a fairly familiar (inter)action. You are having coffee (or tea) with a friend. The friend has her cell phone lying on the table next to her cup. Both of you are engaged in a conversation on a topic that you both care about. Now, your friend's cell phone makes a slight sound. You continue to speak with each other as she picks up the cell phone and reads the message that has arrived. She then sends a brief message back; all the while you are continuing your conversation. Now imagine two scenarios. As your friend reads the message and texts back, you are fully aware that your friend is:

1) Fully engaged in the conversation with you, treating texting more as an aside; or
2) Your friend briefly engages deeply with text messaging and treats your conversation more as an aside.

Both of these instances are equally possible and usually, when people hear this kind of possibility, you are told that you *interpret* the engagement of your friend in either the first or the second way. Interpretation can easily become a point of argument, so that in the example above, one interlocutor (in this case you) may make the claim "*you paid more attention to messaging than to our conversation*" and the other interlocutor easily rejects it by claiming "*that is only your interpretation*". When, however, we get away from the notion of *interpretation* and have a look at an instance like the one in our example, we can make quite strong claims about what people are more and what they are less focused upon.

Modal density is lower-level mediated action density within a higher-level mediated action. That means modal density is produced through *concrete actions* that people take. Actions that people take are visible, audible, or otherwise perceptible. Actions that people take either happen or they do not happen. They are concrete and analyzable through the tool modal density, as lower-level mediated action density. Thus, *modal density is not a matter of interpretation*. Lower-level mediated action density, i.e. *modal density is concrete and thus unmistakably analyzable*. Either a mediated action is produced or not produced. As we transcribe all lower-level mediated actions that social actors produce, when putting them together we arrive at the modal density that is produced in and through the production of the higher-level mediated action that we are analyzing.

Let us revisit the example from above. The person you are conversing and having coffee (or tea) with picks up a cell phone, gazes at it, reads the message, writes a text, and sends it off. These actions may be almost exactly the same in the two instances where:

1) The person continues to focus upon the conversation with you; and
2) The person changes focus and pays more attention to texting.

But, there will be two important differences:

1) The intensity of the texting actions performed will differ.
2) Other lower-level mediated actions that the person is producing will differ. The way the person is sitting, holding their body, head, shoulders, legs, feet, or their facial expression will differ.

In addition, the intensity with which the texting actions are performed will be visible not only in the way the person is performing these, but also and maybe most importantly in the way the person is performing the *other* lower-level mediated actions. This brings us back to the theoretical foundation that all actions a person performs are linked, building *one system of communication*. Because all actions are linked, people always communicate multimodally, not only in what they do or not do in their focus, but also in what they do and not do on other levels of their attention. All actions communicate and all actions can be read by others. However, about conversing with others, we are primed to only believe in what we *hear* but not what we *see* or *feel* (through the mode of touch for example). We are taught from childhood onward to *only* pay attention to the verbal actions that people communicate in conversation, and we are quite incorrectly taught that nonverbal actions that we see or feel or otherwise perceive can only be *interpreted*, but not examined as clearly as verbal actions. *Every action* that is performed can be analyzed. Certainly, just as in language, there will be cross-cultural differences. But just as in language, cross-cultural differences in *all* actions that people perform can be analyzed.

Task 15

Think about the difference in intensity or complexity of lower-level mediated actions when a friend is more focused upon your conversation and when a friend is more focused upon texting. Discuss.

There is much work to be done to investigate the modal density that social actors perform in (inter)action. With this tool, we can analyze when and how two people engaged in a shared focused higher-level mediated action produce modal density differently. When analyzing this difference in modal density, we may also wish to analyze the modal configurations (Analytical Tool 5) that make up the higher-level mediated actions.

Or, we can examine how social actors employ a different modal density altogether so that they display a difference in the attention that each person pays to the shared higher-level mediated action. When using the tool modal density for the analysis of whether or not shared higher-level mediated action also means shared focus, or for the analysis of multiple higher-level mediated actions performed by one or more people, we will want to utilize the tool modal density in connection with the foreground-background continuum of attention/awareness (Analytical Tool 6).

Task 16

When thinking about modal density as displaying the level of attention that a person pays in an (inter)action, we automatically have to think about a variety of attention levels. Discuss why this is so.

Modal density is a tool that allows us to examine all lower-level mediated actions that a participant performs when producing a higher-level mediated action. Modal density thus not only moves us beyond language in use, but also beyond focused attention in (inter)action. This brings us to the connected notion of a foreground-background continuum of attention levels.

Next, we want to relate the concept of modal configuration to the notions of perception and embodiment.

Perception: Modal Density

Social actors perceive modal density when performing a higher-level mediated action. This means, we know which lower-level mediated actions to produce in what way in order to perform a particular higher-level mediated action. Just as we perceive the intensity and/or complexity of the chains of lower-level mediated actions necessary, we can also perceive the modal density of others when they are engaged in a higher-level mediated action. Just think of walking into a room to find someone intensely speaking on the phone. Instantaneously, you perceive that this person is focused upon the phone (inter)action. Just as we can tell (perceive) what someone is focused upon, we can quite aptly perceive what someone is not focused upon. Thus, without knowing anything about lower-level mediated action density (modal density), everyone can perceive modal density. The analytical tool modal density (lower-level action density) thus possesses great practical capability. While all social actors can and do perceive modal density (even without knowing that they do), analysts can utilize the tool modal density in order to systematically and reliably analyze higher-level mediated actions.

Embodiment: Modal Density

Because all mediated actions are embodied, the modal density of the concrete lower-level mediated actions are always embodied. In fact, all chains of lower-level mediated actions are produced by social actors through their physical, cognitive, psychological bodies and the physical environment and objects (through multiple mediation). Since modal density is embodied and at least in part physical, we can analyze the chains of lower-level mediated actions, analyzing how exactly social actor produce the always embodied higher-level mediated actions.

Analytical Tool for Micro Analysis 5: Modal Configuration

Modal Configuration
This analytical tool is used in the following way:
1) Modal configuration allows us to examine the hierarchical ordering of the lower-level mediated actions that make up (or are produced by) a higher-level mediated action.   2) Modal configuration *is* lower-level mediated action configuration within a higher-level mediated action performed by one social actor.   3) Modal configurations may differ greatly from one social actor to another involved in an (ostensibly) same higher-level mediated action.

Modal configuration is defined as the hierarchical ordering of lower-level mediated actions within a higher-level mediated action. We determine this hierarchy through the analysis of the importance of a lower-level mediated action (or chains thereof) for the production of the higher-level mediated action under examination. Thus, in our example of your friend and you having a cup of coffee (or tea) and conversing as she receives a text and texts back, we can examine the modal configuration of each higher-level mediated action. For example, when investigating the higher-level mediated action of her texting, we will find that, the mode of object handling is the hierarchically most important mode since without a having placed the phone within reach (having placed the phone on the table is a frozen mediated action) and without picking up the phone to read the text and respond, there is no higher-level mediated action of texting. Next, we may find that the mode of gaze and the mode of written language are hierarchically right below the mode of object handling. These two modes will build an aggregate in this instance, since your friend cannot read or type the text without looking at it. In this way, we systematically analyze the chains of lower-level mediated actions that make up the higher-level mediated action of texting and see what is absolutely necessary to perform this very action and what is not. For example, her sitting at a table will not be highly relevant to the mediated action of texting since she could also text standing up. However, her sitting at the table is important for the other higher-level mediated action that she is performing simultaneously, namely having coffee (or tea) and conversing with you.

Task 17
Imagine the conversation with your friend and think through the modal configurations of your conversation. What might you be finding? Discuss.

Next, we want to relate the concept of modal configuration to the notions of perception and embodiment.

Perception: Modal Configurations
In some ways, all social actors perceive modal configurations when performing a higher-level mediated action, i.e. we know what is absolutely necessary in order to perform a particular higher-level mediated action. For example, if you want to cook dinner, you need to have the food for your dishes, i.e. you need to have bought groceries (this higher-level mediated action is later frozen in your groceries), need to have access to some kind of kitchen where you can prepare the food, and so on. Thus, we can perceive the relevance of certain mediated actions. We can also perceive which actions are not relevant to a certain kind of higher-level mediated action. For example, it may be pleasant to listen to music while cooking, but listening to music is certainly not important to the higher-level mediated action of cooking, while the groceries certainly are. Whereas every social actor perceives what is needed in order to perform a particular higher-level mediated action, multimodal discourse analysts can analyze the hierarchical positions of the chains of lower-level mediated actions (modal configurations) within a higher-level mediated action. Perception allows us to systematically work through the modal configurations of higher-level mediated actions.

Embodiment: Modal Configurations
Just as all mediated actions are embodied, the modal configurations of the concrete lower-level mediated actions are always embodied. All hierarchically ordered chains of lower-level mediated actions are produced by social actors through their physical,

cognitive, psychological bodies with the physical environment and objects. Because modal configurations are embodied, we can perceive the ordering of the chains of lower-level mediated actions, analyzing how exactly social actors produce higher-level mediated actions. This makes the work of multimodal discourse analysts even more exciting, because we can systematically and scientifically analyze how social actors in everyday lives perform particular higher-level mediated actions by producing specific embodied modal configurations.

Task 18
Read the chapter: Norris, S. (2009a). Modal density and modal configurations: multimodal actions. In: Routledge Handbook for Multimodal Discourse Analysis (ed. C. Jewit), London: Routledge.

Task 19
Discuss how modal density and modal configurations are useful as individual analytical tools and how they are useful as combined analytical tools.

Analytical Tool for Micro Analysis 6: Modal Density Foreground-Background Continuum of Attention/Awareness

Modal Density Foreground-Background Continuum of Attention/Awareness
This analytical tool is used in the following way: 1) The modal density foreground-background continuum of attention/awareness allows us to examine the various levels of attention that a social actor pays to simultaneously performed higher-level mediated actions.

   Once we realize that we can analyze the modal density employed by a social actor in (inter)action when performing a certain higher-level mediated action, we also want to realize that social actors more often than not pay attention to more than one higher-level mediated action at a time. In fact, it is quite rare in everyday life that social actors pay attention to only one higher-level mediated action. This notion of paying attention to only one thing is known as the notion of flow (Csikszentmihalyi 1990). It is a wonderfully fulfilling moment, when we can get lost in one particular higher-level mediated action, performing only that one and not worry about anything else. However, most often, people in their everyday lives, have many things going on, are (inter)acting with many people on different timelines and simultaneously on different levels of attention. For example, a father may be working in his office, but also be highly aware of the time that he needs to leave in order to pick up the children from school. He may be working on a particular task, but also be thinking about dinner, texting his partner in intervals as they are discussing what groceries they need to buy. This all goes on seamlessly, without too much difficulty, and stays in the minds of the social actors on different levels or switches from foreground to mid-ground to background of their attention. Others around them are somewhat aware of what the father is paying attention to, so that a co-worker might make a comment to bring his focus back to work, when he is engaged in texting his partner, or the father may look at the time to see what time it is and how much longer he has to work on the task that he is engaged in before he has to leave to fetch the children. Only focusing on one higher-level mediated action or one (inter)action at a time, i.e. *flow* is nice, but achieving flow is not the most natural thing in our busy lives.

When we realize just how often everybody is performing simultaneous higher-level mediated actions, we realize that analyzing only those actions that participants focus upon paints a quite distorted picture. In order not to fall into the trap of distortion, we thus need to analyze not only what people are (or should be) focused upon, but also that which they mid-ground or background. Social actors are not necessarily focused upon a conversation, and are not necessarily focused upon what we think they should be focused upon. Only through in-depth analysis, can we clearly know what a person is paying most (inter)active attention to. This still leaves out inner thought, but that really is not much of a problem since our interest is not reading people's minds, but analyzing their (inter)actions. When examining the foreground-background continuum of attention and awareness, we want to realize that people also may pay attention to more than three higher-level mediated actions at a time (the most that I have analyzed in one participant were seven simultaneous higher-level mediated actions); similarly, we may find fewer than three higher-level mediated actions being performed.

When we examine (inter)actions, we can analyze those higher-level mediated actions that are in some way concretely produced (such as looking at the clock for picking up the children or texting) while working on a task at the office. This concrete producing of higher-level mediated actions means that we can determine the lower-level mediated action density, i.e. modal density, that a social actor produces in and through these higher-level mediated actions. When examining modal density of each of the simultaneously performed higher-level mediated actions, then we can determine which of these higher-level mediated actions a social actor pays more and which the social actor pays less attention to. The attention levels will, no doubt, fluctuate in everyday life. Sometimes, a person pays more attention to a conversation and sometimes, a person pays more attention to texting. But in either case, the attention level at which a person in (inter)action is engaged in, is always and reliably analyzable through the analysis of modal density (lower-level mediated action density). The higher-level mediated action a social actor is paying most attention to is then positioned at the foreground (or focus) on the foreground-background continuum and the one they pay least attention to is positioned at the background of their attention/awareness levels. The higher-level mediated actions performed with more or less modal density are positioned relationally to the other two. Important to note here is that the foreground-background continuum of attention/awareness is our way of illustrating the amount of attention that a social actor pays to several higher-level mediated actions that they perform simultaneously. *This graph is a heuristic.* This graph does not depict the actual mind of a social actor. All that it depicts is the various higher-level mediated actions that a social actor performs simultaneously at a moment in time and it shows how much attention the social actor pays at that point in time to these various higher-level mediated actions. Thus, when we now revisit the example of your friend texting and you complaining that they were paying more attention to their texting than to the ongoing conversation with you, you could, had you taken a video of the (inter)action, determine exactly when and how your friend paid more attention to the texting.

The modal density foreground-background continuum of attention/awareness allows us to systematically determine which higher-level mediated action a social actor pays more and which they pay less attention to when engaging in simultaneous higher-level mediated actions. The higher the modal density, the more attention is paid to the higher-level mediated action. The lower the modal density, the less attention is paid to the higher-level mediated action.

Task 20

Read the article:
Norris, S. (2006). Multiparty interaction: a multimodal perspective on relevance. *Discourse Studies* 8 (3): 401–421.

Task 21

Draw a two-dimensional graph with just an x- and a y-axis similar to the one in the article and demonstrate on this heuristic what a friend's attention/awareness graph would look like when they are:

1) More focused upon your conversation; and
2) More focused upon texting.

Task 22

Discuss the complexity of attention/awareness when engaging in a multiparty (inter)action.

Next, we want to think about the relevance of perception and embodiment in relation to the analytical tool *modal density foreground-background continuum of attention/ awareness*.

Perception: Modal Density Foreground-Background Continuum of Attention/Awareness

As social actors, we perceive not only what we ourselves are doing, but we also perceive what others are doing. Indeed, as mentioned above, we read modal density quite aptly and correctly without actually knowing or understanding the notion of modal density. If you show someone a video clip of a few people engaged in several higher-level actions, the viewer will tell you quite correctly what each person is paying attention to most and what they are paying attention to least. For years, I have tried this out with various people and always have unsurprisingly had a very successful outcome. People can tell when others are paying focused attention to something and usually will try to refrain from disturbing them. In fact, we learn this from early childhood onward. We also can tell when someone is paying little attention to something (such as a conversation). We may be offended or we may welcome this in others depending upon the situation. But the point here is not that we evaluate others paying more or less attention to a specific higher-level mediated action (even though in everyday life we often do evaluate), the point here is the fact that we perceive the difference. But why and how do we perceive the difference? The answer lies in the notion of embodiment.

Embodiment: Modal Density Foreground-Background Continuum of Attention/Awareness

Modal density is the lower-level mediated action density in a higher-level mediated action performed by a social actor. All mediated actions are embodied. This means that all mediated actions are produced by a social actor through their physical, cognitive, psychological bodies and the physical environment and objects. Because all mediated actions (higher-level, lower-level, and frozen) are embodied, we can perceive the mediated actions as social actors in an actual (inter)action and as social scientists when analyzing mediated actions. The difference between social actors in everyday life and social scientists lies in the fact that as social scientists we employ reliable analytical tools (such as modal density and the foreground-background continuum of attention/awareness) to systematically analyze and illustrate. While social actors in their everyday lives are generally able to read modal density and the attention that social actors pay to specific higher-level mediated actions, social actors are often quite unaware and quite unsure of their own perception. The reason for this, as pointed out earlier, is that we have been brought up to *incorrectly believe* that only words are reliable in communication, while nonverbal means of communication are interpretable, but not knowable. This makes the work of social scientists using the analytical tools of modal density and the foreground-background continuum that much more important, because we can actually systematically and scientifically demonstrate what is going on in any specific and always embodied (inter)action.

Analytical Tool for Micro Analysis 7: Semantic/Pragmatic Means

Semantic/Pragmatic Means
The analytical tool semantic/pragmatic means allows us to examine when a social actor changes their focus. This analytical tool has two simultaneous, but different, dimensions: 1) A semantic dimension for the performer. By performing a pronounced lower-level mediated action that does not belong to a higher-level mediated action, the performer changes their focus upon a different mediated action, producing a change in *meaning*. In this sense, the pronounced lower-level mediated action is semantic.   2) A pragmatic dimension for the performer as well as for others (inter)acting with the performer. By performing the pronounced lower-level mediated action, the performer indicates to themselves and others that they are changing their focus. Others read the pronounced lower-level mediated action in use and react to it. In this sense, the pronounced lower-level mediated action is pragmatic.

Now that we have learned that social actors often perform several higher-level mediated actions simultaneously, paying different levels of attention to them, we want to ask ourselves how we know when somebody changes their focus. In our example of you having coffee (or tea) with your friend, you are well aware that she is focusing on your conversation before she receives the first text. But then, let us say, she focuses on her texting, while she is mid-grounding your conversation. In other words, the higher-level mediated action of texting has moved into your friend's focus. As mentioned earlier, we know that this happens and when it happens in (inter)action. We can read another person's focused and un-focused attention and we can be certain that we can read a shift in focus with accuracy. The reason that we can determine a shift in focus is that we do not *interpret*, but that we in fact *read* another person's pronounced lower-level mediated action that indicates a shift in focus. While the person producing such a pronounced lower-level mediated action is likely unaware of their doing so, and while most people in (inter)action who quite aptly are reading these kinds of pronounced lower-level mediated actions are just as likely unaware of the fact that they are reading them, such pronounced lower-level mediated actions are concrete.

Concrete pronounced lower-level mediated actions that indicate a shift in focus by a social actor are what I call semantic/pragmatic means. Semantic/pragmatic means are pronounced lower-level mediated actions, which neither belong to the higher-level mediated action produced in the focus before a shift occurs, nor do they belong to the newly focused upon higher-level mediated action. They have no meaning in relation to the higher-level mediated actions performed, but rather function as a structuring device in generally two ways:

1) They *structure* the *focus* of the social actor performing the means (semantic function, i.e. relating to *meaning* in the performer); and
2) They indicate to other social actors that the performer is shifting their attention (pragmatic function, i.e. *interactive function* relating to the notion of *in use*).

But, semantic/pragmatic means can also be used by the performer in order to pull the interlocutor's focus of attention to a certain higher-level mediated action (in teaching for example).

Task 23

Read the article:
Norris, S. (2016a). Concepts in multimodal discourse analysis with examples from video conferencing. *Yearbook of the Poznań Linguistic Meeting* 2 (1): 141–165, ISSN (Online) 2449–7525, September 2016. de Gruyter Open.

Now that we have realized that we do not actually interpret a shift in focus, but, contrary to most people's belief, perceive it, we want to think about the notions of perception and embodiment.

Perception: Semantic/Pragmatic Means
Because semantic/pragmatic means are concretely pronounced lower-level mediated actions, we have no problem perceiving them. We may either see them (when they are performed in our field of vision). We may hear them (when they are performed audibly), or we may feel them (when they are performed through touch). In any case, a semantic/pragmatic means is easily perceived (even if not easily recognized as such). Knowing exactly what you perceive is not the same as perceiving it. For example, when a lecturer

sorts their papers at the end of a lecture and knocks them on the lectern to straighten them out, they may not realize that they just performed a semantic/pragmatic means. Neither will the students realize that that is what happened. Yet, as soon as this semantic/pragmatic means is performed, students will begin to pack up their things, i.e. they will react to the semantic/pragmatic means of their lecturer. Just as in this example, people perform and others react to semantic/pragmatic means on a regular basis. Yet few realize that they are simply communicating and/or reading a shift in focused attention. Social actors perceive another's shift in focused attention, and social actors who are performing the semantic/pragmatic means perceive that they are shifting their own focused attention even if only tacitly. For the performer, the semantic/pragmatic means has a structuring function of their own perception. For others, the performance of a semantic/pragmatic means displays that the performer is changing their focused attention. The reason others can perceive this comes about because semantic/pragmatic means are embodied.

Embodiment: Semantic/Pragmatic Means

Since semantic/pragmatic means are pronounced concrete lower-level mediated actions, they are always embodied since all mediated actions are produced by social actors through their physical, cognitive, psychological bodies, and the physical environment and objects. Because semantic/pragmatic means are embodied, we can perceive these pronounced lower-level mediated actions as social actors in an actual (inter) action and as social scientists when analyzing how social actors change their focus from one higher-level mediated action to another. While social actors in their everyday lives are usually able to read semantic/pragmatic means (as we can see that they are reacting to them), social actors are usually unaware of their own perception of these pronounced lower-level mediated actions. This makes the work of multimodal discourse analysts even more exciting, because we can systematically and scientifically analyze how social actors in everyday lives perform *and* react to semantic/pragmatic means.

Task 24

Read the article:
Norris, S. (2009). Tempo, *Auftakt*, levels of actions, and practice: rhythms in ordinary interactions. *Journal of Applied Linguistics* 6 (3): 333–356.

Task 25

Discuss semantic/pragmatic means as performed in everyday life and as performed by instructors.

Task 26

Think about rhythm in higher-level actions and how semantic/pragmatic means can be viewed from this point of view. Discuss.

Step 2: Conducting a Micro Analysis by Utilizing Analytical Tools

In Step 2 of Phase V, we want to use the chosen analytical tool(s) in order to analyze the transcribed data piece. The data has already told a story and you have chosen the data piece that you ended up transcribing in Phase IV. Now, we want to examine it deeper. But once again, we want the data piece to tell us which analytical tool is best to use for its analysis. Maybe, when you transcribed the many modes individually, one mode jumped out at you and presented itself as of particular interest.

Utilizing Analytical Tool for Micro Analysis 1: The Lower-Level Mediated Action

You may wish to utilize the lower-level mediated action as your analytical tool in order to examine the always multiple ways of mediation, for example, when we look at the object handling transcript presented in the last chapter (Chapter 6). Here, you may want to utilize Analytical Tool 1, the lower-level mediated action, and examine the multiple ways the lower-level mediated action of moving the mouse is mediated. Here, we may want to begin by revisiting the object handling transcript as well as the video clip, watching the clip as we are re-reading the transcript. Then, we will want to begin listing the meditational means and cultural tools that are mediating the transcribed chain of lower-level mediated action. The most obvious is the mouse itself and the hand holding and moving it, as well as the surface upon which the movement occurs. We do not want to forget the knowledge of technology, which no doubt mediates the action. But then we also want to realize that the screen and the gaze mediate the movement of the mouse. Now we are starting to get into complexity that shows that there is no simple way of analyzing the multiple ways that a seemingly simple lower-level action is mediated. Thus, now we want to have a look at a gaze transcript of the same (inter)action and see how and when gaze mediates the lower-level action of moving the mouse.

Task 27

Transcribe the mode of gaze for Video 6.6 and collate the two transcripts to gain a better idea of what is going on when the participant moves the mouse.

Task 28

Re-read the article:
Norris, S. (2013). What is a mode? Smell, olfactory perception, and the notion of mode in multimodal mediated theory. *Multimodal Communication* 2 (2): 155–169.

Task 29

Realize that a mode is a concept, while a lower-level mediated action is concrete. Thus, the lower-level mediated action of gaze can certainly also mediate the lower-level mediated action of object handling.

Utilizing Analytical Tool for Micro Analysis 2: The Higher-Level Mediated Action

You may wish to utilize the higher-level mediated action as your analytical tool in order to examine the coming together of always multiple chains of lower-level mediated action. For example, when we look at the gaze and head movement transcripts presented in Chapter 6, you can begin to think through the ways that the higher-level mediated action of working on a task via video conferencing technology is produced. For this, you will want to utilize Analytical Tool 2, the higher-level mediated action and examine which multiple chains of lower-level mediated action come together in this (inter)action. Here, we may want to begin by revisiting not only the transcripts but also the video clip, watching the clip as we are re-reading the transcripts. Then, we will want to begin listing the chains of lower-level mediated action that come about through the production of a higher-level mediated action, which in turn produce the higher-level mediated action. An interesting thing to look at, also, is when certain chains of lower-level mediated actions begin and when they end. When working through the multiple chains of lower-level mediated actions, you will then notice that they do not all originate at the same point in clock time and that they do not all end at the same point in clock time.

Task 30
Watch Video 6.4 and jot down the multiple chains of lower-level mediated action that you can detect. Then, discuss the importance of multimodal transcription.

Utilizing Analytical Tool for Micro Analysis 3: The Frozen Mediated Action

You may wish to utilize the frozen mediated action as your analytical tool in order to examine how previously performed (lower-level or higher-level) mediated actions are frozen in objects or the environment.

   For example, you can look at your desk in front of you and begin to jot down the mediated actions that had to have been performed in order for the objects arranged on it to be present. Then, you can go a step further and try to make sense of what kind of identity these objects speak of. However, here you need to be very careful. While you will know what specific frozen mediated actions embedded in objects mean to you, you cannot assume that other people assign the same identity to the objects. Exploring frozen mediated actions and their identity-telling properties is an interesting and eye-opening experience, where the observer may think of one thing, while the owner may be trying to portray something else. But quite often, the owner of an object is quite unaware of what identity-telling frozen mediated actions others read off of the object and are surprised when you tell them what the frozen mediated action of owning the object tells the viewer about the owner. Here, you may want to look at the frozen mediated actions embedded in your own things and determine what kind of identity they speak about. This can be a nice way to learn something about yourself.

Task 31
Examine some frozen mediated actions embedded in your own belongings and write down what they say about your identity.

Utilizing Analytical Tool for Micro Analysis 4: Modal Density

You may wish to utilize modal density as your analytical tool in order to examine how a person produces a focused higher-level mediated action. For example, you may wish to transcribe a brief moment in Video 6.2 completely for the man in the interaction and then determine how he produces modal density. Does he use some chains of lower-level mediated actions in a particularly intense way (such as pensively reading the printed task) or does he utilize many different chains of lower-level mediated actions in complexly intertwined ways? When you think that he uses modal intensity for an action, show the part to another person and see if they can see it too. As mentioned before, we are very apt in reading what others do; intensity is visible (or audible, etc.). While this notion is always relative to the person and the particular interaction, it is quite obvious.

Task 32

Look at interactions when you take a stroll around town and try to determine what people you encounter focus upon. Even without listening, you can often tell quite clearly what a person is focused upon.

Task 33

Next, still walking around your city or a mall or such, try to see modal intensity and jot down your observations. What do people do when producing some kind of modal intensity? Then do the same for modal complexity.

Utilizing Analytical Tool for Micro Analysis 5: Modal Configuration

You may wish to utilize modal configuration as your analytical tool in order to examine how a higher-level mediated action is modally hierarchically constructed. For example, if you have transcribed a brief moment in Video 6.2 completely for the man in the interaction and you have determined the modal density that he employs, you can now use that work in order to determine which modes (chains of lower-level mediated actions including frozen mediated actions) are hierarchically higher and which are hierarchically lower in the interaction. In order to determine modal configuration, you want to go about it in two ways: first, list what is absolutely necessary for the interaction to unfold as it does and second, list what has little to no relevance for the interaction to unfold as it does. You may find that some lower-level mediated actions are equally important. When that happens, you may have discovered a modal aggregate, i.e. chains of lower-level mediated actions that *have to come together* for the interaction to unfold as it does. Then, hierarchize the modes and modal aggregates.

Task 34

Think through the concept of modal configuration. What can an analysis of modal configuration tell us about an action or interaction? Discuss examples such as teaching, painting, or cooking.

Utilizing Analytical Tool for Micro Analysis 6: Modal Density Foreground-
Background Continuum of Attention/Awareness

You may wish to utilize the modal density foreground-background continuum as your analytical tool in order to examine what a person in a multiparty interaction is focused upon, what they mid-ground and what they background. For example, you can have a look at Video 6.1 (Chapter 6) and determine which interaction the mother of the triplets is focused upon and which interaction she mid-grounds. Does she focus upon the interaction with her brother in Canada or does she focus upon the triplets? How do you know? The answer clearly can be found in the modal density that she employs for each of the interactions. Is her modal density higher in the interaction with her brother via Skype or is her modal density higher in the interaction with her children?

Task 35

Draw a simple two-dimensional graph to depict the mother's focused interaction and her mid-grounded interaction at a particularly clear moment in the video.

Task 36

Discuss how essential multimodal transcription is for a clear determination of *how* modal density is produced.

Task 37

Take a little excursion and watch multiparty interactions. See if you can determine who is focusing upon which interaction. Jot down what you see.

Utilizing Analytical Tool for Micro Analysis 7: Semantic/Pragmatic Means

You may wish to utilize the tool semantic/pragmatic means in order to examine how a person changes their focus. It takes a bit of practice to see (or hear) the pronounced lower-level mediated actions. While we all use them and while we all react to the ones that others use in interaction with us, we are quite unaware of their existence. But of course, that also makes these pronounced lower-level actions very interesting. If you have a video of people engaged over a longer period in time, doing different things, you can most certainly find semantic/pragmatic means at play. Watch and re-watch segments where a person engaged in a focused mediated action then switches to focus upon a different action. In between, usually before they stop their full engagement in the first action or interaction, a semantic/pragmatic means is performed. Only after that, sometimes even five minutes after that, does the person begin to fully focus upon the new action or interaction. Some common semantic/pragmatic means are eyebrow raises, the low bowing of the upper body, large head movements, slapping a leg, or beating an object, or finger on a table top.

Task 38
Watch people at a park or a library and see what they do before they leave the park or library. Note down the pronounced lower-level mediated actions that you see or hear.

Step 3: Selecting Analytical Tools to Put Micro Analyses into a Larger Perspective

In Step 3 of Phase V, we want to select analytical tools that help us to systematically conduct intermediate and macro analyses of specific data pieces. For some analyses, we may want to select just one analytical tool, while for other analyses, we will want to select an analytical tool set, that allows us to gain new insight into our data. In order for you to choose, we now want to learn the three analytical tools or tools sets for intermediate/macro analyses discussed in this book:

1) Scales of action
2) The site of engagement, practices, and discourses
3) Time cycles and rhythms

Analytical Tool for Intermediate/Macro Analyses 1: Scales of Action

Scales of Action
This analytical tool is used in the following way:
1) Scales of action is a tool that helps us identify and illustrate the various mediated actions that participants are engaging in. For example, a social actor may be engaged in the higher-level mediated action of participating in your study. Embedded within this higher-level mediated action, are other higher-level mediated actions of smaller scales, within which are embedded again smaller scale higher-level mediated actions, and so on up to the smallest scales of lower-level mediated actions that a social actor performs.
2) Scales of action is an analytical tool that allows us to demonstrate the various scales of action, allowing us to realize and show where the higher-level mediated action that we investigated in our micro analysis, sits.

Scale of action is defined as the embeddedness of mediated actions. This tool is particularly useful to show how micro actions are a part of a much bigger picture and array of various scales of mediated actions or to demonstrate how some mediated actions are consecutively performed, while they are, however, not at all linked. Thus, when utilizing this tool, we can gain insight into vastly different mediated actions performed as if in order, when in fact they belong to very different mediated actions altogether. When we conduct a micro analysis and then use the analytical tool *scales of action*, we open up our vision past the micro mediated actions and are able to show the embeddedness of such micro mediated actions.

Task 39
Read the article:
Norris, S. (2017). Scales of action: an example of driving and car talk in Germany and North America. *Text & Talk* 37 (1): 117–139.

Task 40

Think about your action of reading this book and begin to draw the embeddedness of this action within all of your actions that you are performing today. Then, indicate which of the higher-level mediated actions shown are linked and which are not linked.

Next, we want to relate the analytical tool scales of action to the notions of perception and embodiment.

Perception: Scales of Action
Social actors perceive scales of action when going about their days. This means, we know which mediated actions belong into what larger scale mediated action or which mediated action is linked to other mediated actions. While we may perform many mediated actions consecutively and just as many or even more simultaneously, we have keen perception to understand which action is related to which other actions. For example, a person may clean the kitchen counter, read a letter about taxes, and walk the dog consecutively. Nobody, not the person performing these actions, nor anybody watching the person performing them will believe that these actions, just because they are performed consecutively, belong together. Next, the same person may feed the dog, turn on their laptop, and read their emails. Without any problem, the person themselves and any other person observing them will determine that walking the dog and feeding the dog are part of an ongoing action of caring for a dog. Even though hardly any person will think in these terms, the perception is certainly there, making the analytical tool grounded in real life and useful for researchers to analyze scales of action.

Embodiment: Scales of Action
Because all mediated actions are embodied, all actions that can be analyzed through the tool scales of action are necessarily embodied. All actions are produced by social actors through their physical, cognitive, psychological bodies and the physical environment and objects through always multiple mediation.

Analytical Tool Set for Intermediate/Macro Analyses 2: Site of Engagement, Practices, and Discourses

Site of Engagement, Practices and Discourses

This analytical tool set is used in the following way:

1) The tool set of the site of engagement, practices (actions with a history), and discourses (practices with an institutional dimension) allows us to gain an understanding of how concrete mediated actions are socially, culturally, and institutionally produced on the one hand and how concrete micro actions produce and shape social, cultural, and institutional practices and discourses on the other.
2) The tool set of the site of engagement, practices, and discourses allows us to put our micro analyses into a larger perspective, demonstrating the relevance, and usefulness of micro analyses within and for our societies. Often, only when we place micro findings into a larger perspective, can we see the social ramifications that our findings may have.

Through the analysis of the site of engagement, which includes the analysis of the micro actions (Step 2) and the analysis of the practices and discourses coming together, we can establish *why* the people we have analyzed acted in specific ways. Only the analysis of the entire site of engagement, the micro analysis, and the practices and discourses at play, allows us to delve into the question of *why people do what they do as they are doing it*. Through the analysis of the site of engagement, then, can we actually begin to answer some very important questions. Through this intricate analysis on different levels that all come together at the site of engagement can we systematically arrive at analyses that are groundbreaking and relevant to today's society.

Task 41

Read the article:
Norris, S. (2014b). The impact of literacy based schooling on learning a creative practice: modal configurations, practices and discourses. *Multimodal Communication* 3 (2): 181–195.

Task 42

Discuss how the analytical tool set, the site of engagement, practices, and discourses allows us to gain greater insight into where and how our micro analyses are relevant to society.

Next, I would like us to think about perception and embodiment with regard to the site of engagement, practices, and discourses.

Perception: Site of Engagement, Practices, and Discourses
When considering a site of engagement, we can probably say that any one social actor usually perceives their own practices and their own discourses that are relevant and play a part in their production of a higher-level mediated action at a site of engagement. This perception, however is more tacit than it is deliberate. I would like to emphasize that practices and discourses are largely outside of the awareness of individuals because they have become part of their historical bodies (Scollon 1998, 2001a), and are (more often than not) little reflected upon. However, perception still plays a part here, as the practices and discourses that are brought into the production of concrete mediated actions, either *feel right* or *feel off* in some ways. Here, the perception is rather geared towards that which does not feel right and the practices and discourses that feel just right are tacitly embraced. This tacit embracing of the practices and discourses that align perfectly with one's mediated actions, are thus still perceived, i.e. through emotion.

Embodiment: Site of Engagement
As noted in Chapter 2, the notion of embodiment refers to the fact that we live as bodies, that these bodies are interconnected with the environment, objects within and with others. Without body, there is no person; without environment, there is no body, since bodies cannot live in a vacuum; without others there is no body, because we cannot grow and live without the care of and interaction with others. Embodiment as described

here demonstrates how concrete actions, practices (actions with a history), and discourses (actions with a history, which link to institutions), are all embodied. Here, we also see that embodiment necessarily is always multimodal and brings with it a direct link to history, memory, emotion, cognition, mediation, or knowledge.

All intersecting concrete mediated actions, practices, and discourses are bound together through embodiment and perception. Because the multimodal framework outlined in this book consists of analytical concepts and tools that allow us to analyze perception and embodiment in great detail, we are able to shed new light upon human action and interaction.

Analytical Tool for Intermediate/Macro Analyses 3: Natural Experienced Time Cycles and Rhythms

---

Natural Experienced Time Cycles and Rhythms

This analytical tool is used in the following way:

1) The tool of time cycles and rhythms allows us to gain an understanding of how concrete mediated actions are rhythmically entrenched in natural time cycles.
2) The tool of time cycles and rhythms allows us to gain an understanding of how concrete mediated actions are rhythmically entrenched in interaction rhythms.
3) In this tool, natural time cycles and interaction rhythms are viewed as being of a same kind since both types of rhythm are natural (i.e. we are not speaking of clock time) and are generally perceived together.

Scollon (2005) discussed various natural time cycles or rhythms that come into play when people perform a mediated action together and that they entrench themselves to. When we conducted the video ethnographic study explicated in Chapters 3.3, 4.3, and 5.3 in this book, I realized that the natural experienced time cycles had a large impact upon international Skype interactions after I had analyzed a representative segment in which a young mother in New Zealand is Skyping with her own mother in Canada. During the call, many times, the young mother turned away from the screen and focused upon her young son. When this happened, her mother in Canada continued the interaction and finished her daughter's sentences. In Norris (2017a), I analyzed an example of this family interaction in detail. At the time of the Skype interaction, it was a rather hot December Saturday morning in New Zealand and a rather cold Friday afternoon in Canada.

While time cycles are usually shared when people interact, I found that not all time cycles or rhythms are, in fact, shared when examining an international Skype session. I analyzed the following specific natural time cycles, which Scollon had examined before me in regard to interaction:

1) The entropic time cycle (the formation and decay of substances, including the formation and decay of the human body, i.e. aging);
2) The solar time cycle (the 365-days revolution of the earth around the sun); and
3) Circadian time cycle (24-hours rotation of the earth around its axis).

While the entropic time cycle between mother and daughter remains to be shared in the interaction, no matter where they are situated on the earth, the other two time cycles are in fact quite different. The solar time cycle, while naturally certainly one, is experienced quite differently in the different hemispheres of the globe (i.e. summer in

New Zealand and winter in Canada). The circadian time cycle, also naturally the same, is experienced quite differently as it is Saturday morning in New Zealand and Friday afternoon in Canada.

For the interaction to come together, the participants had to keep their own time in mind and they also had to keep the other person's time in mind. They needed to keep in mind what they were doing during their own day. Further, each of the participants had to know what the other was doing at a certain time during Saturday morning and Friday afternoon respectively. This keeping one's own rhythms and another person's rhythm in mind is what I called interactive rhythms. Interactive rhythms usually depend on many things such as children's soccer games, grocery shopping, the making of lunches, or dinners, and the like. A Skype call has to fit into these everyday rhythms in order to work. Besides these medium-sized interaction rhythms, I also found that a large interaction rhythm came into play in some Skype interactions. This was a shared parenting interaction rhythm, where the parents of a young mother or father could quite easily understand the rhythm that was going on in a different part of the world. While this may not be the case in all families, such sharing of a parenting cycle can be found in a great number of families (Figure 7.1).

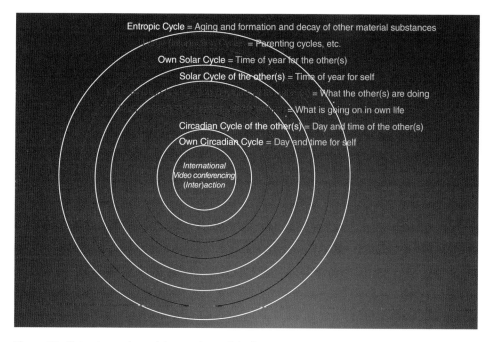

Figure 7.1 Natural experienced time cycles and rhythms.

This analysis showed some quite important ramifications not only for family settings but also for educational and business settings:

1) It is difficult to establish international video conferencing interactions;
2) The further apart, the more complexity is involved;
3) The more people on technical devices, the more complexity is involved; and
4) The more diverse the various locations in the world, the more complexity is involved.

Certainly, this tool, the natural experienced time cycles and rhythms needs to be adapted in ways that are useful for the data that you are examining and the tool, while generally the same, will in fact look differently in different analyses.

Task 43

Read the article:
Norris, S. (2009). Tempo, *Auftakt*, levels of actions, and practice: rhythms in ordinary interactions. *Journal of Applied Linguistics* 6 (3): 333–356.

Or, if you are proficient in German, read the chapter:
Norris, S. (2017). Rhythmus und Resonanz in internationalen Videokonferenzen. In: Resonanz, Rhythmus und Synchronisierung: Erscheinungsformen und Effekte (Hgg. T. Breyer, M. Buchholz, A. Hamburger and S. Pfänder). Bielefeld: transcript-Verlag.

Task 44

Discuss how the analytical tool, natural experienced time cycles and rhythms, allows us to gain insight into micro analyses.

Next, let us think through the notions of perception and embodiment in regard to natural experienced time cycles and rhythms.

Perception: Natural Experienced Time Cycles and Rhythms
Certainly, we can say that everyone perceives time cycles such as the solar time cycle, expressed in the various seasons, or the circadian time cycle, expressed in day-night rhythms. People also perceive their own and other's (inter)action rhythms. All of these are actively perceived in everyday life. Then, we have the entropic rhythm. For people, this is expressed as a process of aging. This rhythm, too is actively perceived, whereas (inter)active rhythms may be quite tacit, expressed for example as the rhythm of parenting, where the grandmother knows just what the daughter is doing when she is parenting her young child; or the daughter knows just how to parent the young child because she has learned some of these ways of parenting from her own mother. Of course, this example will not be true for all families. It is just an example, but an example that we did find in our research. The point here is that even tacit perception of actions and interactions are perceptions after all. The reason that natural experienced time cycles and rhythms are perceptible is the fact that they all are embodied.

Embodiment: Natural Experienced Time Cycles and Rhythms
When we realize that we are our bodies including cognition and emotion, and that our bodies are intricately enmeshed and interconnected with the environment, objects, and with others, then we also realize that natural time and the various rhythms have to be experienced in an embodied way.

Step 4: Putting Micro Analyses into a Larger Perspective by Utilizing Analytical Tools or Tool Sets for Intermediate/Macro Analyses

In Step 4 of Phase V, we want to use the chosen analytical tools or tool sets that allow us to put our micro analyses into a larger perspective. You have already conducted your micro analysis, have learned about the analytical tools or tool sets that will help you to systematically and reliably place your data analysis into a larger frame, and are now ready to utilize the tool.

Utilizing Analytical Tool for Intermediate/Macro Analyses 1: Scales of Action

You may wish to utilize the scales of action as your analytical tool in order to examine where your micro analysis fits into other (inter)actions performed by the participants. For example, when we look at the proxemics transcript of the mother of triplets in New Zealand Skyping with her brother and his two children in Canada, we can place her proxemics actions into a larger picture by using the tool scales of action. We know from the project description that the mother is taking part in a research project. We also know that at least one researcher is present, filming the Skype (inter)action. Without knowing much more, we can already use the tool and draw a diagram to depict the scales of action that we are aware of, showing where the proxemics movements of the mother in New Zealand fits into. By doing this, we can see that our transcript of her minute proxemics movements is a tiny part in a much larger frame. Through this tool, we show where the analysis sits, making sure that we do not inflate micro findings on the one hand, but also, and very importantly so, making sure that we demonstrate the importance of our micro findings in relation to other larger actions.

Task 45

Have another look at the article:
Norris, S. (2017). Scales of action: an example of driving and car talk in Germany and North America. *Text & Talk* 37 (1): 117–139.

Task 46

Draw a graph that depicts some of the scale of actions in relation to our proxemics transcript in Chapter 6.

Utilizing Analytical Tool Set for Intermediate/Macro Analyses 2: Site of Engagement, Practices, and Discourses

You may wish to utilize the tool set site of engagement, practices, and discourses as your analytical tool in order to examine how the concrete mediated actions, no matter how small, are produced by the coming together of practices and discourses at the very same time as these concrete mediated actions reproduce, shape, or change the practices and discourses. For example, you can have a look around the room right now and think about a shared interaction such as an interaction between an instructor and their students. Now, without going into too much detail here and only to illustrate how this tool set is used, draw a site of engagement and place students in one area and the instructor in the other area of the window. Then, begin to think about the practices that one student and the instructor are drawing on. Then, embed the discourses, the practices that have an institutional dimension, that come into play for these two individuals. Here, you will see that the student and the instructor will draw on some of the same practices and discourses but also will draw on practices and discourses that are distinct for each individual. Now, when you are working with your own data, you will see why the participants interact in the way they do, if you place a micro analysis of an interaction into the window of the site of engagement and then add the practices and discourses that intersect. But practices and discourses are not only drawn upon when performing concrete mediated action, they are also re-produced, shaped, or changed. In order to illustrate this back-and-forth between micro, intermediate, and macro, we want to use double arrows.

Task 47

Think through the concept of site of engagement, practices, and discourses. What can an analysis of this tool set tell us about an action or interaction? Discuss examples such as teaching, working in an office, or doctor-patient interactions. Then discuss what other kinds of data other than just video that you would need in order to utilize this tool appropriately.

Utilizing Analytical Tool for Intermediate/Macro Analyses 3: Natural Experienced
Time Cycles and Rhythms
You may wish to utilize the tool natural experienced time cycles and rhythms in order to examine how the concrete mediated actions, no matter how small, are produced as they are intersecting with natural time cycles and rhythms. For example, you may once again turn to your own actions that you are currently producing. You are reading these pages and as you are reading, your reading is embedded in and intersects with a plethora of time cycles and (inter)action rhythms.

Task 48

Think through the analytical tool natural experienced time cycles and rhythms and begin to draw time cycles and rhythms that you are entrenched in as you are reading these pages. Then think through what kind of data besides videos you will need in order to successfully utilize this analytical tool.

Phase V: Summary

In Phase V of systematically working with multimodal data, we gain a deep understanding of particular data pieces, which are first undergoing a micro analysis, and which in turn are placed into a larger perspective. In Phase V you have learned to:

1) Select analytical tools for micro analysis
2) Conduct a micro analysis by utilizing analytical tools

3) Select analytical tools to put micro analyses into a larger perspective
4) Put micro analysis into a larger perspective by utilizing analytical tools or tool sets for intermediate/macro analyses

Now that you have learned the individual analysis steps of Phase V, it is important to realize that in order to truly utilize the tool sets' site of engagement, practice, and discourses as well as the natural experienced time cycles, you will need more than just videos of people producing specific mediated actions. In order to utilize these tools correctly, we need ethnographic and/or interview data in addition to our video data. Otherwise, we cannot know which practices and discourses a person draws on. The reason is that the almost same concrete mediated action can come about by drawing on different practices and discourses. Or, whether a large (inter)action cycle such as a parenting cycle indeed is shared, can only be determined by knowing more about the participants than a snippet of video recorded (inter)action. Using these two analytical tools without having the right kind of (and enough) data would result in interpretation, not however, in theoretically founded analysis.

Thus, the most important aspect to take away from this phase is to learn what each tool has to offer and then to choose the right tool for not only what you would like to do, but to choose the right tool for the data that you have collected. Again, it is important here to work in a data driven way and let the data tell you what it is that needs to be and can be analyzed.

Phase V: Using Analytical Tools – Things to Remember

Things to Remember 1

Before delving into a micro analysis of individual data pieces, we want to make sure that we have a deep understanding of the analytical tools. Each analytical tool allows us to systematically and reliably analyze a different aspect of our data and therefore, choosing the right tool for the data that we are investigating is an important step.

Things to Remember 2

We want to let the data tell the story. In order to truly allow the data to speak to us, we need to have a good grasp of the data piece that we have selected for micro analysis. Thus, you want to re-watch the data piece at intervals as you are choosing your analytical tool(s) to make sure your tool selection is a perfect fit for your data piece(s).

Things to Remember 3

In order to understand how the micro analysis that you have arrived at fits into a larger picture, you next need to select an analytical tool or tool set that allows you to put your data into a larger perspective. Here again, it is important to choose the right tool for the data that you are examining.

Things to Remember 4

Once you have placed your micro analysis of your data piece(s) into a larger perspective, you have arrived at a full multimodal discourse analysis. No doubt, you will have arrived at some groundbreaking findings that will allow us all to better understand human interaction.

Chapter 8

Systematically Working with Multimodal Data: Guides for Instructors

8

A Quick Guide for Instructors

This book has offered a systematic way to collect and analyze multimodal data for the undergraduate and graduate classroom as well as for the researcher new to the field of multimodal discourse analysis. By offering a progression of analysis through phases and steps, where each phase consists of a coherent whole and each step explains a small part of an otherwise very complex analysis process, the book quickly engages the reader in multimodal discourse analysis.

In order to make the book as useful as possible so that a student or researcher can delve right into multimodal discourse analysis without having to first read the vast amount of literature already published on multimodality, the book is limited to one specific analytical framework, Multimodal (Inter)action Analysis (Norris 2004a, 2011a, 2013a). Multimodal (Inter)action Analysis is a holistic multimodal discourse analytical framework, based on socio- and anthropological discourse analysis (Hamilton 1998; Schiffrin 1987; Scollon 1998, 2001a; Tannen 1984) with a theoretical background in sociocultural psychology (Wertsch 1998) and with philosophical notions from Eastern and Western philosophy (Nishida 1958; Yuasa 1987). The framework is readily applicable, and the phases and the Step-by-Step process will allow the reader to gain a quick understanding of how to actually conduct a multimodal discourse analysis. Since we are working here in a data driven way, the reader will find that they are conducting their (outside of this book) background reading not necessarily so much before beginning their analysis, but rather during the analysis process. Again and again, the reader will come up against questions and these questions will guide the reader to the required literature. Because of this, further reading suggestions, which may guide the reader further in their endeavor to learn about the notions of lower-level mediated action, higher-level mediated actions, frozen mediated actions, modal density, levels of attention/awareness, semantic/pragmatic means, modal configurations, scales of action, natural experienced time cycles and rhythms, and the site of engagement including practices and discourses, have been added in Chapter 7. As with the multimodal framework presented, the readings are restricted to the analytical tools presented in this book. With this, classroom use and additional readings in relation to specific concepts have been made even easier for the instructor and the learner alike. Here, in the last chapter, the book offers some suggestions on how it can be used successfully for the undergraduate and graduate classroom as well as for PhD and research seminars. This chapter, just as the first part of Chapter 1, is of particular relevance for instructors teaching multimodal

Systematically Working with Multimodal Data: Research Methods in Multimodal Discourse Analysis,
First Edition. Sigrid Norris.
© 2019 John Wiley & Sons, Inc. Published 2019 by John Wiley & Sons, Inc.
Companion website: www.wiley.com/go/Norris/multimodal-data

discourse analysis and for self-study. But it is noteworthy right up front that the recommendations below are only possible suggestions. Most certainly, what is used for which classes and how fast an instructor will move through the material offered will depend upon the background knowledge of the student body as much as upon the curriculum developed around the book. The suggestions below and the brief summary description of the book may be particularly useful for the instructor when putting together a course and before they teach the material provided in a particular chapter as a quick reminder.

Note 1

The objective of this chapter is to provide instructors with a quick guide:
1) As reference when producing a course outline; and
2) As reference before teaching a new chapter.

A Quick Guide for *Undergraduate-Class* Instructors

Of course, the book can be used in many different ways in the undergraduate classroom. The important thing to note is that Chapters 3.0 and 3.1, 4.0 and 4.1, 5.0, and 5.1 plus Chapters 6 and 7 are meant for the undergraduate reader. But exactly how this material is taught depends upon many factors and will be left for the individual instructor to decide. Instructors, no doubt, will find Chapter 2 valuable for their teaching as well. But undergraduate students can essentially delve straight into Phase I (Chapter 3) and learn about data collection.

Which chapters are used for which courses will vary. For example, Chapter 3 is a relatively long chapter and could be used as reading and practical use for a class just on data collection. Or, depending on the focus of the course, the data collection chapter can be worked through in the first half of the course and the second half of the course can be spent on Phase II (Chapter 4) and Phase III (Chapter 5). Chapter 6, an entire chapter on multimodal transcription, could be a nice stand-alone course or could be taught together with Chapter 7 as a continuation of the previous course offered in Chapters 3 to 5 as its foundation. In either case, I suggest that the instructor uses relevant parts of Chapter 2 to introduce the necessary concepts and their definitions, and the keen student, no doubt, will also find particularly the first part of Chapter 2 highly relevant. Tasks, notes, and definitions given in Chapter 2 could also make for good testing material.

Chapters 3.0 and 3.1
Phase I in Chapters 3.0 and 3.1 takes the undergraduate student through 9 steps of multimodal data collection. The two sections can be read consecutively, so that you first assign Chapter 3.0 and then Chapter 3.1; or they can be read in tandem, so that you may for example want to assign Step 1 in Chapter 3.0 plus Step 1 in Chapter 3.1. In Chapter 3.0, the student learns what each step is about, while in Chapter 3.1 each step is demonstrated with an example from a YouTube video.

In class, you may want to go over what has been learned in Chapter 3.0 and help students work through the tasks, which guide the class to move through Chapter 3.0, whereas, the tasks in Chapter 3.1 guide the students to engage in their own mini research project.

Chapters 4.0 and 4.1

Phase II in Chapters 4.0 and 4.1 takes the undergraduate student through five steps of delineating multimodal data. The two sections can be read consecutively, so that you first assign Chapter 4.0 and then Chapter 4.1; or they can be read in tandem, so that you may for example want to assign Step 1 in Chapter 4.0 plus Step 1 in Chapter 4.1. In Chapter 4.0, the student learns what each step is about, while in Chapter 4.1 each step is demonstrated with an example from a YouTube video.

In class, you may want to go over what has been learned in Chapter 4.0 and help students work through the tasks, which guide the class to move through Chapter 4.0, whereas, the tasks in Chapter 4.1 guide the students to continue working on their own mini research project.

Chapters 5.0 and 5.1

Phase III in Chapters 5.0 and 5.1 takes the undergraduate student through four steps of how to select a multimodal data piece for micro analysis. As in the other two chapters, the two sections can be read consecutively, so that you first assign Chapter 5.0 and then Chapter 5.1, or they can be read in tandem, so that you may for example want to assign Step 1 in Chapter 5.0 plus Step 1 in Chapter 5.1. In Chapter 5.0, the student learns what each step is about, while in Chapter 5.1 each step is demonstrated with an example from a YouTube video.

In class, you may want to go over what has been learned in Chapter 5.0 and help students work through the tasks, which guide the class to move through Chapter 5.0, whereas, the tasks in Chapter 5.1 guide the students to continue working on their own mini research project, helping them to select a data piece for detailed micro analysis.

Chapter 6

Phase IV in Chapter 6 takes the undergraduate student through 11 steps of how to transcribe multimodal data using transcription conventions. This chapter consists of one part in which videos and exercises are offered for the student to engage in multimodal transcription. Here, too, you may want to go over the material that has been learned in Chapter 6 and work through the examples in class.

Chapter 7

Chapter 7 outlines analytical tools. The analytical tools are numbered to make it easier for readers (instructors and students) to find a particular tool. However, they do not need to be used in order. Rather, the student is offered an array of analytical tools to select from. In Chapter 7, an instructor may want to focus on particular analytical tools for students to work with. For the undergraduate classroom, it may make particular sense to focus upon the lower-level mediated action, the higher-level mediated action, modal density, and the modal density foreground-background continuum of attention/awareness. Or, it may be useful to focus upon the lower-level mediated action, the higher-level mediated action, and modal configurations.

A Quick Guide for *Graduate-Course* Instructors

For students to gain a necessary background in order to be able to work systematically with multimodal data, graduate students will want to read about multimodality in general (Chapter 1.1), as well as learn about the theoretical and philosophical background of the framework taught in this book (Chapter 2.1).

Of course, the book can be used in many different ways in the graduate classroom. The important thing to note is that Chapters 3.0 and 3.2, 4.0, and 4.2, 5.0, and 5.2 as well as Chapter 6 and 7 are meant for the graduate reader. But exactly how this material is taught depends upon many factors and will be left for the individual instructor to decide. Instructors, no doubt, will find Chapter 2 valuable for their teaching as well.

Which chapters are used for which courses will vary. For example, Chapter 3 is a relatively long chapter and could be used as reading and practical use for a class only on data collection. A course on data collection would certainly bring in reading from other sources and discuss various ways to collect data in greater depth than we do in this chapter. Or, depending on the focus of the course, the data collection chapter can be worked through in the first half of the course and the second half of the course can be spent on Phase II (Chapter 4) and Phase III (Chapter 5). Chapter 6, an entire chapter on multimodal transcription could be a nice stand-alone course or could be taught together with Chapter 7 as a continuation of the previous course that offered Chapters 3 to 5 as its foundation. In either case, I suggest that the instructor uses the relevant parts of Chapter 2 to introduce the necessary concepts and their definitions.

Chapter 1 from *Multimodality: Some Other Research* Onward
This part of the chapter, offers the student a quick understanding of the vast amount of literature that has already been written on multimodality. While the literature introductions are very brief, they do include a great number of references, which the student can later come back to and follow as they see fit for their own project. The literature and the references offered, however, are by no means comprehensive. Rather, it is just a taster of the literature available. Tasks and discussion points help guide the class. Next, the graduate student will read Chapter 2.

Chapter 2 Up To and Including the Section on the Site of Engagement
This part of Chapter 2 offers the graduate student enough background material to gain a relatively quick, yet deep, theoretical understanding of Multimodal (Inter)action Analysis.

With our extensive focus on perception and embodiment, a theme that runs throughout the book, the student is brought straight into thinking multimodally. Here, main theoretical principles and theoretical notions are introduced and defined. The notes are off-set in gray boxes and definitions are offset in pink boxes to both emphasize their importance and to make it easier for the student to learn and memorize the definitions. Notes and definitions thus make for a good source of learning material that the graduate student can come back to easily when needed. Discussion points, offset in yellow boxes, offer important aspects that students need to think through further. In the graduate classroom, these discussion points should bring about deeper understanding of the concepts and terms. Next, the graduate student will read Chapters 3.0 and 3.2.

Chapters 3.0 and 3.2

In Chapters 3.0 and 3.2 the graduate student learns the 10 steps of multimodal data collection. It may be useful for the graduate student to read the sections consecutively, but that will depend upon your student body. Chapter 3.0 illuminates each step, giving the student the necessary background knowledge for using the steps for their own research project, whereas Chapter 3.2 demonstrates each step, allowing the graduate student to follow the practical application of what was learned in Chapter 3.0. Following the example, the graduate student can relatively quickly move through data collection on their own.

Chapters 4.0 and 4.2

Phase II in Chapters 4.0 and 4.2 takes the graduate student through five steps of delineating multimodal data. The two sections can be either read consecutively, so that you first assign Chapter 4.0 and then Chapter 4.2, or they can be read in tandem, so that you may for example want to assign Step 1 in Chapter 4.0 plus Step 1 in Chapter 4.2. In Chapter 4.0, the student learns what each step is about, while in Chapter 4.2 each step is demonstrated with an example from an experimental study. With these two sections, the graduate student can easily continue working with their own collected material.

Chapters 5.0 and 5.2

Phase III in Chapters 5.0 and 5.2 takes the graduate student through four steps of how to select a multimodal data piece for micro analysis. Like the other two chapters, the two sections can be read consecutively, so that you first assign Chapter 5.0 and then Chapter 5.2; or they can be read in tandem, so that you may for example want to assign Step 1 in Chapter 5.0 plus Step 1 in Chapter 5.2. In Chapter 5.0, the student learns what each step is about, while in Chapter 5.2 cach step is demonstrated with an example from an experimental study. Working through these two sections of Chapter 5, the graduate student will be easily able to continue working with their own data, selecting a multimodal data piece for further detailed micro analysis.

Chapter 6

Phase IV in Chapter 6 takes the graduate student through 11 steps of how to transcribe multimodal data using transcription conventions. Here, videos and transcripts, tasks and notes offer guidance to learn multimodal transcription conventions. While the videos come from various studies, they can be downloaded and used as stand-alone examples. Besides the many examples offered, the chapter engages the graduate student in defining modes and in critically reflecting upon the difference between theoretical concepts and concrete actions.

Chapter 7

Chapter 7 outlines analytical tools. The analytical tools are numbered to make it easier for readers (instructors and students) to find a particular tool. However, they do not need to be used in order. In Chapter 7, an instructor may want to focus on particular analytical tools for students to work with. For the graduate classroom, it may make particular sense to focus upon the lower-level mediated action, the higher-level mediated action, modal density, and the modal density foreground-background continuum of attention/awareness. Or, it may be helpful to focus upon the lower-level mediated action, the higher-level mediated action, and modal configurations. But each time, it will be useful to bring students back to scales of action, the site of engagement including practices and discourses, or naturally experienced cycles or rhythms, which are tools that allow the student to place their micro analyses within a larger picture.

A Quick Guide for *PhD Seminar Instructors and Research Team Leaders*

For scholars to gain a necessary background in order to be able to work systematically with multimodal data, they may want to begin with Chapter 1.1 as well as learn about the theoretical and philosophical background of the framework taught in this book (Chapter 2).

Of course, the book can be used in many different ways for the PhD seminar or for self-study. The important thing to note is that Chapters 3.0 and 3.3, 4.0 and 4.3, and 5.0 and 5.3 as well as Chapters 6 and 7 are meant specifically for the PhD student and scholar. But exactly how this material is taught depends upon many factors and will be left for the individual instructor to decide. Instructors, no doubt, will find Chapter 2 valuable for their teaching as well.

Which chapters are used for which courses will vary. For example, Chapter 3 is a relatively long chapter and could be used as reading and practical use for a class only on data collection. A course on data collection would certainly bring in reading from many other sources and discuss various ways to collect data in greater depth than we do in this chapter. Or, depending on the focus of the course, the data collection chapter can be worked through in the first half of the course and the second half of the course can be spent on Phase II (Chapter 4) and Phase III (Chapter 5). Chapter 6, an entire chapter on multimodal transcription could be a nice stand-alone course or build material for several workshops, but could also be taught together with Chapter 7 as a continuation of the previous course that offered Chapters 3 to 5 as its foundation. In either case, I suggest that the instructor uses the relevant parts of Chapter 2 to introduce the necessary concepts and their definitions. Discussion points offered in Chapter 2 will be good starting points for PhD seminar interaction and group-work.

Chapter 1 from *Multimodality: Some Other Research* Onward

This part of the chapter, offers the reader a quick understanding of the vast amount of literature that has already been written on multimodality. While the literature introductions are very brief, they do include an extensive number of references, which the reader can later come back to and follow as they see fit for their own project. The literature and the references offered however are by no means comprehensive. Rather, it is just a taster of the literature available which will demonstrate that there is much more out there than many scholars not very familiar with the field of multimodality may think. Next, the scholar will be best placed to read Chapter 2.

Chapter 2

The first part of Chapter 2 offers the reader enough background material to gain a relatively quick, yet deep, theoretical understanding of Multimodal (Inter)action Analysis.

With our great focus on perception and embodiment, a theme that runs throughout the book, the reader is brought straight into thinking multimodally. Here, main theoretical principles and theoretical notions are introduced and defined. The notes and definitions are also offset in gray and pink boxes to both emphasize their importance and to make it easily possible for the reader to learn and memorize the definitions. Notes and definitions thus make for a good source of learning material that the reader can return to easily when needed. Discussion points, offset in yellow boxes, offer important aspects that scholars need to think through further. In the PhD seminar, these discussion points should bring about a deeply philosophical and theoretical understanding of the concepts and terms.

Chapter 2.1 moves the reader deeper into the historical origin of our philosophical and theoretical thought. Here, the scholar will learn more about Scollon and his readings of Vygotsky and Nishida. This part of the chapter includes a number of discussion points that lead us deeper into much thinking about philosophical thought and the readings thereof.

Chapters 3.0 and 3.3

In Chapters 3.0 and 3.3 the PhD student learns the 10 steps of multimodal data collection. It may be useful for the scholar to read some sections consecutively, but that will depend upon the student. Chapter 3.0 illuminates each step, giving the student necessary background knowledge to utilize the steps for their own research project, whereas Chapter 3.3 demonstrates each step, allowing the PhD student to follow the practical application of what was learned in Chapter 3.0, engaging in their own video ethnography. Following the example, the student can move through data collection of their own.

Chapters 4.0 and 4.3

Phase II in Chapters 4.0 and 4.3 takes the PhD student through five steps of delineating multimodal data. The reading of the two sections in a PhD seminar is maybe best left to the student to decide. PhD students will also want to have a look at the other chapter sections to gain as clear an understanding of how to work with multimodal data as possible. In Chapter 4.0, the reader learns again what each step is about, while in Chapter 4.3 each step is demonstrated with an example from a video ethnographic study. With these two sections, the PhD student can easily continue working with their own collected material.

Chapters 5.0 and 5.3

Phase III in Chapters 5.0 and 5.3 takes the PhD student through four steps of how to select a multimodal data piece for micro analysis. Like the other two chapters, the order of reading of the two (or four) sections should be left to the scholar to decide. As before, Chapter 5.0 discusses each step, while Chapter 5.3 explicates each step with an example from a video ethnographic study. Working through Chapter 5, the PhD student will be easily able to continue working with their own data, selecting a multimodal data piece for further detailed micro analysis in a systematic manner.

Chapter 6

Phase IV in Chapter 6 takes the PhD student through 11 steps of how to transcribe multimodal data using transcription conventions. Here, videos, transcripts and tasks guide the scholar to learn and engage in multimodal transcription utilizing theoretically founded transcription conventions. This is an important chapter filled with examples which offers downloadable videos that can be used when reading the transcripts as well as for producing transcripts as guided through the tasks in the chapter.

Chapter 7

Chapter 7 outlines analytical tools. The analytical tools are numbered to make it easier for readers (instructors and students) to find a particular tool. However, they do not need to be used in order. In Chapter 7, the scholar learns the function of the analytical tools offered and PhD students may want to work in groups to gain a good grasp of the analytical tools. In particular, the last two tools (always in connection with tools from the previously explained seven analytical tools for micro analysis) will be useful for the advanced researcher, who has collected the kinds of data required for this kind of analysis, namely ethnographic and/or interview data besides the collected videos of (inter) action that they are interested in. With these analytical tools, the scholar can then place their microanalytical findings into a larger picture and demonstrate the relevance and ramifications for society.

References

Abousnnouga, G. and Machin, D. (2010). Analysing the language of war monuments. *Visual Communication* 9 (2): 131–149.

Al Zidjaly, N. (2011a). Multimodal texts as mediated actions: voice, synchronization and layered simultaneity in images of disability. In: *Multimodality in Practice Investigating Theory-in-Practice-Through-Methodology* (ed. S. Norris). London: Routledge.

Al Zidjaly, N. (2011b). Can art (powerpoint) lead to social change? A mediated multimodal inquiry. *Multimodal Communication* 1 (1): 65–82.

Altorfer, A., Jossen, S., Würmle, O. et al. (2000). Measurement and meaning of head movements in everyday face-to-face communicative interaction. *Behaviour Research Methods, Instruments & Computers* 32 (1): 17–32.

Anderson, J.R. (1990). *The Adaptive Character of Thought*. Mahwah, NJ: Erlbaum.

Argyle, M. and Dean, J. (1965). Eye-contact, distance and affiliation. *Sociometry* 28: 289–304.

Auer, P. (2005). Projection in interaction and projection in grammar. *Text: Interdisciplinary Journal for the Study of Discourse* 25 (1): 7–36.

Auer, P., Couper-Kuhlen, E., and Mueller, F. (1999). *Language in Time: The Rhythm and Tempo of Spoken Interaction*, 27–56. Amsterdam: Benjamins.

Auer, P. and Pfaender, S. (eds.) (2011). *Constructions: Emerging and Emergent*. Berlin: Mouton.

Baldry, A. (2004). Phase and transition, type and instance: patterns in media texts as seen through a multi-modal enhancer. In: *Multimodal Discourse Analysis* (ed. K.L. O'Halloran), 83–108. London: Continuum.

Bamberg, M. (2004). Talk, small stories, and adolescent identities. *Human Development* 47: 366–369.

Bamberg, M. (2006). Stories: Big or small: Why do we care? *Narrative inquiry* 16 (1): 139–147.

Bamberg, M., and Georgakopoulou, A. (2008). Small stories as a new perspective in narrative and identity analysis. *Text & Talk* 28 (3): 377–396.

Barton, D. and Hamilton, M. (1998). *Local Literacies: Reading and Writing in One Community*. London: Routledge.

Bateman, J.A. (2008). *Multimodality and Genre: A Foundation for the Systematic Analysis of Multimodal Documents*. London: Palgrave Macmillan.

Bateman, J.A. and Schmidt, K.-H. (2014). *Multimodal Film Analysis: How Films Mean*. London: Routledge.

Systematically Working with Multimodal Data: Research Methods in Multimodal Discourse Analysis, First Edition. Sigrid Norris.
© 2019 John Wiley & Sons, Inc. Published 2019 by John Wiley & Sons, Inc.
Companion website: www.wiley.com/go/Norris/multimodal-data

Bateson, G. (1972). *Steps to an Ecology of Mind*. New York: Ballantine.

Behrends, A., Müller, S., and Dziobek, I. (2012). Moving in and out of synchrony: a concept for a new intervention fostering empathy through interactional movement and dance. *The Arts in Psychotherapy* 39 (2): 107–116.

Bernieri, F.J. and Rosenthal, R. (1991). Interpersonal coordination: behavior matching and interactional synchrony. In: *Fundamentals of Nonverbal Behavior* (ed. R.S. Feldman and B. Rime), 401–432. Cambridge: Cambridge University Press.

Birdwhilstell, R. (1970). *Kinesics and Context: Essays on Body Motion Communication*. Philadelphia: University of Pennsylvania Press.

Bolinger, D. (1964). Around the edge of language: intonation. *Harvard Educational Review* 4: 282–296.

Bourdieu, P. (1977). *Outline of a Theory of Practice*. Cambridge: Cambridge University Press.

Bourdieu, P. (1990). *The Logic of Practice*. Stanford, CA: Stanford University Press.

Bourdieu, P. (1998). *Practical Reason: On the Theory of Action*. Stanford, CA: Stanford University Press.

Bowcher, W.L., Liang, J.Y., and Wen, S. (2013). The multimodal construal of the experiential domain of recipes in Japanese and Chinese. *Semiotica* 197: 233–265.

Breyer, T., Buchholz, M., Hamburger, A., and Pfänder, S. (eds.) (2017). *Resonanz, Rhythmus und Synchronisierung: Erscheinungsformen und Effekte*. Bielefeld: Transcript-Verlag.

Bruner, J. (1986). *Actual Minds, Possible Worlds*. Cambridge, MA: Harvard University Press.

Bruner, J. (1990). *Acts of Meaning*. Cambridge, MA: Harvard University Press.

Bücher, K. (1899). *Arbeit und Rhythmus*. Leipzig: Von B. G. Teubner.

Bucholtz, M. and Hall, K. (2016). Embodied sociolinguistics. In: *Sociolinguistics: Theoretical Debates* (ed. N. Coupland). Cambridge: Cambridge University Press.

Butler, J. (1990). *Bodies That Matter: On the Discursive Limits of "Sex"*. London and New York: Routledge.

Carter, R.E. (1997). *The Nothingness Beyond God: An Introduction to the Philosophy of Nishida Kitaro*. St. Paul, MN: Paragon House Publishers.

de Certeau, M. (1984). *The Practice of Everyday Life*. Berkeley, CA: University of California Press.

Chafe, W. (1992). Prosodic and functional units of language. In: *Talking Data: Transcription and Coding in Discourse Research* (ed. J. Edwards and M. Lampert), 3–31. Hillsdale, NJ: Lawrence Erlbaum Associates.

Chafe, W. (1994). *Discourse, Consciousness, and Time: The Flow and Displacement of Conscious Experience in Speaking and Writing*. Chicago, IL: University of Chicago Press.

Chalmers, D.J. (1996). *The Conscious Mind: In Search of a Fundamental Theory*. Oxford: Oxford University Press.

Chaplin, J.P. (1985). *Dictionary of Psychology*. New York: Laurel.

Christen, H.R. (1980). *Grundlagen der allgemeinen und anorganischen Chemie*. Frankfurt-am-Main: Sauerländer.

Ciccourel, A. (1980). Language and social interaction: philosophical and empirical issues. In: *Language and Social Interaction* (ed. D. Zimmerman and C. West), 1–30. *Special Issue of Sociological Inquiry*, 50 (3/4). San Francisco: Jossey Bass.

Collins, A.M. and Quillian, M.R. (1969). Retrieval time from semantic memory. *Journal of Verbal Learning and Verbal Behavior* 8: 240–247.

Condon, W.S. and Ogston, W.D. (1967). A segmentation of behavior. *Journal of Psychiatric Research* 5: 221–235.

Couper-Kuhlen, E. (1993). *English Speech Rhythm: Form and Function in Everyday Verbal Interaction*. Amsterdam: John Benjamins.

Csikszentmihalyi, M. (1990). *Flow*. New York: Harper and Row.

Descartes, R. (1984). *The Philosophical Writings of Descartes* (trans. J. Cottingham, R. Stoothoff, and D. Murdoch). Cambridge: Cambridge University Press.

Dittman, A.T. (1987). The role of body movement in communication. In: *Nonverbal Behavior and Communication* (ed. A.W. Siegman and S. Feldstein). Hillsdale, NJ: Lawrence Erlbaum Associates.

Djonov, E. and van Leeuwen, T. (2011a). The semiotics of texture: from tactile to visual. *Visual Communication* 10 (4): 541–564.

Djonov, E. and van Leeuwen, T. (2011b). Normativity and software: a multimodal social semiotic approach. In: *Multimodality in Practice Investigating Theory-in-Practice-Through Methodology* (ed. S. Norris). London, England: Routledge.

Djonov, E. and van Leeuwen, T. (2013). Between the grid and composition: layout in PowerPoint's design and use. *Semiotica* 2013 (197): 1–34.

Dray, N.L. and McNeill, D. (1990). Gestures during discourse: the contextual structuring of thought. In: *Meaning and Prototypes: Studies in Linguistic Categorization* (ed. S.L. Tsohatzidis), 466–488. London and New York: Routledge.

Duignan, B. 2014. www.britannica.com/topic/postmodernism-philosophy (accessed on 12 March 2017).

Duranti, A. and Goodwin, C. (eds.) (1992). *Rethinking Context: Language as an Interactive Phenomenon*. Cambridge: Cambridge University Press.

Eco, U. (1972). *Einführung in die Semiotic*. Munich: UTB.

Efron, D. (1941). *Gesture and Environment*. New York: King's Crown Press.

Ehlich, K. (1993). Diskursanalyse. In: *Metzler-Lexikon Sprache* (ed. H. Glück), 145–146. Stuttgart: Metzler.

Ekman, P. (1979). About brows: emotional and conversational signals. In: *Human Ethology* (ed. M. von Cranach, K. Foppa, W. Lepenies and D. Ploog). Cambridge: Cambridge University Press.

Ekman, P. (ed.) (2006). *Darwin and Facial Expression: A Century of Research in Review*. Cambridge, MA: Major Books.

Ekman, P. and Friesen, W.V. (1969). The repertoire of nonverbal behavior: categories, origins, usage, and coding. *Semiotica* 1: 49–98.

Engeström, Y. (1987). *Learning by Expanding: An Activity-Theoretical Approach to Developmental Research*. Helsinki: Orienta- Konsultit.

Engeström, Y. and Middleton, D. (eds.) (1998). *Cognition and Communication at Work*. Cambridge: Cambridge University Press.

Erickson, F. (1980). *Timing and Context in Children's Everyday Discourse: Implications for the Study of Referential and Social Meaning, Sociolinguistic Working Paper*, vol. 67, 1–43. Austin, TX: Southwest Educational Development Laboratory.

Erickson, F. (1982). Money tree, lasagna bush, salt and pepper: social construction of topical cohesion in a conversation among Italian-Americans. In: *Analyzing Discourse: Text and Talk, Georgetown University Round Table on Languages and Linguistics* (ed. D. Tannen), 43–70. Washington, DC: Georgetown University Press.

Erickson, F. (1990). The social construction of discourse coherence in a family dinner table conversation. In: *Conversational Organization and Its Development* (ed. B. Dorval), 207–238. Norwood, NJ: Ablex.

Erickson, F. and Schultz, J. (1977). When is a context? *Institute for Comparative Human Development Newsletter* 1 (2): 5–10.

Exline, R. and Fehr, B.J. (1982). The assessment of gaze and mutual gaze. In: *Handbook of Methods in Nonverbal Behavior Research* (ed. K.R. Scherer and P. Ekman). Cambridge: Cambridge University Press.

Fairclough, N. (2001). Critical discourse analysis as a method in social scientific research. In: *Methods in Critical Discourse Analysis* (ed. R. Wodak and M. Meyer), 121–138. London: Sage.

Fairclough, N. and Wodak, R. (1997). Critical discourse analysis: an overview. In: *Discourse as Social Interaction* (ed. T. van Dijk). London: Sage.

Fasold, R. (1990). *Sociolinguistics of Language*. Oxford: Blackwell.

Ferre, G. (2014). Multimodal hyperbole. *Multimodal Communication* 3 (1): 25–50.

Finnegan, R. (2002). *Communicating: The Multiple Modes of Human Interconnection*. London: Routledge.

Flewitt, R., Hampel, Hauck, R.M., and Lancaster, L. (2009). What are multimodal data and transcription? In: *The Routledge Handbook of Multimodal Analysis* (ed. C. Jewitt), 40–53. New York and London: Routledge.

Fodor, J. (1975). *The Language of Thought*. Cambridge, MA: Harvard University Press.

Forceville, C. (1994). Pictorial metaphor in advertisements. *Metaphor and Symbolic Activity* 9: 1–29.

Foucault, M. (1993). *Die Ordnung des Diskurses*. Frankfurt-am-Main: Fischer.

Fox, J. and Artemeva, N. (2011). The cinematic art of teaching university mathematics: chalk talk as embodied practice. *Multimodal Communication* 1 (1): 83–103.

Frielund, A.J., Ekman, P., and Oster, H. (1987). Facial expression of emotion. In: *Nonverbal Behavior and Communication* (ed. A.W. Siegman and S. Feldstein). Mahwah, NJ: Lawrence Erlbaum Associates.

Garfinkel, H. (1967). *Studies in Ethnomethodology*. Englewood Cliffs, NJ: Prentice-Hall.

Garfinkel, H. (1974). On the origins of the term "ethnomethodology". In: *Ethnomethodology* (ed. R. Turner), 15–17. Harmondsworth: Penguin.

Garfinkel, H. and Sacks, H. (1970). On formal structures of practical action. In: *Theoretical Sociology* (ed. J.C. McKinney and E.A. Tiryakian), 338 366. New York: Appleton-Century-Crofts.

Garrod, S. and Pickering, M.J. (2009). Joint action, interactive alignment, and dialog. *Topics in Cognitive Science* 1: 292–304.

Geenen, J. (2013a). Actionary pertinence: space to place in kitesurfing. *Multimodal Communication* 2 (2): 123–153.

Geenen, J. 2013b. Kitesurfing: action, (Inter)action and mediation. Unpublished PhD Thesis, Auckland, NZ: AUT University.

Geenen, J. (2017). Show (and sometimes) Tell: identity construction and the affordances of video-conferencing. *Multimodal Communication* 6 (1): 1–18.

Geenen, J. 2018. The acquisition of interactive aptitudes: A microgenetic case study. *Pragmatics & Society* 9 (4): 519–546.

Geenen, J., Norris, S., and Makboon, B. (2015). Multimodal discourse analysis. In: *International Encyclopedia of Language and Social Interaction*. Hoboken: NJ: Wiley-Blackwell.

Giddens, A. (1979). *Central Problems in Social Theory: Action, Structure, and Contradiction in Social Analysis.* Berkeley and Los Angeles, CA: University of California Press.

Giddens, A. (1984). *The Constitutio of Society: Outline of a Theory of Structuration.* Berkeley: University of California Press.

Gill, S.P. (2011). Rhythmic synchrony and mediated interaction: towards a framework of rhythm in embodied interaction. *AI & Society* 27 (1): 111–127.

Goffman, E. (1959). *The Presentation of Self in Everyday Life.* New York: Doubleday.

Goffman, E. (1961). *Asylum.* New York: Anchor Press.

Goffman, E. (1963). *Behavior in Public Places.* New York: Free Press of Glencoe.

Goffman, E. (1974). *Frame Analysis.* New York: Harper & Row.

Goffman, E. (1979 [1976]). *Gender Advertisements.* London: Macmillan.

Goffman, E. (1981). *Forms of Talk.* Philadelphia, PA: University of Pennsylvania Press.

Goodwin, C. (1979). *Conversation and Organization.* New York: Academic Press.

Goodwin, C. (1980). Restarts, pauses, and the achievement of mutual gaze at turn beginning. *Sociological Inquiry* 50 (3–4): 272–302.

Goodwin, C. (1981). *Conversational Organization: Interaction Between Speakers and Hearers.* New York: Academic Press.

Goodwin, C. (1986). Gestures as a resource for the organization of mutual orientation. *Semiotica* 62: 29–49.

Goodwin, C. (1994). Professional vision. *American Anthropologist* 96 (3): 606–633.

Goodwin, C. (1995). Seeing in depth. *Social Studies of Sciences* 25: 237–274.

Goodwin, C. (1996). Practices of color classification. *Ninchi Kagaku Cognitive Studies: Bulletin of the Japanese Cognitive Science Society* 3 (2): 62–82.

Goodwin, C. (2000). Action and embodiment within situated human interaction. *Journal of Pragmatics.* 32 (10): 1489–1522.

Goodwin, C. (2001). Practices of seeing visual analysis: an ethnomethodological approach. In: *Handbook of Visual Analysis* (ed. T. van Leeuwen and C. Jewitt). London: Sage.

Goodwin, C. and Goodwin, M.H. (1992). Assessment and the construction of context. In: *Rethinking Context: Language as an Interactive Phenomienon* (ed. A. Duranti and C. Goodwin). Cambridge: Cambridge University Press.

Goodwin, C. and Heritage, J. (1990). Conversation analysis. *Annual Review of Anthropology* 19: 283–307.

Gumperz, J. (1981). The linguistic bases of communicative competence. In: *Analyzing Discourse: Text and Talk, Georgetown University Round Table on Languages and Linguistics* (ed. D. Tannen), 323–334. Washington, DC: Georgetown University Press.

Gumperz, J. (1982). *Discourse Strategies.* Cambridge: Cambridge University Press.

Habermas, J. 1984. *The Theory of Communicative Action, Vol. 1, Reason and the Rationalization of Society* (trans. T. McCarthy). Boston, MA: Beacon Press.

Habermas, J. (1999a). *Moralbewusstsein und kommunikatives Handeln.* Frankfurt-am-Main: Suhrkamp.

Habermas, T. (1999b). *Geliebte Objekte: Symbole und Instrumente der Identitätsbildung.* Frankfurt-am-Main: Suhrkamp.

Haddington, P., Mondada, L., and Nevile, M. (2013). Being mobile: interaction on the move. In: *Interaction and Mobility, Language and the Body in Motion* (ed. P. Haddington, L. Mondada and M. Nevile). Berlin and Boston: De Gruyter.

Hall, E.T. (1959). *The Silent Language.* Garden City, NY: Doubleday.

Hall, E.T. (1966). *The Hidden Dimension.* New York: Doubleday.

Hall, E.T. (1983). *The Dance of Life: The Other Dimension of Time*. New York: Anchor.

Halliday, M.A.K. (1973). *Explorations in the Functions of Language*. London: Edward Arnold.

Halliday, M.A.K. (1974). The place of Wfunctional sentence perspectiveW in the systems of linguistic description. In: *Papers on Functional Sentence Perspective* (ed. F. Danes). The Hague: Mouton.

Halliday, M.A.K. (1978). *Language as a Social Semiotic*. London: Edward Arnold.

Halliday, M.A.K. (1985). *An Introduction to Functional Grammar*. London: Edward Arnold.

Hamilton, H.E. (1998). Reported speech and survivor identity in on-line bone marrow transplantation narratives. *Journal of Sociolinguistics* 2 (1): 53–67.

Hasko, V. (2012). Qualitative corpus analysis. In: *The Encyclopedia of Applied Linguistics*. Hoboken, NJ: John Wiley Online Library.

Haviland, J. (1993). Anchoring, iconicity, and orientation in Guugu Yimidhirr pointing gestures. *Journal of Linguistic Anthropology* 3 (1): 3–45.

Haviland, J. (2000). Pointing, gesture spaces, and mental maps. In: *Language and Gesture: Window into Thought and Action* (ed. D. McNeill), 13–46. Cambridge: Cambridge University Press.

Hegel, G.W.F. (1988). *Phänomenologie des Geistes*. Hamburg: Felix Meiner Verlag.

Heidegger, M. (1962). *Being and Time* (trans. J. Macquarrie and E. Robinson). New York: Harper & Row.

Heims, S.P. (1977). Gregory Bateson and mathematicians: from interdisciplinary interaction to social functions. *Journal of the History of the Behavioral Sciences* 13: 141–159.

Heisig, J.W. (2001). *Philosophers of Nothingness*. Honolulu: University of Hawai'i Press.

Hofinger, A. and Ventola, E. (2004). Multimodality in operation: language and picture in a museum. In: *Perspectives on Multimodality* (ed. E. Ventola, C. Charles and M. Kaltenbacher), 193–208. Amsterdam and Philadelphia, PA: John Benjamins Publishing.

Holler, J. and Wilkin, K. (2011). Co-speech gesture mimicry in the process of collaborative referring during face-to-face dialogue. *Journal of Nonverbal Behavior* 35 (2): 133–153.

Holmes, J. and Marra, M. (2002). Having a laugh at work: how humour contributes to workplace culture. *Journal of Pragmatics* 34: 1683–1710.

Holquist, M. and Emerson, C. 1981. In: *Glossary for The Dialogic Imagination: Four Essays* (ed. M.M. Bakhtin and M. Holquist, trans. M. Holquist and C. Emerson). Austin, TX: University of Texas Press.

Husserl, E. 1991. *On the Phenomenology of the Consciousness of Internal Time (1893 1917)* (trans. J.B. Brough). Dordrecht: Kluwer.

Husserl, E. 1999. *Cartesian Meditations: An Introduction to Phenomenology* (trans. D. Cairns). Dordrecht: Kluwer.

Husserl, E. 2006. *The Basic Problems of Phenomenology: From the Lectures Winter Semester 1910–1011* (trans. I. Farin and J.G. Hart). Dordrecht: Springer.

Hymes, D. (1972a). Toward ethnographies of communication: the analysis of communicative events. In: *Language and Social Context* (ed. P. Giglioli), 21–43. Harmondsworth: Penguin (Excerpts from Hymes, D. (1966). Introduction: toward ethnographies of communication. *American Anthropologist* 66 (6): 12–25).

Hymes, D. (1972b). Models of the interaction of language and social life. In: *Directions in Sociolinguistics: the Ethnography of Communication* (ed. J. Gumperz and D. Hymes), 35–71. New York: Holt, Rinehart and Winston.

Hymes, D. (1974a). Toward ethnographies of communication. In: *Foundations in Sociolinguistics: An Ethnographic Approach*, 3–28. Philadelphia, PA: University of Pennsylvania Press.

Hymes, D. (1974b). *Foundations in Sociolinguistics: an Ethnographic Approach*. Philadelphia, PA: University of Pennsylvania Press.

Iedema, R. (2003). Multimodality, resemiotization: extending the analysis of discourse as multi-semiotic practice. *Visual Communication* 1 (3): 29–57.

Jefferson, G. (1974). Error correction and interactional resources. *Language in Society* 3: 181–199.

Jewitt, C. (2002). The move from page to screen: the multimodal reshaping of school English. *Visual Communication* 1 (2): 171–196.

Jewitt, C. (2008). Multimodality and literacy in school classroom. *AERA Review of Research in Education* 32: 241–267.

Jewitt, C. (2009). *Routledge Handbook of Multimodal Analysis*. London: Routledge.

Jewitt, C. and Kress, G. (eds.) *Multimodal Literacy*. New York: Peter Lang.

Jewitt, C. and Oyama, R. (2001). Visual meaning: a social semiotic approach. In: *Handbook of Visual Analysis* (ed. T. Van Leeuwen and C. Jewitt), 134–156. London: Sage.

Jocuns, A. (2007). Semiotics and classroom interaction: mediated discourse, distributed cognition, and the multimodal semiotics of Maguru Panggul pedagogy in two Balinese Gamelan classrooms in the United States. *Semiotica* 2007 (164): 123–151.

Johnston, A. (2004). Files, forms and fonts: mediational means and identity negotiation in immigration interviews. In: *Discourse and Technology: Multimodal Discourse Analysis, Georgetown University Round Table on Languages and Linguistics* (ed. P. Levine and S. Scollen), 116–127. Washington, DC: Georgetown University Press.

Jones, R. (2004). The problem of context in computer mediated communication. In: *Discourse and Technology: Multimodal Discourse Analysis, Georgetown University Round Table on Languages and Linguistics* (ed. P. LeVine and R. Scollon), 20–33. Washington, DC: Georgetown University Press.

Jones, R.H. (2005). Sites of engagement as sites of attention: time, space and culture in electronic discourse. In: *Discourse in Action: Introducing Mediated Discourse Analysis* (ed. S. Norris and R. Jones), 141–154. London: Routledge.

Jones, R.H. (2009). Technology and sites of display. In: *The Routledge Handbook of Multimodal Analysis* (ed. C. Jewitt), 114–126. New York and London: Routledge.

Jones, R. (2014). The multimodal dimension of claims in food packaging. *Multimodal Communication* 3 (1): 1–11.

Jones, R.H. and Norris, S. (2005a). Discourse as action/discourse in action. In: *Discourse in Action: Introducing Mediated Discourse Analysis* (ed. S. Norris and R. Jones), 3–14. London: Routledge.

Jones, R.H. and Norris, S. (2005b). Introducing mediational means/cultural tools. In: *Discourse in Action: Introducing Mediated Discourse Analysis* (ed. S. Norris and R. Jones), 49–51. London: Routledge.

Jones, R.H. and Norris, S. (2005c). Introducing practice. In: *Discourse in Action: Introducing Mediated Discourse Analysis* (ed. S. Norris and R. Jones), 97–99. London: Routledge.

Jones, R.H. and Norris, S. (2005d). Introducing agency. In: *Discourse in Action: Introducing Mediated Discourse Analysis* (ed. S. Norris and R. Jones), 167–171. London: Routledge.

Jossen, S., Käsermann, M., Altorfer, A. et al. (2000). The study of emotional processes in communication: II. Peripheral blood flow as an indicator of emotionalization. *Behaviour Research Methods, Instruments and Computers* 32 (1): 47–55.

Kahneman, D. (1973). *Attention and Effort*. Englewood Cliffs, NJ: Prentice Hall.

Kant, I. (1973 [1787]). *Immanuel Kant's Critique of Pure Reason* (trans. N.K. Smith), 20–33. London: Macmillan.

Käsermann, M., Altdorfer, A., Foppa, K. et al. (2000). The study of emotional processes in communication: I. Measuring emotionalization in everyday face-to-face communicative interaction. *Behaviour Research Methods, Instruments and Computers* 32 (1): 33–46.

Kastberg, P. (2007). Knowledge communication: the emergence of a third order discipline. In: *Kommunikation in Bewegung: Multimedialer Und Multilingualer Wissenstransfer in Der Experten-Laien-Kommunikation Festschrift Für Annely Rothkegel* (ed. C. Villiger and H. Gerzymisch-Arbogast), 7–24. Bern: Peter Lang.

Kendon, A. (1967). Some functions of gaze-direction in social interaction. *Acta Psychologica* 26: 22–63.

Kendon, A. (1972). Some relationships between body motion and speech: an analysis of an example. In: *Studies in Dyadic Communication* (ed. A.W. Siegman and B. Pope). New York: Pergamon Press.

Kendon, A. (1974). Movement coordination in social interaction: some examples described. In: *Nonverbal Communication* (ed. S. Weitz), 150–168. New York: Oxford University Press.

Kendon, A. (1977). *Studies in the Behavior of Social Interaction*. Bloomington: Indiana University Press.

Kendon, A. (1978). Looking in conversation and the regulation of turns at talk: a comment on the papers of G. Beattie and D.R. Rutter et al. *British Journal of Social and Clinical Psychology* 17: 23–24.

Kendon, A. (1980). Gesticulation and speech: two aspects of the process of utterance. In: *Nonverbal Communication and Language* (ed. M.R. Key). The Hague: Mouton.

Kendon, A. (1981). Geography of gesture. *Semiotica* 37: 129–163.

Kendon, A. (1982). A study of gesture: some observations on its history. *Semiotic Inquiry* 2: 45–62.

Kendon, A. (1990). *Conducting Interaction: Patterns of Behaviour in Focused Encounters*. Cambridge: Cambridge University Press.

Kendon, A. (1992). The negotiation of context in face-to-face interaction. In: *Rethinking Context: Language as an Interactive Phenomenon* (ed. A. Duranti and C. Goodwin). Cambridge: Cambridge University Press.

Kendon, A. (1994). Introduction to the special issue: gesture and understanding in social interaction. *Research in Language and Social Interaction* 27 (3): 171–174.

Kendon, A. (1997). Gesture. *Annual Review of Anthropology* 26: 109–128.

Kendon, A. (2004). *Gesture: Visible Action as Utterance*. Cambridge: Cambridge University Press.

Kendon, A. and Ferber, A. (1973). A description of some human greetings. In: *Comparative Ecology and Behavior of Primates* (ed. R.P. Michael and J.H. Crook), 591–668. London: Academic Press.

Kintsch, W. (1988). The role of knowledge in discourse comprehension: a construction-integration model. *Psychological Review* 95: 163–182.

König, B. and Lick, E. (2014). Wine labels in Austrian food retail stores: a semiotic analysis of multimodal red wine labels. *Semiotica* 200 (1/4): 313–334.

Kozulin, A. (1990). *Vygotsky's Psychology: A Biography of Ideas*. Cambridge, MA: Harvard University Press.

Kress, G. (1993). Against arbitrariness: the social production of the sign as a foundational issue in critical discourse analysis. *Discourse & Society* 4: 169–191.

Kress, G. (2000). Design and transformation: new theories of meaning. In: *Multiliteracies: Literacy Learning and the Design of Social Futures* (ed. B. Cope and M. Kalantzis), 153–203. London: Routledge.

Kress, G. (2005). Gains and losses: new forms of texts, knowledge and learning. *Computers and Composition* 22: 5–22.

Kress, G. (2009). What is a mode? In: *The Routledge Handbook of Multimodal Analysis* (ed. C. Jewitt), 54–67. New York and London: Routledge.

Kress, G., Jewitt, C., Ogborn, J., and Tsatsarelis, C. (2001). *Multimodal Teaching and Learning: the Rhetorics of the Science Classroom*. London: Continuum.

Kress, G. and van Leeuwen, T. (1996). *Reading Images: The Grammar of Visual Design*. London: Routledge.

Kress, G. and van Leeuwen, T. (1998). Front pages: (the critical) analysis. In: *Approaches to Media Discourse* (ed. A. Bell and P. Garrett), 186–219. Oxford and Maiden, MA: Blackwell.

Kress, G. and Van Leeuwen, T. (2001). *Multimodal Discourse: The Modes and Media of Contemporary Communication*. London: Edward Arnold.

Kress, G. and van Leeuwen, T. (2002). Colour as a semiotic mode: notes for a grammar of colour. *Visual Communication* 1: 343–368.

Kusmierczyk, E. (2013). Critical points in the negotiation of understanding: multimodal approach to job interviews in NZ context. *TESOLANZ Journal: The Journal of the TESOL Association of Aotearoa New Zealand* 21: 57–77.

Labov, W. (2006 [1966]). *The Social Stratification of English in New York City*. Cambridge: Cambridge University Press.

Ladd, D.R. (1980). *The Structure of Intonational Meaning: Evidence from English*. Bloomington: Indiana University Press.

Ladefoged, P. (1975). *A Course in Phonetics*. Orlando, FL: Harcourt Brace.

Lakoff, R.T. (1972). Language in context. *Language* 48: 907–927.

Latour, B. (1994). On technical mediation. *Common Knowledge* 3 (2): 29–64.

Latour, B. (1996). Do scientific objects have a history? Pasteur and Whitehead in a bath of lactic acid. *Common Knowledge* 5 (1): 76–91.

Latour, B. (2005). *Reassembling the Social: An Introduction to Actor-Network-Theory*. Oxford: Oxford University Press.

Lave, J. and Wenger, E. (eds.) (1991). *Situated Learning: Legitimate Peripheral Participation*. Cambridge: Cambridge University Press.

Lemke, J. (1998). Multiplying meaning: visual and verbal semiotics in scientific text. In: *Reading Science* (ed. J. Martin and R. Veel). London: Routledge.

Lemke, J. (2000a). Across the scales of time: artifacts, activities, and meanings in ecosocial systems. *Mind, Culture, and Activity* 7 (4): 273–290.

Lemke, J. (2000b). Introduction: language and other semiotic systems in education. *Linguistics and Education* 10 (3): 307–334.

Lemke, J. (2000c). Opening up closure: semiotics across scales. In: *Closure: Emergent Organizations and Their Dynamics, Annals of the New York Academy of Sciences*, vol. 901 (ed. J.L.R. Chandler and G. Van de Vijver), 100–111. New York: New York Academy of Sciences.

Lemke, J. (2000d). Material sign processes and ecosocial organization. In: *Downward Causation: Self-organization in Biology, Psychology, and Society* (ed. P.B. Andersen, C. Emmeche and N.O. Finnemann-Nielsen), 181–213. Aarhus: Aarhus University Press.

Lemke, J. (2002). Travels in hypermodality. *Visual Communication* 1 (3): 299–325.

Levine, P. and Scollon, R. (2004). Multimodal discourse analysis as the confluence of discourse and technology. In: *Discourse and Technology: Multimodal Discourse Analysis* (ed. P. Levine and R. Scollon), 1–6. Washington, DC: Georgetown University Press.

Levinson, S. (1983). *Pragmatics*. Cambridge: Cambridge University Press.

Lieberman, M. and Prince, A. (1977). On stress and linguistic rhythm. *Linguistic Inquiry* 8: 249–336.

Lindgren, R. and Johnson-Glenberg, M. (2013). Emboldened by embodiment: six precepts for research on embodied learning and mixed reality. *Educational Researcher* 42 (8): 445–452.

Loenhoff, J. and Schmitz, W.H. (2015). *Telekommunikation gegen Isolation: Kommunikationswissenschaftliche Studien aus einem Modellprojekt in einer Klinik*. Wiesbaden: Springer.

Lou, J.J. (2017). Spaces of consumption and senses of place: a geosemiotic analysis of three markets in Hong Kong. *Social Semiotics* 27 (4): 513–531.

Luhmann, N. (1998). *Gesellschaftsstruktur und Semantik*. Frankfurt-am-Main: Suhrkamp.

Machin, D. (2013). Towards a social semiotics of rhythm in popular music. *Semiotica* 197 (1/4): 119–140.

Maier, C.D. (2012). Closer to nature: a case study of the multifunctional selection of moving images in an environmental corporate video. *Multimodal Communication* 1 (3): 233–250.

Maier, C.D., Kampf, C., and Kastberg, P. (2007). Multimodal analysis: an integrative approach for scientific visualizing on the web. *Journal of Technical Writing and Communication* 37 (4): 453–478.

Makboon, B. (2013). The "chosen Cne": depicting religious belief through gestures. *Multimodal Communication* 2 (2): 171–194.

Makboon, B. (2015). *Communicating Religious Belief: Multimodal Identity Production of Thai Vegetarians*. Auckland: AUT University.

Margolis, E. (1999). Class pictures: representation of race, gender and ability in a century of school photography. *Visual Sociology* 14: 7–38.

Martinec, R. (1998). Cohesion in action. *Semiotica* 120 (1–2): 161–180.

McCloud, S. (1993). *Understanding Comics: The Invisible Art*. Northampton, MA: Tundra.

McNeill, D. (1981). Action, thought and language. *Cognition* 10 (1–3): 201–208.

McNeill, G.H. (1992). *Hand and Mind: What Gestures Reveal About Thought*. Chicago, IL: University of Chicago Press.

Mead, G.H. (1974). *Mind, Self, and Society from the Standpoint of a Social Behaviorist*. Chicago, IL: University of Chicago Press.

Merleau-Ponty, M. (1963). *The Structure of Behaviour*. Boston, MA: Beacon Press.

Merleau-Ponty, M. (2012). *Phenomenology of Perception*. London: Routledge.

Merritt, M. (1976). On questions (in service encounters). *Language in Society* 5: 315–357.

Metz, C. (1974). *Language and Cinema*. The Hague: Mouton.

Mey, J.L. (2001). *Pragmatics: An Introduction*. Oxford: Blackwell.

Michiko, Y. (2002). *Zen and Philosophy: An Intellectual Biography of Nishida Kitaro*. Honolulu: University of Hawai'i Press.

Milroy, L. (1987). *Observing and Analyzing Natural Language*. Oxford: Blackwell.

Mondada, L. (2006). Participants' online analysis and multimodal practices: projecting the end of the turn and the closing of the sequence. *Discourse Studies* 8 (1): 117–129.

Mondada, L. (2014). Instructions in the operating room: how the surgeon directs their assistant's hands. *Discourse Studies* 16 (2): 131–161.

Mondada, L. (2017). Walking and talking together: questions/answers and mobile participation in guided visits. *Social Sciences Information* 56 (2): 220–253.

Mondada, L. (2018). Greetings as a device to find out and establish the language of service encounters in multilingual settings. *Journal of Pragmatics* 126: 10–28.

Müller, C., Fricke, E., Cienki, A., and McNeill, D. (2013). *Body – Language – Communication*. Berlin and New York: Mouton.

Murray, G., Fujishima, N., and Uzuka, M. (2014). The semiotics of place: autonomy and space. In: *Social Dimensions of Autonomy in Language Learning* (ed. G. Murray), 81–95. London: Palgrave Macmillan.

Newell, A. and Simon, H.A. (1976). Computer science as empirical enquiry. *Communications of the ACM* 19: 113–126.

Nishida, K. (1958). *Intelligibility and the Philosophy of Nothingness: Three Philosophical Essays*. Honolulu: East-West Center Press.

Nishida, K. 1990. *A Inquiry into the Good* (trans. A. Masao and C. Ives). New Haven, CT: Yale University Press.

Nishitani, K. 1991. *Nishida Kitaro* (trans. Y. Seisaku and J.W. Heisig). Berkley and Los Angeles, CA: University of California Press.

Nolan, Francis. 2014. Intonation. www.ling.cam.ac.uk/francis/FN_inton_prepub.pdf

Norris, S. 2002a. A theoretical framework for multimodal discourse analysis presented via the analysis of identity construction of two 2omen Living in Germany. Dissertation. Department of Linguistics, Georgetown University.

Norris, S. (2002b). The implication of visual research for discourse analysis: transcription beyond language. *Visual Communication* 1 (1): 97–121.

Norris, S. (2004a). *Analyzing Multimodal Interaction: A Methodological Framework*. London: Routledge.

Norris, S. (2004b). Multimodal discourse analysis: a conceptual framework. In: *Discourse and Technology: Multimodal Discourse Analysis* (ed. P. Levine and R. Scollon), 101–115. Washington, DC: Georgetown University Press.

Norris, S. (2005). Habitus, social identity, the perception of male domination – and agency? In: *Discourse in Action: Introducing Mediated Discourse Analysis* (ed. S. Norris and R. Jones), 183–197. London: Routledge.

Norris, S. (2006). Multiparty interaction: a multimodal perspective on relevance. *Discourse Studies* 8 (3): 401–421.

Norris, S. (2007). The micropolitics of personal national and ethnicity identity. *Discourse and Society* 18 (5): 653–674.

Norris, S. (2008). Some thoughts on personal identity construction: a multimodal perspective. In: *Advances in Discourse Studies* (ed. V. Bhatia, J. Flowerdew and R.H. Jones), 132–147. London and New York: Routledge.

Norris, S. (2009a). Modal density and modal configurations: multimodal actions. In: *Routledge Handbook for Multimodal Discourse Analysis* (ed. C. Jewit). London: Routledge.

Norris, S. (2009b). Tempo, Auftakt, levels of actions, and practice: rhythms in ordinary interactions. *Journal of Applied Linguistics* 6 (3): 333–356.

Norris, S. (2011a). *Identity in (Inter)action: Introducing Multimodal (Inter)action Analysis*. Berlin and Boston: Mouton.

Norris, S. (2011b). Practice-based research: multimodal explorations through poetry and painting. *Multimodal Communication* 1 (1): 31–46.

Norris, S. (2011c). Three hierarchical positions of deictic gesture in relation to spoken language: a multimodal interaction analysis. *Visual Communication* 10 (2): 129–147.

Norris, S. (2012a). Teaching touch/response-feel: a first step to an analysis of touch from an (inter)active perspective. In: *Multimodality and Technology: Theory, Method, Practice* (ed. S. Norris). London: Routledge.

Norris, S. (2012b). The creation of a community artist in everyday life: long-duration process and creative actions. In: *Discourse and Creativity* (ed. R.H. Jones). Harlow: Pearson Education.

Norris, S. (ed.) (2012c). *Multimodality and Practice: Investigating Theory-in-Practice-Through-Method*. New York: Routledge.

Norris, S. (2013a). What is a mode? Smell, olfactory perception, and the notion of mode in multimodal mediated theory. *Multimodal Communication* 2 (2): 155–170.

Norris, S. (2013b). Multimodal (inter)action analysis: an integrative methodology. In: *Body – Language – Communication* (ed. C. Müller, E. Fricke, A. Cienki and D. McNeill). Berlin and New York: Mouton.

Norris, S. (2013c). Multimodal (inter)action analysis. In: *New Methods in Literacy Research* (ed. P. Albers, T. Holbrook and A.S. Flint). London and New York: Routledge.

Norris, S. (2014a). Learning tacit classroom participation. WCLTA. *Procedia Social and Behavioral Sciences* 141: 166–170. New York: Elsevier.

Norris, S. (2014b). The impact of literacy based schooling on learning a creative practice: modal configurations, practices and discourses. *Multimodal Communication* 3 (2): 181–195.

Norris, S. (2014c). Developing multimodal (inter)action analysis: a personal account. In: *Interactions, Images and Texts: A Reader in Multimodality* (ed. S. Norris and C.D. Maier). Berlin and Boston, MA: Mouton.

Norris, S. (ed.) (2015a). General introduction to multimodality. In: *Multimodality: Critical Concepts in Linguistics*, 1e, vol. I, 1–7. Abingdon: Routledge.

Norris, S. (ed.) (2015b). Introduction to Volume I. Some forerunners of multimodality and early multimodality. In: *Multimodality: Critical Concepts in Linguistics*, 1e, vol. I, 8–10. Abingdon: Routledge.

Norris, S. (ed.) (2015c). Introduction to Volume II. A call for multimodal theory, early multimodality: 2000 and 2001, building a foundation: 2002–2004, and developments: 2004–2005. In: *Multimodality: Critical Concepts in Linguistics*, 1e, vol. II, xiii–2. Abingdon: Routledge.

Norris, S. (ed.) (2015d). Introduction to Volume III. Multimodality becomes more established: 2006–2011. In: *Multimodality: Critical Concepts in Linguistics*, 1e, vol. III, xiii–2. Abingdon: Routledge.

Norris, S. (ed.) (2015e). Introduction to Volume IV: 2012–2014. In: *Multimodality: Critical Concepts in Linguistics*, 1e, vol. IV, xi–2. Abingdon: Routledge.

Norris, S. (ed.) (2015f). *Multimodality: Critical Concepts in Linguistics*, 1e, vol. I–IV, 1,714. Abingdon: Routledge.

Norris, S. (2016a). Concepts in multimodal discourse analysis with examples from video conferencing. *Yearbook of the Poznań Linguistic Meeting* 2 (1): 141–165. ISSN (Online) 2449-7525, DOI: 10.1515/yplm-2016-0007, September 2016. De Gruyter Open.

Norris, S. (2016b). Multimodal interaction – language and modal configurations. In: *Handbook 'Language in Multimodal Contexts'* (ed. N.-M. Klug and H. Stöckl), 121–142. Berlin and Boston: De Gruyter Mouton.

Norris, S. (2017a). Rhythmus und Resonanz in internationalen Videokonferenzen. In: *Resonanz, Rhythmus & Synchronisierung: Erscheinungsformen und Effekte* (ed. T. Breyer, M. Buchholz, A. Hamburger and S. Pfänder). Bielefeld: Transcript-Verlag.

Norris, S. (2017b). Scales of action: an example of driving and car talk in Germany and North America. *Text and Talk* 37 (1): 117–139.

Norris, S., Geenen, J., Metten, T., and Pirini, J. (2014). Collecting video data: role of the researcher. In: *Interactions, Images and Texts: A Reader in Multimodality* (ed. S. Norris and C.D. Maier). Berlin and Boston, MA: Mouton.

Norris, S. and Jones, R.H. (eds.) (2005a). *Discourse in Action: Introducing Mediated Discourse Analysis*. London: Routledge.

Norris, S. and Jones, R.H. (eds.) (2005b). Introducing mediated action. In: *Discourse in Action: Introducing Mediated Discourse Analysis*, 15–19. London: Routledge.

Norris, S. and Jones, R.H. (eds.) (2005c). Methodological principles and new directions in MDA. In: *Discourse in Action: Introducing Mediated Discourse Analysis*, 201–206. London: Routledge.

Norris, S. and Jones, R.H. (eds.) (2005d). Introducing sites of engagement. In: *Discourse in Action: Introducing Mediated Discourse Analysis*, 139–140. London: Routledge.

Norris, S. and Maier, C.D. (eds.) (2014a). *Interactions, Texts and Images: A Reader in Multimodality*. Berlin and Boston, MA: Mouton.

Norris, S. and Maier, C.D. (eds.) (2014b). Introduction. In: *Interactions, Images and Texts: A Reader in Multimodality*. Berlin and Boston, MA: De Gruyter Mouton.

Norris, S. and Maier, C.D. (eds.) (2014c). Concluding remarks. In: *Interactions, Images and Texts: A Reader in Multimodality*. Berlin and Boston, MA: De Gruyter Mouton.

Norris, S. and Makboon, B. (2015). Objects, frozen actions, and identity: a multimodal (inter)action analysis. *Multimodal Communication* 4 (1): 43–60.

Norris, S. and Pirini, J. (2017). Communicating knowledge, getting attention, and negotiating disagreement via videoconferencing technology: a multimodal analysis. *Organizational Knowledge Communication* 3 (1): 23–48.

O'Halloran, K.L. (1999). Towards a systemic functional analysis of multisemiotic mathematics texts. *Semiotica* 124 (1/2): 1–29.

O'Halloran, K.L. (2007). Systemic functional multimodal discourse analysis (SF-MDA) approach to mathematics, grammar and literacy. In: *Advances in Language and Education* (ed. A. McCabe, M. O'Donnell and R. Whittaker), 75–100. London: Continuum.

O'Halloran, K., Podlasov, A., Chua, A., and Marissa, K.L.E. (2012). Interactive software for multimodal analysis. *Visual Communication* 11 (3): 363–381.

Ochs, E. (1979). Transcription as theory. In: *Developmental Pragmatics* (ed. E. Ochs and B.B. Schieffelin). New York: Academic Press.

O'Toole, M. (1994). *The Languages of Displayed Art*, 3–31. London: Leicester University Press.

O'Toole, M. (2004). Opera ludentes: the Sydney Opera House at work and play. In: *Multimodal Discourse Analysis* (ed. K.L. O'Halloran), 11–27. London and New York: Continuum.

Pahl, K. (2007). Creativity in events and practices: a lens for understanding children's multimodal texts. *Literacy* 41: 86–92.

Pan, Y. (2014). Nexus analysis. In: *Interactions, Images and Texts: A Reader in Multimodality* (ed. S. Norris and C.D. Maier). Berlin and Boston: De Gruyter Mouton.

Peirce, C.S. (1955). Logic as semiotic: the theory of signs. In: *Philosophical Writings of Peirce* (ed. J. Buchler), 98–119. New York: Dover Publications.

Piaget, J. (1976). *The Grasp of Consciousness: Action and Concept in the Young Child*. Cambridge, MA: Harvard University Press.

Piaget, J. (1978). *Success and Understanding*. Cambridge, MA: Harvard University Press.

Pietikäinen, S., Lane, P., Salo, H., and Laihiala-Kankainen, S. (2011). Frozen actions in the Arctic linguistic landscape: a nexus analysis of language processes in visual space. *International Journal of Multilingualism* 8 ((4): 277–298.

Pike, K.L. (1967). *Language in Relation to a Unified Theory of the Structure of Human Behavior*. The Hague: Mouton.

Pirini, J. (2013a). Analysing business coaching: using modal density as a methodological tool. *Multimodal Communication* 2 (2): 195–216.

Pirini, J. (2013b). Analysing business coaching: using modal density as a methodological tool. *Multimodal Communication* 2 (2): 195–215.

Pirini, J. (2014a). Producing shared attention/awareness in high school tutoring. *Multimodal Communication* 3 (2): 163–179.

Pirini, J. (2014b). Introduction to multimodal (inter)action analysis. In: *Interactions, Images and Texts: A Reader in Multimodality* (ed. S. Norris and C.D. Maier), 77–92. Boston and Berlin, MA: De Gruyter Mouton.

Pirini, J. 2015. Research into tutoring: exploring agency and intersubjectivity. Unpublished doctoral dissertation. Auckland: AUT University.

Pirini, J. (2016). Intersubjectivity and materiality: a multimodal perspective. *Multimodal Communication* 5 (1): 1–14.

Pirini, J. (2017). Agency and co-production: a multimodal perspective. *Multimodal Communication* 6 (2): 1–20.

Pirini, J., Norris, S., Geenen, J., and Matelau, T. (2014). Studying social actors: some thoughts on ethics. In: *Interactions, Images and Texts: A Reader in Multimodality* (ed. S. Norris and C.D. Maier), 233–242. Berlin, Boston, MA: De Gruyter Mouton.

Randolph, T. 2000. *Why we act: Agency in mediated discourse*. AAAL. Bristol, UK.

Raskin, J. (2000). *The Human Interface: New Directions for Designing Interactive Systems*. New York: W.W. Norton.

Reckwitz, A. (2002). Toward a theory of social practices: a development in culturalist theorizing. *European Journal of Social Theory* 5 (2): 243–263.

Rish, R.M. (2015). Researching writing events: using mediated discourse analysis to explore how students write together. *Literacy Discussion* 49 (1): 12–19.

Robinson, H. 2003. *Stanford Encyclopedia of Philosophy*. https://plato.stanford.edu/archives/fall2003/entries/dualism/ (accessed 15 March 2017).

Rowsell, J., Kress, G., and Street, B. (2013). Visual optics: interpreting body art, three ways. *Visual Communication* 12 (1): 97–122.

Royce, T. (1998). Synergy on the page: exploring intersemiotic complementarity in page-based multimodal text. *Japan Association Systemic Functional Linguistics Occasional Papers* 1: 25–50.

Ruesch, J. and Kees, W. (1956). *Nonverbal Communication: Notes on the Visual Perception of Human Relations*. Berkeley, CA: University of California Press.

Sacks, H. (1973). On some puns with some imitations. In: *Sociolinguistics: Current Trends and Prospects, 23rd Annual Round Table on Languages and Linguistics* (ed. R.W. Shuy), 135–144. Washington, DC: Georgetown University Press.

Sacks, H. (1974). An analysis of the course of a joke's telling in conversation. In: *Explorations in the Ethnography of Speaking* (ed. R. Bauman and J. Sherzer), 337–353. Cambridge: Cambridge University Press.

Sacks, H., Schegloff, E., and Jefferson, G. (1974). A simplest systematics for the organization of turn-taking for conversation. *Language* 50: 696–735.

de Saint-Georges, I. (2004). Materiality in discourse: the influence of space and layout in making meaning. In: *Discourse and Technology: Multimodal Discourse Analysis, Georgetown University Round Table on Languages and Linguistics* (ed. P. Levine and S. Scollen), 101–115. Washington, DC: Georgetown University Press.

de Saint-Georges, I. and Norris, S. (2000). Nationality and the European Union: competing identities in the visual design of four European cities. *Visual Sociology* 15: 65–78.

Sapir, E. (1921). *Language*. New York: Harcourt, Brace, and World.

Sapir, E. (1933). Communication. *Encyclopedia of the Social Sciences* 4: 78–81.

de Saussure, F. (1959 [1915]). In: *Course in General Linguistics* (ed. C. Bally and A. Sechehaye, trans. W. Baskin). New York: Philosophical Library.

Schafer, R.M. (1977). *The Soundscape: Our Sonic Environment and the Tuning of the World*. Rochester, VT: Destiny Books.

Schatzki, T.R. (1996). *Social Practices: A Wittgensteinian Approach to Human Activity and the Social*. Cambridge: Cambridge University Press.

Scheflen, A.E. (1964). The significance of posture in communication systems. *Psychiatry* 27: 316–331.

Scheflen, A.E. (1974). *How Behaviour Means*. Garden City, NY: Doubleday.

Schegloff, E. (1972). Sequencing in conversational openings. In: *Directions in Sociolinguistics* (ed. J. Gumperz and D. Hymes), 346–380. New York: Holt, Rinehart and Winston.

Schiffrin, D. (1977). Opening encounters. *American Sociological Review* 42 (4): 671–691.

Schiffrin, D. (1981). Handwork as ceremony: the case of the handshake. In: *Nonverbal Communication, Interaction and Gesture* (ed. A. Kendon), 237–250. The Hague: Mouton.

Schiffrin, D. (1985). Multiple constraints on discourse options: a quantitative analysis of causal sequences. *Discourse Processes* 8 (3): 281–303.

Schiffrin, D. (1986). Turn-initial variation: structure and function in conversation. In: *Diversity and Diachrony* (ed. D. Sankoff), 367–380. Philadelphia, PA: John Benjamins Press.

Schiffrin, D. (1987). *Discourse Markers*. Cambridge: Cambridge University Press.

Schiffrin, D. (1988a). Conversation analysis. In: *Linguistics: The Cambridge Survey* (ed. F. Newmeyer), 251–276. Cambridge: Cambridge University Press.

Schiffrin, D. (1988b). Sociolinguistic approaches to discourse. Topic and reference in narrative. In: *Linguistic Contact and Variation* (ed. K. Ferrera et al.), 1–28. Austin, TX: University of Texas Press.

Schiffrin, D. (1990). Conversational analysis. *Annual Review of Applied Linguistics* 11: 3–19.

Schiffrin, D. (1994). *Approaches to Discourse*. Oxford: Blackwell.

Schiffrin, D., Tannen, D., and Hamilton, H.E. (eds.) (2001). *Handbook of Discourse Analysis*. Oxford: Blackwell.

Schmidt, R. (2001). Attention. In: *Cognition and Second Language Instruction* (ed. P. Robinson). Cambridge: Cambridge University Press.

Scollon, R. (1979). A real early stage: an unzipped condensation of a dissertation on child language. In: *Developmental Pragmatics* (ed. E. Ochs and B.B. Schieffelin), 215–227. New York: Academic Press.

Scollon, R. (1981). *Tempo, Density, and Silence: Rhythm in Ordinary Talk*. Fairbanks, AK: Centre for Cross-Cultural Studies, University of Alaska.

Scollon, R. (1982). The rhythmic integration of ordinary talk. In: *Analyzing Discourse: Text and Talk, Georgetown University Round Table on Languages and Linguistics 1981* (ed. D. Tannen), 335–349. Washington, DC: Georgetown University Press.

Scollon, R. (1997). Handbills, tissues, and condoms: a site of engagement for the construction of identity in public discourse. *Journal of Sociolinguistics* 1 (1): 39–61.

Scollon, R. (1998). *Mediated Discourse as Social Interaction: A Study of News Discourse*. London: Longman.

Scollon, R. (2001a). *Mediated Discourse: The Nexus of Practice*. London: Routledge.

Scollon, R. (2001b). Action and text: toward an integrated understanding of the place of text in social (inter)action. In: *Methods of Critical Discourse Analysis* (ed. R. Wodak and M. Meyer), 139–183. London: Sage.

Scollon, S. (2001c). Habitus, conciousness, agency and the problems of intention: how we carry and are carried by political discourses. *Folia Linguistica* XXXV (1–2): 97–129.

Scollon, R. (2005). The rhythmic integration of action and disocurses: Work, the body and the earth. In: *Discourse in Action: Introducing mediated Mediated discourse Discourse analysisAnalysis* (ed. S. Norris and R.H. Jones), 201–206. London: Routledge.

Scollon, R. and Scollon, S.W. (2003). *Discourses in Place: Language in the Material World*. London: Routledge.

Searle, J. (2001). *Geist, Sprache und Gesellschaft*. Suhrkamp: Frankfurt-am-Main.

Simonsen, K. (2012). In quest of a new humanism: embodiment, experience and phenomenology as critical geography. *Progress in Human Geography* 37 ((1): 10–26.

Sklar, L. (1977). *Space, Time, and Spacetime*. Berkeley, CA: University of California Press.

Sloetjes, H. and Wittenburg, P. (2008). Annotation by category – ELAN and ISO DCR. In: *Proceedings of the 6th International Conference on Language Resources and Evaluation* (*LREC 2008*).

Smith, D.W. (2016). Phenomenology. In: *The Stanford Encyclopedia of Philosophy* (Winter 2016 Edition) (ed. E.N. Zalta). Stanford, CA: Stanford University.

Sperber, D. and Wilson, D. (1986). *Relevance: Communication and Cognition*. Cambridge, MA: Harvard University Press.

Stenglin, M. (2009). Space odyssey: towards a social semiotic model of three-dimensional space. *Visual Communication* 8 (1): 35–64.

Stöckl, H. (2001). Texts with a view: windows onto the World. Notes on the textuality of pictures. In: *Text – Varieties – Translation*, ZAA Studies: Language, Literature, Culture, vol. 5 (ed. W. Thiele, A. Neubert and C. Todenhagen), 81–107.

Stöckl, H. (2005). Typography: body and dress of a text – a signing mode between language and image. *Visual Communication* 4 (2): 204–214.

Streeck, J. (1988). The significance of gesture: how it is established. *IPRA Papers in Pragmatics* 2 (1): 60–83.

Streeck, J. (1993). Gesture as communication I: its coordination with gaze and speech. *Communication Monographs* 60 (4): 275–299.

Streeck, J. (1994). Gesture as communication II: the audience as co-author. *Research on Language and Social Interaction* 27 (3): 223–238.

Streeck, J. (1996). How to do things with things: objects trouvés and symbolization. *Human Studies* 19: 365–384.

Tannen, D. (1979). What's in a frame? Surface evidence of underlying expectations. In: *New Directions in Discourse Processing* (ed. R. Freedle), 137–181. Norwood, NJ: Ablex Publishing.

Tannen, D. (1984). *Conversational Style: Analyzing Talk Among Friends*. Norwood, NJ: Ablex.

Tannen, D. (1989a). *Talking Voices: Repetition, Dialogue, and Imagery in Conversational Discourse*. Cambridge: Cambridge University Press.

Tannen, D. 1989b. Interpreting interruption in conversation. *Papers from the 25th Annual Regional Meeting of the Chicago Linguistics Society*, 266–287 Chicago.

Tannen, D. and Wallat, C. (1997). Interactive frames and knowledge schemas in interaction: examples from a medical examination/interview. In: *Framing in Discourse* (ed. D. Tannen), 57–76. New York and Oxford: Oxford University Press.

Tapio, E. (2014). The marginalisation of finely tuned semiotic practices and misunderstandings in relation to (signed) languages and deafness. *Multimodal Communication* 3 (2): 131–142.

Trochim, W.M. (2006). *The Research Methods Knowledge Base*, 2e. Web Center for Social Research Methods www.socialresearchmethods.net/kb (version current as of 20 October 2006). (accessed 3 December 2017).

Trudge, J. (1990). Vygotsky, the zone of proximal development, and peer collaboration: implications for classroom practice. In: *Vygotsky and Education: Instructional Implications and Applications of Sociohistorical Psychology* (ed. L.C. Moll), 155–172. Cambridge: Cambridge University Press.

Tulving, E. (1983). *Elements of Episodic Memory*. Oxford: Oxford University Press.

Unger-Hamilton, C., Fairbairn, N., and Walters, D. (1979). *Die Musik: Menschen, Instrumente und Ereignisse in Bildern und Dokumenten*. Munich: Christian Verlag.

Van Dijk, T. (1977). *Text and Context: Explorations in the Semantics and Pragmatics of Discourse*. London: Longman.

Van Dijk, T. (1980). *Textwissenschaft: Eine interdisziplinäre Einführung*. Munich: DTV.

Van Leeuwen, T. (1983). Impartial speech: observations on the intonation of radio newsreaders. *Australian Journal of Cultural Studies* 2 (1): 84–98.

Van Leeuwen, T. (1984). Rhythmic structures of the film text. In: *Discourse and Communication – New Approaches to the Analysis of a Media Discourse and Communication* (ed. T.A. van Dijk), 216–232. Berlin: Walter de Gruyter.

Van Leeuwen, T. (1999). *Speech, Music, Sound*. London: Macmillan.

Van Leeuwen, T. (2005). Multimodality, genre and design. In: *Discourse in Action: Introducing Mediated Discourse Analysis* (ed. S. Norris and R.H. Jones), 73–93. London: Routledge.

Van Leeuwen, T. and Jewitt, C. (2001). *Handbook of Visual Analysis*. London: Sage.

Van Leewen, T. (2009). The world according to Playmobil. *Semiotica* 2009 (173): 299–315.

Van Lier, L. (1995). Some features of a theory of practice. *TESOL Journal* 4 (1): 6–10.

Van Lier, L. (1996). *Interaction in the Language Curriculum: Awareness, Autonomy and Authenticity*. London: Longman.

Ventola, E. (2004). Multimodality in operation: language and picture in a museum. In: *Perspectives on Multimodality* (ed. E. Ventola, C. Charles and M. Kaltenbacher). Amsterdam and Philadelphia: John Benjamins Publishing.

Vygotsky, L.S. (1978). *Mind in Society: The Development of Higher Psychological Processes* (ed. M. Cole, V. John-Steiner, S. Scribner and E. Souberman). Cambridge, MA: Harvard University Press.

Vygotsky, L.S. (1981). The instrumental method in psychology. In: *The Concept of Activity in Soviet Psychology* (ed. J.V. Wertsch), 134–143. Armonk, NY: M.E. Sharpe.

Vygotsky, L.S. (1986 [1962]). *Thought and Language* (new edition A. Kozulin). Cambridge, MA: MIT.

Weis, E. and Belton, J. (eds.) (1985). *Film Sound: Theory and Practice*. New York: Columbia University Press.

Wertsch, J.V. (ed.) (1981). *The Concept of Activity in Soviet Psychology*. Armonk, NY: M.E. Sharpe.

Wertsch, J.V. (ed.) (1985a). *Culture, Communication and Cognition: Vygotskian Perspectives*. New York: Cambridge University Press.

Wertsch, J.V. (ed.) (1985b). *Vygotsky and the Social Formation of Mind*. Cambridge, MA: Harvard University Press.

Wertsch, J.V. (1998). *Voices of the Mind: A Sociocultural Approach to Mediated Action*. Cambridge, MA: Harvard University Press.

Whalen, J., Whalen, M., and Henderson, K. (2002). Improvisational choreography in teleservice work. *The British Journal of Sociology* 53: 239–258.

White, P. (2010). Grabbing attention: the importance of modal density in advertising. *Visual Communication* 9 (4): 371–397.

Whorf, B.L. (1956 [1940]). Science and linguistics. In: *Language, Thought, and Reality* (ed. J.B. Carroll), 207–219. Cambridge, MA: MIT Press.

Wickens, C. (1984). Processing resources in attention. In: *Varieties of Attention* (ed. R. Parasuraman and D.R. Davis), 63–102. New York: Academic Press.

Wickens, C. (1989). Attention and skilled performance. In: *Human Skills* (ed. D. Holding), 71–105. New York: Academic Press.

Wildfeuer, J. (2012). Intersemiosis in film: towards a new organisation of semiotic resources in multimodal filmic text. *Multimodal Communication* 1 (3): 277–303.

Winograd, T. (1972). *Understanding Natural Language*. New York: Academic Press.

Wittgenstein, L. (1998). *Abhandlung Tractatus logico-philosophicus*. Frankfurt-am-Main: Suhrkamp.

Wodak, R. (1989). *Language, Power and Ideology*. Amsterdam: Benjamins.

Wodak, R. (1995). Critical linguistics and critical discourse analysis. In: *Handbook of Pragmatics: Manual* (ed. J. Verschueren, J.-O. Östman and J. Blommaert), 204–210. Amsterdam: Benjamins.

Wodak, R. (2001). What CDA is about: a summary of its history, important concepts and its developments. In: *Methods of Critical Discourse Analysis* (ed. R. Wodak and M. Meyer), 1–13. London: Sage.

Wohlwend, K.E. and Lewis, C. (2011). Critical literacy, critical engagement, and digital technology: convergence and embodiment in glocal spheres. In: *Handbook of Research on Teaching the English Language Arts: Co-Sponsored by the International Reading Association and the National Council of Teachers of English* (ed. D. Lapp and D. Fisher). New York: Routledge.

Wohlwend, K.E., Peppler, K.A., Keune, A., and Thompson, N. (2017). Making sense and nonsense: comparing mediated discourse and agential realist approaches to materiality in a preschool makerspace. *Journal of Early Childhood Literacy* 17 (3): 444–462.

Yuasa, Y. (1987). In: *The Body: Toward an Eastern Mind-Body Theory* (ed. T.P. Kasulis, trans. S. Nagatomo and T.P. Kasulis). Albany: State University of New York Press.

Zemel, A. and Koschmann, T. (2014). Put your fingers right in here: learnability and instructed experience. *Discourse Studies* 16 (2): 163–183.

Index

Systematically Working with Multimodal Data: Research Methods in Multimodal Discourse Analysis, First Edition. Sigrid Norris.
© 2019 John Wiley & Sons, Inc. Published 2019 by John Wiley & Sons, Inc.
Companion website: www.wiley.com/go/Norris/multimodal-data